A Theological Introduction to the

PENTATEUCH

A Theological Introduction to the
PENTATEUCH

INTERPRETING THE TORAH AS CHRISTIAN SCRIPTURE

EDITED BY

RICHARD S. BRIGGS
AND JOEL N. LOHR

B
Baker Academic
a division of Baker Publishing Group
Grand Rapids, Michigan

© 2012 by Richard S. Briggs and Joel N. Lohr

Published by Baker Academic
a division of Baker Publishing Group
P.O. Box 6287, Grand Rapids, MI 49516-6287
www.bakeracademic.com

Printed in the United States of America

Library of Congress Cataloging-in-Publication Data
A theological introduction to the Pentateuch : interpreting the Torah as Christian Scripture
/ edited by Richard S. Briggs and Joel N. Lohr.
        p.   cm.
    Festschrift for Walter Moberly.
    Includes bibliographical references (p.   ) and indexes.
    ISBN 978-0-8010-3912-6 (pbk.)
    1. Bible. O.T. Pentateuch—Theology. I. Briggs, Richard, 1966– II. Lohr, Joel N.
III. Moberly, R. W. L.
BS1225.52.T54 2012
222'.1061—dc23   2011043228

Scripture quotations are based on the New Revised Standard Version of the Bible, copyright © 1989, by the Division of Christian Education of the National Council of the Churches of Christ in the United States of America. Used by permission. All rights reserved. Instances of "the LORD" have been adjusted to "YHWH," and in places the authors have modified the NRSV or provided their own translation to clarify a specific issue under discussion.

Scripture quotations labeled NASB are from the New American Standard Bible®, copyright © 1960, 1962, 1963, 1968, 1971, 1972, 1973, 1975, 1977, 1995 by The Lockman Foundation. Used by permission.

Scripture quotations labeled NIV are from the Holy Bible, New International Version®. NIV®. Copyright © 1973, 1978, 1984, 2011 by Biblica, Inc.™ Used by permission of Zondervan. All rights reserved worldwide. www.zondervan.com

Scripture quotations labeled NJPS are from the New Jewish Publication Society Version © 1985 by The Jewish Publication Society. All rights reserved.

The internet addresses, email addresses, and phone numbers in this book are accurate at the time of publication. They are provided as a resource. Baker Publishing Group does not endorse them or vouch for their content or permanence.

12   13   14   15   16   17   18   7   6   5   4   3   2   1

green
press
INITIATIVE

To R. Walter L. Moberly
Teacher, Mentor, Colleague, Christian
on the occasion of his sixtieth birthday, March 2012

Contents

Preface

The present volume aims to offer a concise introduction to some of the many and various practices that might be described as "theological interpretation of the Pentateuch." It presents a review of key issues and also models good interpretive practice. To this end, each chapter combines a discussion of theological themes and issues in the theological interpretation of its chosen pentateuchal book, followed by detailed exploration of one or two case studies, offering theological exegesis of a passage or two from the book.

All the contributors are either former research students or Durham colleagues of Professor Walter Moberly, and all are indebted, in a variety of ways, to his own careful and creative theological work in Old Testament interpretation. The volume is dedicated to Walter Moberly, therefore, as something of a small-scale *festschrift*. Our only regret in such a project is that he was unable to offer his unique brand of wisdom, advice, attention to detail, and generously constructive critique to these pieces.

We thank the contributors for their enthusiasm in cooperating on the project and for much engaging international email correspondence about the nature of theological interpretation. Several of us would like to acknowledge more specific debts: Joel Lohr thanks the Priscilla and Stanford Reid Trust for funding that allowed him to devote extra time to this project; Richard Briggs is indebted to research leave awarded by the council of St. John's College, Durham University; and Nathan MacDonald and Rob Barrett gratefully acknowledge the support of the Alexander von Humboldt Foundation and the German Federal Ministry of Education and Research. Finally, as editors, we are pleased to record our very real thanks to all the helpful staff at Baker Academic, and in particular to Jim Kinney for sharing our enthusiasm for such a book as this.

Richard S. Briggs
Joel N. Lohr

Contributors

Rob Barrett
Postgraduate Research Fellow
Theologische Fakultät, Georg-August-Universität, Göttingen, Germany

Richard S. Briggs
Lecturer in Old Testament; Director of Biblical Studies
Cranmer Hall, St. John's College, Durham University, England

Joel N. Lohr
Assistant Professor of Religious Studies
Trinity Western University, Canada
Visiting Scholar
Wycliffe College, University of Toronto, Canada

Nathan MacDonald
Reader in Old Testament
University of St. Andrews, Scotland
Leader of the Sofja-Kovalevskaja Research Team
Theologische Fakultät, Georg-August-Universität, Göttingen, Germany

Jo Bailey Wells
Associate Professor of the Practice of Christian Ministry and Bible; Director
of Anglican Studies
Duke Divinity School, Duke University, Durham, North Carolina, United States

Abbreviations

*	With verse/chapter numbers = only some parts of the indicated passages
//	Parallel to
ANE	Ancient Near East/Eastern
ANET	*Ancient Near Eastern Texts Relating to the Old Testament*. Edited by J. B. Pritchard. 1950. 3rd ed. Princeton, NJ: Princeton University Press, 1969.
BCE	Before the Common Era
CE	Common Era
D	The Deuteronomist—a pentateuchal source
DDD	*Dictionary of Deities and Demons in the Bible*. Edited by K. van der Toorn, B. Becking, and P. W. van der Horst. Leiden: Brill, 1995.
E	The Elohist—a pentateuchal source
J	The Yahwist (Jahwist)—a pentateuchal source
JEDP	Pentateuchal sources combined; *see each letter*
LXX	Septuagint
MT	Masoretic Text
NASB	New American Standard Bible
NIB	*New Interpreter's Bible*. Edited by Leander E. Keck. 12 vols. plus index. Nashville: Abingdon, 1994–2004.
NIDB	*New Interpreter's Dictionary of the Bible*. Edited by Katharine Doob Sakenfeld. 5 vols. Nashville: Abingdon, 2006–2009.
NIV	New International Version (2011)
NJPS	New Jewish Publication Society (translation of the Tanakh)
NRSV	New Revised Standard Version

NT   New Testament

OT   Old Testament

P   The Priestly source—a pentateuchal source

TDOT *Theological Dictionary of the Old Testament*. Edited by G. Johannes
        Botterweck and Helmer Ringgren. Translated by John T. Willis et
        al. 15 vols. Grand Rapids: Eerdmans, 1974–2006.

v./vv. verse/verses

VTE   *The Vassal-Treaties of Esarhaddon*. Edited and translated by Donald
        J. Wiseman. London: British School of Archaeology in Iraq, 1958.

Introduction

Reading the Pentateuch as Christian Scripture

RICHARD S. BRIGGS AND JOEL N. LOHR

The Pentateuch is the five-book collection that stands together at the head of the sacred Scriptures of both Judaism and Christianity. At the beginning of his introductory article on the Pentateuch, Walter Moberly captures two key aspects of how these texts have been and are approached: "This material has captured the imagination—and challenged the understanding—of both Jews and Christians down the ages. . . . Yet for all their importance, the question of how to read these texts well is not straightforward."[1] First of all, these are cherished texts. Second, they are frequently difficult texts. It is tempting to many interpreters to see these two observations as being in tension. Many have sacrificed imaginative understanding (let alone constructive engagement) in the face of the complexities of trying to read the Pentateuch well. In our view, theologically interested interpretation will not want to make that choice. In fact, it may be that it is precisely among the difficulties posed by these texts that we see most clearly their enduring value and are provoked to read them well. Yet, of course, a great deal of interpretive dispute boils down to the key question of what it means to read well.

In this chapter we map out some of the key issues in these areas and provide the reader with a brief outline of the approach we take in this book. First, we discuss what makes our approach in this book "theological." This is conducted with reference to several of the ways in which we have learned

---

1. R. W. L. Moberly, "Pentateuch," *NIDB* 4:430–38, here 4:430.

1

from Walter Moberly what it might mean to read Scripture well. In particular, we could not resist subtitling this book as we have and titling this introductory chapter "Reading the Pentateuch as Christian Scripture." Many works of biblical and theological study emerging from his watchful supervision at Durham have begun (and in some cases have ended) with a title such as "Reading X as Christian Scripture."[2] Second, we move on to a consideration of how one might understand "theological interpretation" in relation to two other prominent ways of characterizing one's approach: the historical and the literary. We aim to show that theological interpretation can be distinctive at the same time as being deeply interrelated to other angles of approach. Last, we discuss the format of the present volume. Here we highlight the unique contribution of each author and provide a rationale for our decision to use focused case studies—which engage with particular passages in each pentateuchal book—rather than attempt to survey the content of the Pentateuch in full.

Introducing the Pentateuch: A Theological Approach

George Steiner once memorably asked, "What worthwhile book after the Pentateuch has been written by a committee?"[3] Such a question certainly challenges a project like this one, a book about the Pentateuch written, if not by a committee, at least by a group of people working together. Furthermore, there are many ways one could conceive of an introduction to the Pentateuch being organized. Correspondingly, many good introductions to the Pentateuch already exist. Why another? What makes this one different?

We have tried to bring together an introduction that is self-consciously theological in approach. Many of the ways in which we understand this task, which is sometimes called "theological interpretation," are heavily indebted to the approach to biblical interpretation and theology practiced in the wide-ranging work of Walter Moberly, the honoree of this volume. At the end of this book is an appendix that reviews some of his work in the field of pentateuchal interpretation. Here at the beginning, however, it seems appropriate to sketch out some of the factors that have weighed upon us in bringing this volume together. The slight risk is that it might look as if we are commending the idea of needing to start with a theoretical discussion before the moment of actual engagement with the biblical text. That is not our intention. Rather, all the points that follow are broad convictions and practices that we have taken from Moberly's work and influence. Put together, they offer a set of

2. For a recent example, see Douglas S. Earl, *Reading Joshua as Christian Scripture*, Journal of Theological Interpretation: Supplement Series 2 (Winona Lake, IN: Eisenbrauns, 2010).

3. George Steiner, *Real Presences: Is There Anything* in *What We Say?* (London: Faber & Faber, 1989), 36.

working guidelines for how one might envisage the practices of theological interpretation at the present time.

First, it is important to take the text with full imaginative seriousness. The emphasis is to fall equally on the *imagination* and the *seriousness*. This means working with the text's details, its oddities, and its unwillingness to fit into paradigms we ourselves might find rather more straightforward or congenial. But in seeking to enter imaginatively into the world of the text, and in particular in being willing to follow where the text leads, the interpreter is working on the assumption that there should be "no exception whatever to the principle that any reading must be sustained or overturned by generally recognized canons of exegesis."[4]

Second, however, the question of what it means to read well requires more than just the deployment of exegetical methods, no matter how well attuned any such methods may be. The situation of the interpreter of the biblical text is also a key element, and this immediately raises the question of the purposes for which any reading of the Bible is carried out. In a key quotation at the beginning of his striking work *The Old Testament of the Old Testament*, Moberly suggests that "the crucial question, which is prior to questions of method and sets the context for them, is that of purpose and goal. To put it simply, *how we use the Bible depends on why we use the Bible.* In practice, many of the disagreements about how are, in effect, disagreements about why, and failure to recognize this leads to endless confusion."[5]

If this is so, and we think it is, then our interests as interpreters of Christian Scripture will be shaped in certain significant ways by Christian theological concerns. What is envisaged here is a dialogue between the theological thinking brought to the text and the pressure exerted by the text itself, pressure that in turn will shape and reshape that theology.[6] Despite frequent criticisms to the contrary, this does not mean that theological interpretation is the taming of the text to deliver precisely those theological conclusions that the interpreter already held most dear before reading the text. The goal, rather, is a kind of theologically creative work that is shaped in key ways by Scripture. As is often the case, examples of this practice perhaps do a better job of defining what it is than any attempt to map out particular criteria in advance. Walter Moberly's students have long been encouraged to seek such examples in the works of theologians such as Nicholas Lash, Rowan Williams, or—in certain

4. R. W. L. Moberly, *Prophecy and Discernment*, Cambridge Studies in Christian Doctrine 14 (Cambridge: Cambridge University Press, 2006), 38–39n62.

5. R. W. L. Moberly, *The Old Testament of the Old Testament: Patriarchal Narratives and Mosaic Yahwism*, Overtures to Biblical Theology (Minneapolis: Fortress, 1992), 2.

6. The image of the text's exerting "pressure" is helpfully articulated in C. Kavin Rowe, "Biblical Pressure and Trinitarian Hermeneutics," *Pro ecclesia* 11 (2002): 295–312. Rowe in turn attributes that image to Brevard Childs.

ways—Karl Barth, as much as in the more familiar terrain of biblical studies within which many Old Testament interpreters more commonly operate.[7]

Third, the two points above are to be held together. Theological interpretation at the present time, as we have conceived of it, is not a retreat from the rigors of critical analysis to a premodern practice pure and simple. Neither is the deployment of critical canons of exegesis pure and simple. Rather, it is the interweaving of concerns both traditional and modern, which may be both theologically orthodox and robustly critical, but all the while alert to the fact (a social as well as theological fact) that these texts have remained sacred Scripture for many centuries. As such, it is clear that we are not the first to read them or wrestle with their interpretation; therefore the long history of reception, both within and outside the church and synagogue, offers important resources, insights, corrections, and contributions to any attempt to read Scripture today.

Fourth, in the light of this awareness of our historical and theological location in a great chain of interpreters (which stretches back to the texts themselves), we are acutely aware that Christians who read these texts from the Pentateuch, and the Christian Old Testament, are also reading texts that constitute Jewish Torah and Jewish Scripture for Jews. In some ways this is a specific case of the point made above, that one's reading is framed by the concerns that bring one to read this literature in the first place. Jewish readings of the Torah overlap, as well as contrast strikingly, with Christian readings of the Pentateuch.[8] Our work aims to be informed by both perspectives, even while as Christians we cannot but read Jewish Scripture (or Tanakh) as *Old Testament*. This point is helpfully explored by Moberly, perhaps precisely because of his deep interests in Jewish-Christian dialogue.[9] The goal is to read this literature not at the cost of its status in contemporary Judaism or in a way that negates its value for present-day Jews. As Moberly states, "The Christian should no more denigrate the Torah-centered religion of the Old Testament, or the Judaism that grows out of it and stands in basic continuity with it, than that Torah-centered religion (i.e., Mosaic Yahwism) itself denigrated patriarchal religion [which it does not]."[10] To put it simply, as Christians we live and read

7. For examples, see the commendations in Moberly, *Prophecy and Discernment*, 36–37; see especially his discussions here and elsewhere of Nicholas Lash's *The Beginning and the End of "Religion"* (Cambridge: Cambridge University Press, 1996). As a result, works such as Moberly's *Prophecy and Discernment* can be characterized as being "in biblical studies but not of it" (so Richard S. Briggs, "Christian Theological Interpretation of Scripture Built on the Foundation of the Apostles and the Prophets: The Contribution of R. W. L. Moberly's *Prophecy and Discernment*," *Journal of Theological Interpretation* 4 [2010]: 309–18, here 317).

8. Here we refer the reader to Joel S. Kaminsky and Joel N. Lohr, *The Torah: A Beginner's Guide* (Oxford: Oneworld, 2011), a book written by a Jew and a Christian to explore precisely this dynamic and to learn from each other's tradition.

9. See esp. Moberly, *Old Testament of the Old Testament*, 147–75.

10. Ibid., 163.

these Scriptures in some relationship to Judaism even while our interests and concerns are not identical. In this book we engage with Jewish interpretation more on an ad hoc basis than in any programmatic way. However, such an approach is also one way to affirm that we should learn from anywhere and everywhere wisdom may be found.

A fifth point concerns whether one can offer a succinct definition of "theological interpretation." Many attempts have been made in recent years to do just this, including a helpful one by Moberly himself.[11] His own working definition of the practice, offered in grateful dialogue with a range of differently worded proposals, is this: "Theological interpretation is reading the Bible with a concern for the enduring truth of its witness to the nature of God and humanity, with a view to enabling the transformation of humanity into the likeness of God."[12] Though many such attempts offer something of value, the risk is that any statement short enough to be memorable is probably going to be a simplification in one way or another. It is not our intention to wade into this literature of conceptual clarification, and neither is the purpose of this introduction to suggest that one must sort out the theoretical issues in advance of engaging with the text theologically.[13] If pressed, one might suggest that the theoretical/hermeneutical issues are always under consideration right alongside the careful consideration of the text, rather than being either prolegomena or a methodological statement of the steps one must take in interpretation. Nevertheless, for the benefit of readers who do wish to think about this conceptual question, it does seem appropriate to clarify in what sense this book operates with a notion of "theological interpretation," and perhaps more specifically, to elaborate a little on how the notion does or does not overlap with other ways of engaging with the text. In the next section, therefore, we give further attention to this particular area.

Finally, by way of clarifying the nature of this "introduction," all the contributors are indebted to the model that Moberly has himself practiced, of requiring attention to the specifics of the particular biblical texts. The appendix on his work, at the end of this book, gives many examples of this with regard to the Pentateuch. We recognize the temptation for introductions to talk about the biblical text without ever getting around to actually reading it. At the same time, if our readings are to engage in a careful, critical, and constructive way with the text, asking some of the framework questions we have been discussing, and offering serious hermeneutical and theological reflection, then we cannot do more than read a fraction of the pentateuchal text in any detail. We have chosen to follow a style much in debt to the practice of Moberly

11. R. W. L. Moberly, "What Is Theological Interpretation of Scripture?" *Journal of Theological Interpretation* 3 (2009): 161–78.

12. Ibid., 163 (originally in italics).

13. For a brief and elegant entrée into this area, see Stephen E. Fowl, *Theological Interpretation of Scripture*, Cascade Companions (Eugene, OR: Wipf & Stock, 2009).

himself. Instead of seeking to cover a host of texts or surveying the content of each biblical book in full, in this book each contributor allots about half their chapter to the detailed consideration of one or two texts from their book *as a model* of what theological engagement with the book in question might look like. Readers may find that there are "family resemblances" between the interpretive studies in the book without finding in them a simple unity of method or purpose that could clearly map out "the right way of doing theological interpretation." In this too we have appreciated an elegant maxim offered by Moberly: "Too much ink has been spilt in arguing the merits of approaches to the Bible that, rightly or wrongly, have been advocated or perceived as *the* way. Since such debates are ultimately futile, I have no desire to add to them here."[14] Neither do we.

These six points, then, offer some sense of what a theological approach to the Pentateuch might entail. It would be nice to have a suitably symbolic seven points to make at the beginning of a book about the Old Testament, so let us add one more, in the shape of a more personal note. It has seemed appropriate to offer this collection of chapters in honor of Walter Moberly in the form of an "introduction." Walter's long-term work in Durham University has always retained a deep commitment to combining research and writing with the fundamental vocation of teaching. He is a committed, enthusiastic, and highly respected teacher, who has long suggested that one of the most demanding tasks in Old Testament studies today is to teach well at the *introductory* level: to lead students into the joys and complexities of the discipline while at the same time giving them an understanding of *why* the subject matters and how best to contribute to it. We have sought to model this volume in ways that reflect that commitment: this is not a random collection of essays but an attempt to produce a work that will inform and encourage those engaging with the Pentateuch to grapple with the many and varied tasks of theological interpretation. In the spirit of constructive theological work, this book is intended neither as the first word nor the last word, but as an attempt to offer a next word in our ongoing work with the biblical text.

Reading the Pentateuch as Scripture: A Question of Frameworks

On the Complex Nature of Interpretation

Doubtless the best way to learn how to interpret any biblical book, whether theologically or in any other way, is by doing it. Those who have pondered how to teach scriptural texts will surely resonate with the observation of Ellen Davis: "The only way I know to teach people to read the Bible is to read it

---

14. Moberly, *Old Testament of the Old Testament*, 4.

myself, afresh, in their presence."[15] Some readers, therefore, will be inclined to move on at this point to consider the individual chapters on the books of the Pentateuch. But others, as noted above, will want to probe a little further the question of what is at stake in interpreting the Pentateuch theologically. The following discussion is offered to that end.

As a rough and approximate model at this point, let us say that there are various angles of approach to most biblical texts, depending on how one characterizes the main focus, or "leading edge," of interpretive inquiry. Thus one might read with pronounced literary, historical, sociopolitical, or theological leanings, and indeed many other presenting perspectives too, since such complex and richly resonant texts as we find in the Pentateuch rightly deserve full attention from a large number of perspectives. All these angles must also be pursued "critically"—in other words, with care, self-reflection, and the appropriate hermeneutical mixture of trust and suspicion, which together make for rigorous and yet open reading.[16]

Theological interpretation, understood in the mix of these complex and interweaving interpretive practices, is perhaps then to be understood as one aspect of an integrated practice of reading the text, as carefully and reflectively as possible, but recognizing that among the many "leading edges" that can occupy the interpreter, one wishes to arrive at consideration of the theologically significant angles as a matter of some urgency. This way of characterizing the task may allow us to explain how it is that so much commentary in the nineteenth and twentieth centuries remained theologically alert and engaged all the while operating within (what now appear to be) somewhat underdeveloped interpretive frameworks. Frequently one would find that significant theological matters were often too easily assimilated to prior understandings (whether popular or ecclesiological) or were deferred to the point of not being considered at all (as in some kinds of commentary that seemed determined to bracket out all manner of personal, hermeneutical, or "existential" engagement with the text). Such commentary could still be theological, or at least contain theological elements, even while its concerns were primarily shaped by other matters.

In considering this topic, it is all too easy to reduce the options to polarized and mutually exclusive alternatives: historical-critical or theological, objective or confessional, public or private, and so on. Likely such an unweaving of the integrated practice of interpretation will always be reductive, and the inappropriate privileging of any one polarized alternative *to the exclusion*

15. Ellen F. Davis, "Entering the Story: Teaching the Bible in the Church," in *Sharper Than a Two-Edged Sword: Preaching, Teaching, and Living the Bible*, ed. Michael Root and James J. Buckley (Grand Rapids: Eerdmans, 2008), 44–62, here 49.

16. See Richard S. Briggs, "Juniper Trees and Pistachio Nuts: Trust and Suspicion as Modes of Scriptural Imagination," *Theology* 112 (2009): 353–63, which draws from the work of Paul Ricoeur to explore these points.

of the other will in the end also impoverish the chosen angle of approach. Thus, for example, an exclusion of the theological dimensions of interpretive inquiry will impoverish a historically oriented reading of a text by limiting the conceptuality of what is at stake in the historical context. The same is true when one's cultural horizons limit or reduce the scope for understanding the literary artistry of the ancient text. Problems of this type can be multiplied. As soon as one allows that many different angles of inquiry must critically interact in the handling of the text, the specter of one kind of approach having its prejudiced way with the text in a gloomy exercise of self-justification should be set aside. We must recognize that interpretation requires probing *self*-examination alongside probing *textual* examination in an open-ended process where key questions and insights are conceptualized and reconceptualized many times. Theological interpretation of the Pentateuch, then, is not a method nor the execution of a program (even an interpretive program), but is the self-conscious decision to bring questions of ongoing theological vitality to the fore, amid the many and various legitimate avenues of interpretive inquiry.

To demonstrate what is at stake in this way of characterizing the issues, we will consider the overlapping perspectives of two or three approaches to the Pentateuch, and in particular one or two examples from the book of Genesis. There are many angles of approach we could consider. A current series of guides to the interpretation of biblical books, *Methods in Biblical Interpretation*, typically takes a handful of approaches such as "rhetorical criticism," "feminist criticism," "postcolonial criticism," or "genre criticism" and explores what each angle brings to the reading.[17] The volume on Genesis planned for the series burst its banks and ended up being published separately, offering no fewer than ten approaches, including chapters on "cultural memory," "rabbinic interpretation," and "translation."[18] Clearly such a book on "methods for the Pentateuch" could be indefinitely long, and we cannot undertake such an overview here. So at the risk of oversimplification, let us make a practical distinction between approaches that are in some sense predominantly interested in (1) history, those dominated by (2) literary concerns, and those with more specifically (3) theological or canonically oriented interests. Many (though not all) reading strategies can be thought of in terms of how they navigate this range of interests. As long as we remember that this is not meant to be a threefold map of all the possibilities, we should not be led too far astray. In what follows we seek to show that historically oriented readings can range across a variety of sorts of theological engagement, not all of which would

---

17. See, e.g., Thomas B. Dozeman, ed., *Methods for Exodus*, Methods in Biblical Interpretation (Cambridge: Cambridge University Press, 2010). The sample approaches listed above are among those used in this volume.

18. Ronald Hendel, ed., *Reading Genesis: Ten Methods* (Cambridge: Cambridge University Press, 2010). It also contains a chapter, "Modern Theology," by John J. Collins (196–214), which is a (largely nontheological) review of accounts offered by other theologians.

really be best understood as "theological interpretation," and the same can be said of literary readings. Conversely, although we do not discuss it directly, self-declared theological interpretations may be characterized by a variety of practices with regard to historical or literary interpretive judgments.

Historical Frameworks

The rise of "historical consciousness"[19] remains perhaps the key defining feature of modern-era readings of biblical and other texts. One does not have to search far to find statements such as this, in a recent account of Genesis 1: "I have proposed a reading of Genesis that I believe to be faithful to the context of the original audience and author."[20] As it happens, this comes from a study that is concerned to dispute certain unhelpfully restrictive readings of that chapter with regard to modern interpretive frameworks, but the assumption, widely shared, is that correct interpretation depends upon correct understanding of the originating context. Now if such a principle is granted, then the hunt is clearly on for original contexts within which Genesis (and likewise the whole Pentateuch) was written or received. The problem is that the best we can do here is to offer hypotheses that try to make the most compelling sense of the evidence. On the one hand, it makes considerable sense to say that the Pentateuch was finally brought together in the Persian period (i.e., around the fifth century BCE),[21] but on the other hand, this observation must be coupled with the recognition that individual elements within it have a variety of original provenances or settings. Thus while "the original context" may be a helpful interpretive framework to consider, there are often going to be several such contexts, some of them more determinable than others. Also, our understanding of the ways in which the individual elements of the Pentateuch have been incorporated into the finished whole has been in considerable flux in recent years.

During the past two centuries pentateuchal criticism has been dominated by the classic JEDP theory. This theory, concerning the authorship of separate written documents subsequently combined together, attempted to give a comprehensive explanation for the differences in language and literary styles in the Pentateuch and to explain the various tensions, contradictions, and

19. On the general hermeneutical issue, see, e.g., Hans-Georg Gadamer, "The Problem of Historical Consciousness," in *Interpretive Social Research: A Reader*, ed. Paul Rabinow and William M. Sullivan (Berkeley and Los Angeles: University of California Press, 1979), 103–60; contingency and specificity are key issues.

20. John H. Walton, *The Lost World of Genesis One: Ancient Cosmology and the Origins Debate* (Downers Grove, IL: InterVarsity, 2009), 7.

21. For an up-to-date discussion of various aspects of this debate, see Gary N. Knoppers and Bernard M. Levinson, eds., *The Pentateuch as Torah: New Models for Understanding Its Promulgation and Acceptance* (Winona Lake, IN: Eisenbrauns, 2007).

differences of outlook found therein. There are many versions of this theory at the detailed level, and our goal is not to expound them all here.[22] In outline, the Yahwist (or Jahwist) source (J) was dated to the ninth century BCE, giving a southern-kingdom perspective on the history of Israel in its life with YHWH. Then J was supplemented by a later, eighth-century, northern-kingdom account written by the Elohist (E), so-called because he most often spoke of God as *Elohim*. After this came the work of the Deuteronomist (D), which in most early versions of the theory was simply the book of Deuteronomy. This "book" (or scroll) was understood to be the product of scribes seeking reform in 622 BCE, in conjunction with King Josiah, whose story is told in 2 Kings 22–23. Subsequent to this, a third continuous account came into being and formed the fourth document, called the Priestly source (P). This text was thought to be incorporated into the other three in such a way that it framed the finished work as a whole. Thus P was dated to postexilic times and was understood to be the source that emphasized ritual and legal aspects of life with YHWH. It was Julius Wellhausen (1844–1918) who formulated the most well-known version of the theory by arguing that the shift from a relatively unstructured faith in YHWH (J) toward a reliance on law and ritual (P) was to be understood as a decline into "legalism," and hence that the four sources were to be put in the order J-E-D-P. This ordering of the sources was Wellhausen's great contribution, overturning the previously held view that P, which provided the overall structure of the finished Pentateuch, must therefore have been (relatively) early. Today it is clear that this value judgment tells us more about Wellhausen than about ancient Israel, and it is clearly related to what has been a common tendency for (mainly Protestant) Christians to read law and ritual texts as less significant than other texts.[23] Nevertheless, this became the JEDP theory as it has been known and passed on to generations of students ever since.

More recently, however, the notion of continuous sources has fallen out of favor, although the idea of a Priestly source, P, remains something of a constant in pentateuchal criticism. Today it is more common to envisage separate (i.e., noncontinuous) blocks of tradition being edited together at a later stage to form a single continuous narrative. This move, proposed by Rolf Rendtorff and his students, now holds considerable sway, although perhaps more in Europe than in North America.[24] It finds eloquent expression in the work of Konrad Schmid, especially his *Genesis and the Moses Story*, who suggests that the book of Genesis is basically an alternative story of origins that developed separately from the Moses traditions of Exodus–Deuteronomy, and that the two are brought together shortly after the composition of P, in the first half

22. An elegant review of the topic, setting it in a broader historical context, is offered by Jean-Louis Ska, *Introduction to Reading the Pentateuch* (Winona Lake, IN: Eisenbrauns, 2006), 96–126.

23. Joel N. Lohr's chapter on Leviticus, below, explores this point in greater depth.

24. See Ska, *Introduction to Reading the Pentateuch*, 127–64.

of the fifth century BCE.[25] Schmid adduces various reasons for thinking that Genesis was not originally written to lead into Exodus; and especially at the key juncture between Genesis 50 and Exodus 1 he finds cause to remove certain verses as later editorial additions designed to effect such a merging of traditions.[26] Why did this happen? Schmid's lengthy answer, offering multiple insights into many details of texts in and beyond the Pentateuch, revolves around the notion of a fundamental diversity of theological conceptualizations of the ways of God in Israel's life and history: "The ancestors and the exodus not only mark two sequential stations for the beginnings of Israel's history (as the Bible reports), they also stand for two different theological perspectives showing how Israel interpreted its bond with God."[27]

At the risk of oversimplifying a subtle thesis, one could say that Schmid sees the ancestor narratives (i.e., Gen. 12–50) as emphasizing Israel's foundation upon the promises to, and covenants with, Abraham and others in Genesis, whereas the "Moses traditions" lean toward the significance of the law and the correct observance of the requirements for worship and priesthood. Schmid acknowledges that there are "mediating positions," although he tends to present any such mediation as leaning one way or the other.[28]

Arguably, though, such a tendency to operate with one or the other view as "basic" is a product of his interpretive model. It is precisely a presenting oddity of the finished Pentateuch that one finds these contrasting perspectives merged together. Although it is a solution of sorts to parcel them out to different historical traditions, it effectively removes the problem rather than resolving it: it displaces the problem and reduces things to a question of the development of the history of religious traditions, rather than leaving it as a fundamental theological question about the pentateuchal text. In the words of Moberly, discussing the relationship of Genesis to the rest of the Pentateuch and in particular the "classic problem" of how the life and faith of the ancestors relates to the Torah:

> Remarkably, this classic problem almost entirely receded from focus in 19th- and 20th-cent. pentateuchal criticism as scholars reconceptualised the theological

25. Konrad Schmid, *Genesis and the Moses Story: Israel's Dual Origins in the Hebrew Bible*, trans. James D. Nogalski, Siphrut: Literature and Theology of the Hebrew Scriptures 3 (Winona Lake, IN: Eisenbrauns, 2010), esp. 224–59. This book is a minor updating and translation of Schmid's *Erzväter und Exodus: Untersuchungen zur doppelten Begründung der Ursprünge Israels innerhalb der Geschichtsbücher des Alten Testaments*, Wissenschaftliche Monographien zum Alten und Neuen Testament 81 (Neukirchen-Vluyn: Neukirchener Verlag, 1999).

26. This crux is also key to many of the essays in Thomas B. Dozeman and Konrad Schmid, eds., *A Farewell to the Yahwist? The Composition of the Pentateuch in Recent European Interpretation*, SBL Symposium Series 34 (Atlanta: Society of Biblical Literature, 2006); not all of these essayists are persuaded by Schmid's thesis.

27. Schmid, *Genesis*, 333.

28. Ibid., 328–33.

issue as a problem of religious history to be tackled by historical-critical methods. . . . Scholars ceased to ask about the status of pre-Mosaic religion in relation to Mosaic norms. . . .

This change in focus illustrates the implications of differences of approach to
interpreting the Pentateuch. The questions one asks and the answers that appear
plausible are inseparable from the wider frame of reference and assumptions
within which one works.[29]

In other words, the properly *theological* question regarding the subject matter of the text ends up being approached by historical and literary methods
"without remainder": the problem is deemed explained if the growth of the
texts is accounted for.

This is not the place for a full evaluation of Schmid's work.[30] Yet it is perti-
nent to ask how one might characterize his approach in the light of Moberly's
observations above. Clearly, in one sense Schmid is very much engaged with
theological issues, though his study does not exemplify "theological interpretation" in the sense that we have been describing it. He is more interested in
providing an account of the development of the texts as we now have them,
rather than engaging with the resultant theological conceptualization once
the texts have reached their final form. There is considerable difference, for
example, in understanding promise and obedience as developing from divergent
traditions rather than as being simultaneous theological claims about life with
YHWH. In a brief discussion Schmid does say that the combining of Genesis
with Exodus places the "salvation-history" of the final canonical text "under
the sign of the promise," and thus he suggests that the Genesis perspective is in
some way the overarching one.[31] Schmid is hopeful, however, that in the future
the final "mixed" texts of the Pentateuch will receive the theological attention
they deserve. It is open to debate whether that attention will be theologically
richer thanks to a theory of how the finished text developed.[32]

In short, the historically oriented aspects of pentateuchal criticism exempli-
fied by Schmid's book could be construed, in different places and with respect to
different interpretive issues, as either hospitable or problematic to the concerns
of theological interpretation. This should certainly warn against too dogmatic
a pronouncement concerning the historical nature or otherwise of theological
interpretation. Instead, we find what we have anticipated: historical concerns
interweave with theological interests in many and unpredictable ways. The two
are different but not separable. It would be helpful if theologically interested
interpreters in general avoided exaggerated claims about "historical criticism"

29. Moberly, "Pentateuch," 434.
30. For sample critiques, one might consult the essays by Van Seters and Carr in *Farewell
to the Yahwist?*
31. Schmid, *Genesis*, 265–67, and, more generally, 259–81.
32. Ibid., 281.

and its supposed (or real) shortcomings. Equally, of course, historical critics should avoid suggesting that one can proceed as if theological questions make no difference to one's interpretive approach.

Literary Readings

Literary readings, sometimes known in biblical studies as examples of "new literary criticism" (to distinguish them from older concerns about literary sources and so forth), are typically characterized by attention to such matters as narrative, plot, characterization, point of view, and tropes such as irony. In so doing, they tend to be concerned with "final form" readings of the biblical text (that is, readings of the text as we now have it, not as it may have been in earlier hypothesized forms). Such approaches naturally invite consideration of the reader's role in interpretation. Genesis in particular has been fertile ground for this. Its long narrative form and strong characterization have allowed all manner of literary analyses to flourish.

One should not underestimate the significance of one of the first such readings of any biblical narrative, Erich Auerbach's famous consideration of Abraham and Isaac (Gen. 22) in his *Mimesis*.[33] In Auerbach's striking phrase, the tale is "fraught with background," by which he means that it is sparely underwritten, thus requiring any reader who wishes to understand it to enter into the process of exploring its "lacunae" (gaps, obscurities), imagining how the psychological and personal aspects of the tale must be understood. In this way the reader is drawn into the world of the text.

In what sense, then, might such approaches be understood theologically? Several kinds of cases might be considered, revealing a range of possible answers. A reading such as that offered by Laurence Turner shows how the book of Genesis can be analyzed in terms of plot, in particular by comparing how the story develops with what he terms "announcements of plot" (such as 1:28; 12:1–3; 25:23; and others). Turner concludes that "the Announcements are misleading indicators of how the plot of Genesis will develop. Too many other factors impinge upon the narrative for these to be taken as predetermining plot."[34] Although Turner wants to affirm that "Genesis is a sophisticated piece of literature,"[35] his literary perspective forecloses on some significant theological dimensions of interpretation. Most significantly, he decides that he will not import theological perspectives external to the text into his reading. Hence "YHWH" becomes another character in a narrative rather than the God worshiped in Israel.

---

33. Erich Auerbach, *Mimesis: The Representation of Reality in Western Literature* (Princeton, NJ: Princeton University Press, 1953), 3–23; on "Odysseus' Scar," see esp. 8–18.

34. Laurence A. Turner, *Announcements of Plot in Genesis*, Journal for the Study of the Old Testament: Supplement Series 96 (Sheffield: JSOT Press, 1990), 181; cf. esp. 13–19 for his programmatic statement.

35. Ibid., 182.

Regardless of the merits of such an approach in terms of literary-critical methodology, this is a prime example of foreclosing on some relevant aspects of the interpretation of scriptural texts. The problem is that such an approach does not permit the integrated work of multifaceted interpretation to draw upon theological perspectives that might otherwise contribute to a wise reading. This is not to say that one must interpret Genesis in such a way that one's prior theology is affirmed, but it does suggest that there is more to bring to the question of whether YHWH is fair *in Genesis*, say, than simply concluding that the narrative of Genesis does not allow us to answer this question. For one thing, the storyteller does seem to assume that YHWH is a character already known to the reader, and one might argue, as Moberly has in another context, that from the very first chapter of Genesis the story assumes that this YHWH, known to the reader, is good and can be trusted.[36] The point is that one's very reading of the narrative might be productively shaped by critical reflection on all sorts of other perspectives regarding the sense in which fairness can be attributed to YHWH.[37] A thoroughgoing execution of this problematic kind of literary approach to Genesis may be found in W. Lee Humphrey's reading of God as simply a character in the narrative.[38] The great merit of such approaches is that they pay careful attention to the details of the text. But even in Humphrey's direct consideration of the character of God (which turns out to be "complex and at points conflicted"),[39] the possibility of substantive theological conclusions is more or less entirely ruled out by the literary methods chosen. In one sense, then, his reading is "theological." In another, it is not the kind of "theological interpretation" we are seeking to describe.

One of the most striking ways of putting this comes from George Steiner, a literary critic who has spent a great deal of time in thinking through questions of how texts do or do not change our world. He was asked to review Robert Alter and Frank Kermode's *Literary Guide to the Bible*, which is full of the kinds of readings we have just been considering, combined with a tendency to bring Scripture down to the level of the common and the everyday. Steiner was unimpressed and unleashed a poetic tour de force of critical reflection:

> The question is: Does this *Literary Guide* help us to come to sensible grips with the singularity and the overwhelming provocations of the Bible—a singularity

36. See R. W. L. Moberly, "Did the Serpent Get It Right?" *Journal of Theological Studies* 39 (1988): 1–27; and his follow-up article, "Did the Interpreters Get It Right? Genesis 2–3 Reconsidered," *Journal of Theological Studies* 59 (2008): 22–40.

37. This particular example is handled all too briefly by Turner, *Announcements*, 113.

38. W. Lee Humphreys, *The Character of God in the Book of Genesis: A Narrative Appraisal* (Louisville: Westminster John Knox, 2001).

39. Ibid., 256.

and a summons altogether independent of the reach of current literary-critical fashions? Does it help us to understand in what ways the Bible and the demands of answerability it puts upon us are like no others? Of this tome—and I repeat that it contains much that is enlightening, convincing, and finely argued—a terrible blandness is born. . . . Holy Scripture as it is cocooned in the academic poise and urbanity of these commentaries . . . emerges as might a fair number of other great books of high antiquity and stylistic variousness. We hear of "omelettes," of "pressure cookers," not of the terror, of the *mysterium tremendum*, that inhabits man's endeavors to speak to and speak of God.[40]

Again, to reiterate, literary readings can offer tremendous help to theological concerns when they are pursued as keys to reading the text carefully, but not when their methodological commitments cause the interpreter to ignore or foreclose on allowing exploration of key theological notions (such as the character of God, to take the obvious example we have been discussing). Thus to characterize a reading of the Pentateuch as "literary" in itself leaves open the question of how theological it is.

Theological Interpretation

Hopefully we have by now said enough to begin to indicate how the historical and literary concerns of interpretation—to use just two examples—should not be played off against theological interests. With regard to theological interpretation, what matters is that the interpreter engages with issues of theological substance, drawing both from a broad range of theological concerns that the reader might bring to the text, as well as paying careful attention to the theological subject matter of the text itself. The manner by which one arrives at such issues is perhaps of secondary significance, and in the chapters that follow various different ways of proceeding are explored and modeled.

Each contributor to the present volume seeks to introduce one book of the Pentateuch with eyes clearly set upon the kind of theological interpretation we have been discussing in this introduction. This is done in two main ways. In the first half of each chapter, the author will introduce the book by way of prominent themes and issues, as well as by looking at some of the hermeneutical questions arising from the book. In the second half of the chapter, each author will engage in an exercise in theological interpretation, examining a particular focal passage (or passages) from that book in detail. We hope that our reasons for structuring things in this way will be self-evident, so that such an approach allows the reader to see exactly how historical, literary, and other concerns play differing roles in each discussion and in each passage. Further,

40. George Steiner, "The Good Books," *The New Yorker*, January 11, 1988; repr. in *Religion and Intellectual Life* 6 (1989): 9–16, here 14–15.

such examples permit the reader to see careful theological interpretation being exercised in practice. Some of the different ways in which this task is approached are as follows:

- For Genesis, Richard Briggs explores the Babel story in Genesis 11:1–9, paying particular attention to literary questions about the text, but noting that historical questions contribute to the reader's thinking about the role of the text in its canonical context, which he explores through the twin themes of blessing and limitation.
- Jo Bailey Wells looks at Exodus 19:1–8, engaging with its literary shape and texture, and showing that Israel's covenantal status as a "kingdom of priests" entails that Israel is invested with the character of YHWH for the world.
- For Leviticus, Joel Lohr examines what some call the center of the book, the Yom Kippur (or Day of Atonement) passage of Leviticus 16, asking how modern (and particularly Protestant) biases against ritual and priesthood make reading this literature difficult, even if, as he suggests, the New Testament cannot be understood apart from it.
- Nathan MacDonald examines Numbers 20–21 and shows how a careful engagement with recent pentateuchal criticism can shed light on the theological dynamics between Numbers 20–21 and the rest of the book; he also shows how the book of Numbers bridges the Priestly corpus (Genesis–Leviticus) with Deuteronomy, theologically as well as literarily.
- Rob Barrett considers two different texts in Deuteronomy (Deut. 8 and 15:1–11) and argues that the two passages illustrate the book's vision of covenantal issues of loyalty to YHWH, the dynamics of blessing and curse, and the nature of the law; in particular, he shows how the claims of Deuteronomy still speak powerfully on matters of economic significance today.

The decision to engage with one or two passages in each book is intended to illuminate what is at stake in theological interpretation in practice, as well as to exemplify (in a range of different ways) the approach that Walter Moberly has often taken in reading biblical books and indeed the larger Old Testament as a whole. And like Moberly, we do so by drawing from multiple interpretive perspectives in order to illuminate the text for the work of Christian theology. Theological interpretation is not just one thing; it includes a coherent set of practices that overlap with many other critical modes of engagement with the biblical text. The chapters that follow seek to lead the reader in understanding the promise and possibilities of consciously theological interpretation. Our hope is that they will in turn provoke further readings of these pentateuchal texts as Christian Scripture.

FURTHER READING

The Works of Walter Moberly

Walter Moberly is the author of the following books:

At the Mountain of God: Story and Theology in Exodus 32–34. Journal for the
   Study of the Old Testament: Supplement Series 22. Sheffield: JSOT Press, 1983.

From Eden to Golgotha: Essays in Biblical Theology. University of South Florida
   Studies in the History of Judaism. Atlanta: Scholars Press, 1992.

The Old Testament of the Old Testament: Patriarchal Narratives and Mosaic
   Yahwism. Overtures to Biblical Theology. Minneapolis: Fortress, 1992; repr.,
   Eugene, OR: Wipf & Stock, 2002.

Genesis 12–50. Old Testament Guides. Sheffield: JSOT Press, 1992. Reissued (with
   updating) in Genesis and Exodus, by John W. Rogerson, R. W. L. Moberly, and
   William Johnstone (with an introduction by John Goldingay), 99–179. Sheffield:
   Sheffield Academic Press, 2001.

The Bible, Theology, and Faith: A Study of Abraham and Jesus. Cambridge Studies
   in Christian Doctrine 5. Cambridge: Cambridge University Press, 2000.

Prophecy and Discernment. Cambridge Studies in Christian Doctrine 14. Cambridge: Cambridge University Press, 2006.

The Theology of the Book of Genesis. Old Testament Theology. Cambridge:
   Cambridge University Press, 2009.

In addition he has written many significant articles in the area of theological
interpretation. See the appendix to this book for a survey of those writings
that focus in some way on the interpretation of the Pentateuch and its individual texts.

Introductions to the Pentateuch

If it is true, as suggested above, that there are many ways of introducing
the Pentateuch, then it is also true that a range of books will provide helpfully complementary understandings of the task of reading the Pentateuch
well. The following are all strong guides to some of the multiple historical,
literary, and theological tasks involved, though some focus more on one aspect than others.

Blenkinsopp, Joseph. The Pentateuch: An Introduction to the First Five Books of
   the Bible. Anchor Bible Reference Library. New York: Doubleday, 2000.

Clines, David J. A. The Theme of the Pentateuch. Journal for the Study of the
   Old Testament: Supplement Series 10. Rev. ed. Sheffield: Sheffield Academic
   Press, 1997.

Fretheim, Terence E. The Pentateuch. Interpreting Biblical Texts. Nashville: Abingdon, 1996.

Kaminsky, Joel S., and Joel N. Lohr. *The Torah: A Beginner's Guide*. Oxford: Oneworld, 2011.

Ska, Jean-Louis. *Introduction to Reading the Pentateuch*. Translated by Pascale Dominique. Winona Lake, IN: Eisenbrauns, 2006.

van Wijk-Bos, Johanna W. H. *Making Wise the Simple: The Torah in Christian Faith and Practice*. Grand Rapids: Eerdmans, 2005.

Wenham, Gordon. *Exploring the Old Testament*. Vol. 1, *The Pentateuch*. London: SPCK, 2003.

Whybray, R. Norman. *Introduction to the Pentateuch*. Grand Rapids: Eerdmans, 1995.

Translations

In addition to standard Bible translations, it is also worth knowing about fresh translations of the Pentateuch, including the following:

Alter, Robert. *The Five Books of Moses: A Translation with Commentary*. New York: Norton, 2004.

Fox, Everett. *The Five Books of Moses: A New Translation with Introductions, Commentary, and Notes*. The Schocken Bible. Vol. 1. Dallas: Word, 1995.

1

The Book of Genesis

RICHARD S. BRIGGS

On any account of Christian (and Jewish) Scripture, the book of Genesis stands out. Whether one approaches the book from the perspectives of popular culture, of science, of ethics, of history, or from any theological angle, the book of Genesis is a text that invites, and has long received, serious attention. It remains a fixture of general public awareness of the Bible long after most of the rest of the Old Testament (and much of the New) has receded from cultural prominence. Its stories retain their power through media ranging from the literary, such as in Steinbeck's famous *East of Eden*,[1] to the musical, most famously in the long-running *Joseph and His Amazing Technicolor Dreamcoat*. Its simple and elegant account of creation retains its startling value against any and all other accounts of origins, provoking controversy as much today as it doubtless did when it was written. Its notion of humans in the image of God continues to invite all manner of ethical, psychological, and philosophical reflection. And then in the wideranging fields of biblical studies, Genesis has long been the proving ground of many theories attempting to explain the origins and development of the Old Testament as a literary collection of texts.

I am delighted to be able to dedicate this chapter to Walter Moberly in grateful thanks for his wisdom and friendship over our several years as colleagues in Durham. In particular, the present chapter is indebted to his many writings on the book of Genesis.

1. On this and many others, see the fascinating study by Terry R. Wright, *The Genesis of Fiction: Modern Novelists as Biblical Interpreters* (Aldershot, UK: Ashgate, 2007). Also note the startling comic book adaptation by Robert Crumb, *The Book of Genesis Illustrated*, trans. Robert Alter (New York: Norton, 2009).

The book's impact is related to its extraordinary scope, ambition, and placement as the opening text of sacred Scripture. The very familiarity of Genesis can obscure some of its most striking features. It paints on a canvas designed to encompass all of human history, from the beginning to a specific point on the cusp of the narrative of Israel, stopping short of Moses and Israel's exodus from Egypt. It opens with its narratives of "Adam" ("man") and "Eve" ("mother of living"), of Cain ("I have gotten") and Abel ("breath"), of Enosh ("human") and the sons of God who "take" daughters of men as wives (6:2). Barely six chapters later, a cataclysmic flood appears to reset the narrative and return us to a new beginning, with Noah heading up a new "first family," as one might say. All of these, along with many other aspects of the opening chapters of the book, play no further role in the Old Testament; they are not even mentioned. And then it becomes specific and focuses on one man, Abram (exalted father), and the trials and successes of him and his family and the generations that follow after him. The book becomes an extended tale of an extended family, focusing on themes of blessing (12:1–3), covenant (chs. 15 and 17), and the pursuit of a land that is barely in view by the end of its closing chapter. Indeed, its lengthy final narrative of Joseph and his brothers relocates the setting to Egypt and seems to put the major hopes of the Israelites in a fairly precarious state, raising instead the issues of how the people of God are to understand and act within the circumstance of finding themselves a long way from home, and equally far from the fulfillment of the promise. Some of these features of the book are key to understanding it well. At the same time, like any great narrative, it will always remain more probing and productive of fresh insight than any analysis of its constituent parts or themes.

Hermeneutical theory offers us the insight that there is a difference to be pondered here between the tasks of *understanding* Genesis and of *explaining* Genesis.[2] Explanations typically seek to offer an account of the text in such a way that all of it is fitted into the explanatory framework, which can then sometimes replace the text itself with its own paraphrase or theoretical way of looking at it. Thus, for example, one could suggest that the Joseph story was written to respond to life in exile as it was later experienced in the sixth century BCE, and then go on to interpret all the details of the story to fit this hypothesis. In contrast, understandings offer ways of looking at the text that draw out some aspects of its purpose and coherence from some readers' perspectives, without necessarily prejudging other ways of interpreting that would draw out other aspects. Hence, to understand the Joseph story in the way just noted need not mean that one

---

2. The difference is theorized in various (incompatible!) ways, but most helpful to my mind is Paul Ricoeur, *Interpretation Theory: Discourse and the Surplus of Meaning* (Fort Worth: Texas Christian University Press, 1976), 71–88, who urges that interpretation (of written texts) is the dialectic of both understanding and explanation.

has *the* correct account of the historical origin of the written narrative. In turn, understandings can often generate further insights into new possible explanations—leading in turn to ways of reading that will also render coherent the text before us. If one pursues explanations alone, key though they are to accurate handling of the textual data, it can tend to offer the spectacle of a "survival of the fittest" as old theories fall by the wayside. In my judgment, theological interest in the scriptural text invites us to focus at least as much on understandings as on explanations, enabling one to move on from an account of how the text came to be before us, toward asking how one might read it well today. In this chapter we will seek the path of theological understanding of (some aspects of) the book of Genesis: inevitably partial and open to development, but nevertheless focused on highlighting aspects of its theological coherence and challenge for today's readers. In the words of Mark Brett, "The laconic style of Genesis, and its opacities and ambiguities, suggest that we can engage with it only partially: we can never exhaust . . . its meaning."[3]

Outline of Genesis

The book begins with creation. In particular, it offers a story-poem of a seven-day creation of "the heavens and the earth" (1:1), carefully structured to bring out the order and fittingness of the ecosystem described. The unfortunate chapter break after the creation of humanity on the sixth day obscures the more likely intention of marking the climax of creation as the Sabbath, the day of rest, the seventh and final day of the story (whereas, as the chapters now stand, it is easy to read Genesis 1 as suggesting that humans were the high point). Creation points to God, and God deems it very good. Indeed, so strong is this overall impression that it persists even if one observes that Genesis 1:3–5 leaves the strong sense that the darkness is not good, perhaps as an indicator of the "chaos" against which creation is set.[4]

There follows immediately a phrase that will recur throughout the book: "These are the generations (*toledot*) of . . ." (2:4). The plural noun *toledot* derives from the verb *yld*, "to give birth to or bear," or, more traditionally, "to beget," although many modern translations offer a range of words across the book such as "generations," "descendants," or "story." Its elevenfold repetition through the book seems to create a sense of literary episodes occurring in a

3. Mark G. Brett, *Genesis*, Old Testament Readings (London and New York: Routledge, 2000), 3–4.
4. On such a reading, creation is life brought out of the "nothing" of unformed chaos; cf. Jon D. Levenson, *Creation and the Persistence of Evil: The Jewish Drama of Divine Omnipotence*, rev. ed. (Princeton, NJ: Princeton University Press, 1994). For light in Gen. 1 as divine (uncreated) light, see Mark S. Smith, *The Priestly Vision of Genesis 1* (Minneapolis: Fortress, 2010), 71–79.

carefully structured narrative.[5] The phrase is more or less absent elsewhere.[6] It is common for analyses of Genesis to rely in some way or other on these "generational markers." However, despite the obvious appeal of this move on a formal or structural level, it is not straightforwardly apparent how the phrase meaningfully orders the account as a whole. Certainly it serves to underline a coherence between chapters 1 and 11 and 12 and 50, though it has been debated as to whether this is to highlight a continuity between them or rather to draw them into the same frame of reference, for the purpose of emphasizing contrasting perspectives.[7] One function of the "generations of" formula is perhaps to emphasize the focus on the particular people through whom the narrative unfolds, gradually narrowing the notion of a chosen people as the book progresses.[8]

In terms of what takes up the bulk of the narrative, a simpler set of divisions might capture the basic movement of the finished book, whereby chapters 1–11 constitute a so-called primeval narrative, set outside the parameters of Israel as a focus; and then chapters 12–50 offer "ancestral narratives," focusing on three major figures in one family line: Abraham (chs. 12–25), Jacob (27–35), and Joseph (37–50). Walter Brueggemann structures his commentary around this fourfold division and thematizes it as concerning the core notion of "the call of God." That call is "sovereign" in the opening chapters; "embraced" by Abraham; "conflicted" in the life and experience of Jacob; and then "hidden" in the Joseph narrative in that, as is often observed, the God who has spoken and interacted with all the major characters thus far is not represented as speaking directly with Joseph.[9] Although one need not want to characterize the four sections in precisely this way, this is a helpful example of a reading that tries to discern some key theological aspects of the text. Of all the characters in the book, Abraham represents the original model of obedience to God's word alongside receipt of God's promise; while in certain senses Jacob is Israel personified. For Jacob, one should note especially a narrative like 32:22–32, wherein he "wrestles with God" but will not let his adversary go without being blessed by him (v. 26). During this contest he is specifically given the name "Israel" (v. 28). It has always been something of a puzzle why

---

5. In Gen. 2:4; 5:1; 6:9; 10:1; 11:10; 11:27; 25:12; 25:19; 36:1; 36:9; 37:2. Note that 5:1 reads, "This is the book/list [sefer] of the toledot of . . ."

6. The only other OT occurrences are Num. 3:1; Ruth 4:18; and (with "their") 1 Chron. 1:29.

7. See the helpful discussion of Josef Schreiner, "תולדות [toledot]," TDOT 15: 582–88; he works with the standard scholarly assumption that all occurrences of the word are from P.

8. For an exploration of this idea, see Nathan MacDonald, "Did God Choose the Patriarchs? Reading for Election in the Book of Genesis," in Genesis and Christian Theology, ed. Nathan MacDonald, Mark W. Elliott, and Grant Macaskill (Grand Rapids: Eerdmans, forthcoming). MacDonald notes that such a view of the book is more commonly held by Jewish interpreters than Christian ones.

9. Walter Brueggemann, Genesis, Interpretation (Atlanta: John Knox, 1982), 8–10, and throughout.

the book ends with such a long, continuous narrative about Joseph, who is only rarely mentioned outside Genesis. However, here it might be observed that the final "generations" marker in the text is at 37:2, and in fact describes this section of the book as "the *toledot* of Jacob" (which the NRSV deals with by translating as "the story of the family of Jacob"). Perhaps this gives a clearer idea of the way this story is understood to fit into the larger scheme of Genesis, as a story with a "corporate focus."[10] We shall return to the theme of family below.

Two final notes on this discussion. First, some stories disrupt any attempt to offer an overly simplistic map of the narrative as a whole (such as the story of Tamar and Judah in ch. 38). Second, and more generally, it is odd that so much biblical commentary is concerned to provide analytical charts of how a book is "structured." The narrative of Genesis does not have a single structure within it, if only because narrative in general does not work that way. On another occasion such an assertion might invite some theoretical justification before the massed ranks of those who like to "chart" or "outline" their biblical books (a practice that probably makes sense mainly on structuralist assumptions). Yet here we shall note only the relatively straightforward point made by Peter Leithart, that "multiple structure is virtually inescapable, especially in narratives and poetry," and that there are in general a wide variety of possible structures depending on the point being brought into focus.[11]

Genesis in the Canon

Genesis comes first. Its canonical location is both so striking and yet so obvious that one almost forgets to reflect on the significance of its placement. But since the work of Brevard Childs and others, part of the changing frame of reference in Old Testament studies involves adding a "canonical perspective" to all the other ways in which the text invites the reader's engagement.[12] Such a focus presumes upon the point that the production of the book of Genesis was long and drawn out before finally being brought together at some point in Israel's history. Sometimes this has taken the form of arguments about the integration of different narrative "cycles" into the finished whole. The model

---

10. So Terence E. Fretheim, "The Book of Genesis," in *NIB* 1:319–674, esp. 592, also 598. Yet this possibility is not particularly supported by a comparison of the other "generations" headings: it is striking that none of the headings mention Abra(ha)m, for example.

11. See the elegant discussion by Peter J. Leithart, *Deep Exegesis: The Mystery of Reading Scripture* (Waco: Baylor University Press, 2009), 141–71, here 143.

12. The key text remains Brevard S. Childs, *Introduction to the Old Testament as Scripture* (Philadelphia: Fortress, 1979). A fine analysis of what is at stake in the area is offered by Christopher R. Seitz, "The Canonical Approach and Theological Interpretation," in *Canon and Biblical Interpretation*, Scripture and Hermeneutics Series 7, ed. Craig Bartholomew et al. (Grand Rapids: Zondervan and Carlisle: Paternoster 2006), 58–110.

for this process has sometimes focused on the integration of literary sources (as in the JEDP hypothesis), and at other times on the oral traditions by which stories have been passed down in Israel from generation to generation (before being drawn into literary units), the focus of Hermann Gunkel's significant work on Genesis.[13] On either account, the book we have at the beginning of the canon is the achievement of some redactor(s), and in addition there is clear evidence of editorial adjustment occurring over a period of time, such as in the asides to the readers like Genesis 12:6, "At that time the Canaanites were in the land." Although this is not the place for a discussion of all these issues, the overall conclusion is clear, as stated by Childs in his introduction to Genesis: "It has become increasingly obvious that a complex literary history preceded the present structure."[14]

Once granted, such a perspective opens up the possibility of reflecting on why the book has been given the shape and position in the canon that it now occupies. With regard to shape, Childs follows the above observation with "Yet it is also clear that the present order has often assigned a different role to a passage from that which it originally performed."[15]

With regard to canonical location, the case of Genesis is simplified by the basic observation that it has always and only come first. But as with the analysis of the composition of Genesis, so also with the composition of the whole Old Testament: that Genesis comes first is not the same as saying that it was written first. In fact, as noted above, many of its most famous stories and figures appear either not at all or relatively little in the rest of the Old Testament. One of the simplest ways to account for this historically is to suppose that there was no "book of Genesis" quite as we now have it, standing at the head of any collection of holy scriptures that might have been around in preexilic Israel. Scholars who have dated the book (in its final written form) to the Persian period, perhaps in the fifth century BCE, are offering an account that makes good sense of the fact that these stories are not appealed to elsewhere in the canon. This is particularly true of Genesis 1–11; yet with the notable exception of Psalm 105, relatively few Old Testament texts mention many of the other characters from elsewhere in Genesis either. And where they do, it is not to point to any sort of narrative or structuring of the accounts of their exploits (which in some ways Ps. 105 *does* do) so much as to draw on what could well be independent "story units" referring, with little narrative context, to Abraham or Jacob.[16] Such references point to the circulation of

13. On JEDP, see the brief account in the introduction to the present volume. Gunkel's work is found in the introduction to his major 1901 commentary on Genesis translated as Hermann Gunkel, *Genesis*, trans. Mark E. Biddle, Mercer Library of Biblical Studies (Macon, GA: Mercer University Press, 1997).

14. Childs, *Introduction*, 149.

15. Ibid.

16. Examples include Isa. 51:2 (for Abraham) and Hosea 12:2–4 (for Jacob).

stories that later become part of the canonical Genesis, but not to an early completed book of Genesis. All this shows that canonical readings are deeply implicated in various sorts of historical investigation, and in the process they open up productive theological lines of inquiry. A canonical approach suggests that instead of just "being first," and being a book of "beginnings" somewhat by default, the book of Genesis is deliberately first, placed there for (perhaps) some theological reasons.

How then might one reflect on the book's present canonical location? We may consider several examples of how some theological issues are thrown into sharper relief when seen this way. Creation itself is an obvious example. Whatever one concludes with regard to the historical rise of a belief in creation in Israel, which is usually dated relatively late in its development, and which takes different forms at different times, the net effect of beginning Scripture with Genesis 1 is to realign the overall perspective in strongly creation-focused terms. In the midst of many other things that a careful reader of the Old Testament will want to say about creation, the inherently peaceful and ordered account of Genesis 1 is given an undeniable prominence by its canonical location.[17] Second, Genesis is somewhat unusual in the Old Testament for its largely familial frame of reference. Does this suggest an emphasis on the significance of theological reflection on family life? We shall consider this particular topic later.

Other points of theological reflection are also given canonical emphasis. Is the book, and especially chapters 1–11, designed to provoke the reader of Scripture to retain a wider (global?) frame of reference as the setting of the story of Israel? For much of Israel's history, it may have been conceptually straightforward to think of YHWH as the God of Israel, and indeed of the land of Israel, but around the time of the exile, one can see how Israel's sense of its own position among the nations of the world would have been a pressing question. It is striking to reflect that Israel's Scriptures did not begin with any claim that it was the first nation, or the original location of God's walking the earth, or the location of the creation of the first people. Other examples of canonical emphasis could be given: consider the way that having Genesis first foregrounds questions of blessing, covenant, land, pilgrimage, and so forth.

Another level at which a canonical analysis is relevant concerns the ways in which Genesis is deliberately taken up in the New Testament. Christian and Jewish perspectives clearly pull in somewhat different directions at this point.[18] Here, in contrast to its historically late position in the Old Testament (relatively speaking), Genesis does stand at the head of Scripture when the

---

17. See William P. Brown, *The Seven Pillars of Creation: The Bible, Science, and the Ecology of Wonder* (New York: Oxford University Press, 2010), 6 (and passim), for reflection on the differing emphases in different situations (and 33–77 on Gen. 1); cf. also Levenson, *Creation*.

18. One might suggest that they part company entirely, but it is preferable to say that what remains "canonical" in Christian terms is treated as part of the (still-illuminating) later reception of the texts in Jewish terms.

New Testament writers think their way theologically through the issues at hand. Genesis 1 finds resonance in various discussions of creation in the New Testament, notably John 1. The phrase "image of God" is taken up and applied to Jesus (Col. 1:15). Paul draws considerable theological mileage out of a comparison between Adam as the first man and Christ as a second Adam (Rom. 5:12–21; 1 Cor. 15). First Timothy 2 makes notorious use of Adam and Eve in its discussion of men and women. First John 3 reflects upon the Cain and Abel story. Both Jesus and the letters of Peter try to impress upon their hearers the urgency of the present moment by appeal to the "days of Noah" and the story of the flood (Matt. 24:36–44//Luke 17:26–27; 1 Pet. 3:18–22; 2 Pet. 2 and 3). There are also several other references and allusions to aspects of Genesis 1–11 in the New Testament, such as Jesus' reference to Genesis 2:24 in his discussion of divorce (Matt. 19:5//Mark 10:7), or the sending out of the seventy (or seventy-two) in Luke 10, which perhaps envisages a geographical mission to match the spread of the table of nations from Genesis 10.[19] With regard to the later ancestral narratives, space does not permit an account of the major significance of Abraham in the New Testament. While no other characters are discussed at anything like that length, there is significant reflection upon the characters of Sarah, Hagar, Lot, Jacob, Esau, Isaac, and even, in Hebrews 5–7, Melchizedek. In addition to all of these references, we also find two narrative recountings of much of the overall story of Genesis, in Acts 7:2–16 and Hebrews 11:2–22, each bringing out different elements for their own purposes.

So embedded is this network of references and resonances throughout Scripture that it is impossible to imagine the Bible today without the theological contribution made by its first book.

What Keeps Genesis in Focus? Genesis and Its Readers

Several factors have kept Genesis as the focus of scholarly attention through the history of its interpretation. First, some of these factors are concerns driven by the world in which the book's interpreters live. So, for instance, the Genesis accounts of creation pitch it squarely into the arena now occupied by perennial science-versus-faith debates, which provoke ever-renewed attention to matters of chronology and geology as they are illuminated (or otherwise!) in the text.[20]

Second, the global purview of Genesis 1–11 renders its accounts of such topics as sin, death, guilt (or better, shame)—as well as the ecological issues

19. The contested nature of some NT appeals to the OT should not obscure the nevertheless impressive quantity of such allusions. For overviews of the various issues on a case-by-case basis, see G. K. Beale and D. A. Carson, eds., *Commentary on the New Testament Use of the Old Testament* (Grand Rapids: Baker Academic, 2007).

20. See now some of the essays gathered in Stephen C. Barton and David Wilkinson, eds., *Reading Genesis after Darwin* (New York: Oxford University Press, 2009).

foregrounded in the flood narrative—as matters of more or less direct concern to those in today's world. This is true even for those who harbor no direct interests or opinions on matters of Judeo-Christian identity and tradition, but who nevertheless live every day with exactly these sorts of wider issues impinging on their consciousness. In this sense, Genesis 1–11 at least remains a text of relevance to all, alongside other accounts of creation and its ongoing significance that survive from anywhere else. One could broaden this second area with reference to many particular matters of ethical significance that continue to elicit dialogue with specific texts from the whole of Genesis. One thinks, for example, of the ongoing attention paid to the Sodom story (Gen. 19) in attempts to understand the evaluation of sexual activity in same-sex settings. Whatever one concludes about this text or its relevance at the end of such a study, the fact is that scholarship persists with such endeavors.[21]

A third factor securing the continued focus of attention on Genesis is its relevance to interfaith discussions. Insofar as the Qur'an interrelates with Judeo-Christian Scripture, it is the book of Genesis that is especially in view. On the simplest level, Abraham is a figure of huge significance to Jews, Christians, and Muslims. A probing study of the way in which this significance is drawn out in the three differing faith traditions is offered by Jon Levenson, who ably shows that each tradition (perhaps unsurprisingly) focuses on the aspects of the Abraham story that best fit its own framework for understanding life and faith before God in more general terms. Thus Christians, following Paul (and perhaps often Luther), tend to emphasize that the promise precedes the righteous requirements of obedience found in the Torah, with the result that faith in the promise and the life required in response are sometimes *contrasted* rather than held together. Jewish scholars, however, have often focused on precursors of just such righteous requirements as they are found in the Abraham story (e.g., as in Gen. 18:17–19). Levenson concludes, "Efforts to refashion Abraham in the image of the religions that claim him have been the norm."[22] Genesis thus remains a text at the very center of the ongoing interfaith study project known as "Scriptural Reasoning," where Christian, Jewish, and Islamic scholars gather around scriptural texts together.[23] This is only likely to become an increasing emphasis amid the developing religious and political realities of the twenty-first-century world.

21. For a balanced assessment of the relevance of its "testimony" (her term) on this matter, see Phyllis A. Bird, "The Bible in Christian Ethical Deliberation concerning Homosexuality: Old Testament Contributions," in *Homosexuality, Science, and the "Plain Sense" of Scripture*, ed. David L. Balch (Grand Rapids: Eerdmans, 2000), 142–76, esp. 147–49.

22. See Jon D. Levenson, "The Conversion of Abraham to Judaism, Christianity, and Islam," in *The Idea of Biblical Interpretation: Essays in Honor of James L. Kugel*, ed. Hindy Najman and Judith Newman (Leiden: Brill, 2004), 3–40, here 18.

23. A useful orientation to this project is given in David F. Ford and C. C. Pecknold, eds., *The Promise of Scriptural Reasoning* (Oxford: Blackwell, 2006).

However, there are other reasons why Genesis remains a focus of scholarly attention—reasons driven by patient attention to the text itself, rather than by other commitments in the interpreter's frame of reference today. Among the many such issues, it is to those of a more overtly theological nature that we now turn.

Some Theological Interests of Genesis

The book of Genesis has been unusually well served for theologically oriented commentary, not just through the centuries but also notably in the heyday of the modern period. Twentieth-century commentaries by Westermann, von Rad, Sarna, Brueggemann, and Fretheim could all, in their different ways, be called theologically interested.[24] What is it that has facilitated such engagement? Is it partly due to the fact that in Genesis, God is a direct actor in so much of the narrative? While this does in turn raise many probing questions about how best to understand the text when it talks of God's action and speech (and indeed God's speech as action), it does mean that commentary on Genesis, at least when it has wanted to stay within the contours of the world imagined by the text, has tended to contain a pronounced theological element.

Recently this has taken the form of a full-scale theological reflection on the book in Russell Reno's "Theological Commentary," which models a practice of thinking through the text of Genesis in a manner that self-consciously explores how Genesis both illuminates and is illuminated by Christian tradition.[25] Reno's discussion ranges over points where the two are in notable harmony (e.g., with respect to the significance accorded to the Sabbath),[26] as well as points of tension or disharmony—one thinks of his spirited discussion of "creation ex nihilo" as a framework for rightly reading Genesis 1.[27] Reno's work is interesting because it explicitly seeks to harness Genesis to the church's theological task. Perhaps it is more of a work of theology in dialogue with aspects of the text of Genesis rather than a commentary per se, and arguably it is none the worse for that.

However, if the goal is theological interpretation *of the text* rather than just theology in dialogue with the text, it is important to understand the integrated

24. See the brief recommendations of these and other works in R. W. L. Moberly, *The Theology of the Book of Genesis*, Old Testament Theology (Cambridge: Cambridge University Press, 2009), 247–49.

25. Russell R. Reno, *Genesis*, Brazos Theological Commentary on the Bible (Grand Rapids: Brazos, 2010).

26. Ibid., 60–64.

27. Ibid., 39–46. Levenson, *Creation*, perhaps still offers the best way of thinking about how Gen. 1 might be read as a creation ex nihilo text, by rethinking what "nothing" might mean (cf. n. 4 above).

nature of this task as it pertains to theological and exegetical study. Theological interest, in short, need not be understood as bypassing critical engagement with the text. In his introduction to the theology of the book, Walter Moberly suggests that the various dimensions of the interpretive task be woven together in what he labels "a" (rather than "the") canonical approach: "The most fruitful approach for theology, I suggest, is to try to recapture the traditional premodern issue, which relates to the role of Genesis as it has been preserved within the Pentateuch, in a way that also takes seriously the religio-historical insights of characteristic modern scholarship, which relates to the possible origins, development, and ancient function of the Genesis text."[28]

Such an observation still leaves open many different angles of approach, as we shall see in a brief discussion of some themes of theological interest in reading Genesis. We shall first consider two of the many topics brought before us in the text of Genesis: family and blessing. Much also depends, though, on the frameworks within which one is reading the book. So we then consider two such broader concerns where the presenting issue is in some ways brought into focus by reading the book in a broader context: first with regard to a comparison between God and the life of faith in Genesis as against the rest of the Old Testament; and second with regard to the unusual nature of Genesis 1–11, which we shall consider as a prologue, or introduction, to the whole of Scripture.

Genesis and the Family

We have already recognized the unusual prominence given to the family in the book. In his major commentary Claus Westermann drew out interesting aspects of this in his overview of the "patriarchal narratives,"[29] which make up chapters 12–50. He suggested that the three main textual units we identified earlier (relating broadly to Abraham, Jacob, and Joseph) represent three stages, deliberately composed together in this way, that draw out different aspects of "what was permanent and typical of the family": the focus in the Abrahamic narratives is on the parent-child relationship, with a theme of life and death (and in particular, barrenness); then in the Jacob-Esau section is the turn to consider the many conflicting aspects of the brother-brother relationship; and finally in the Joseph narrative is the additional dimension of one brother's relating to many others, alongside concerns with kingship and state.[30] Linked to the familial setting of the narratives are many of the distinctive themes of Genesis in the Old Testament: that the father figure in the family serves in

28. Moberly, *Theology of the Book of Genesis*, 130–31.

29. Gender sensitivity—and the fact that these narratives so closely follow not only the fathers but also the mothers of Israel—has led to this term "ancestral narratives" in recent discussion.

30. Claus Westermann, *Genesis 12–36: A Commentary*, trans. John J. Scullion (Minneapolis: Fortress, 1985), 29.

the priestly role, being the one to bless or withhold blessing; and that worship and sacrifice can take place wherever and however the head of the family chooses. As von Rad expressed it, the family is the common factor of all these narratives, and the family in Genesis is understood as "the total sphere of all human communal life; it is the framework of all human activity, politics and economics as well as religion."[31] Though von Rad's interests lay elsewhere, in tracing the tradition-history of these family reflections, he did thereby powerfully describe how these family narratives had been molded and shaped through their transmission. Thus in Genesis they formed a literary work that looked back precisely in order to provoke the readers' thoughts about their own lives with God. Such texts then "become the witness of a past, and at the same time completely contemporary, act of God."[32]

As it happens, the Genesis witness to a God at work in human families takes on unexpected resonance in today's world, not least in part due to the ways in which Christian readers shape their preunderstanding of the text with strong convictions about family life, or "family values," as the politically loaded term has it. In his article "Genesis and Family Values," David Petersen took precisely this theme in his reading of Genesis as a kind of "family novel."[33] The first book of Holy Scripture, he notes, does not look like much of a mandate for what often passes as "family values" today, and yet it still speaks profoundly to many of the same concerns that do motivate current reflection on the family. Petersen draws out three points in particular: first, Genesis values humanity as a family, in an expansive (nonnuclear) view (referring in particular to 12:1–3); second, Genesis emphasizes the continuity of the family over time; and third, throughout there is a noteworthy focus on conflict and resolution. This last point is clearly one with tremendous resonance today. Petersen comments, pointedly, that for all the moral problems readers today have with Old Testament texts, the book of Genesis steadfastly testifies to family conflict resolution without physical violence in a world where such resolution is repeatedly much needed.

It is also often noted that the narrative development through Genesis does not smoothly follow the expected line of family progression, from father to firstborn son at the turn of each generation. Rather, the expected recipient of any such blessing is often not the one who turns out to be favored, and frequently Genesis tells the story of the "unfavored" figure first before turning to its next focal figure: Ishmael before Isaac, Esau before Jacob, in a pattern found in chapters 1–11 as well (e.g., the story of the wicked people of the earth in ch. 6 before the story of righteous Noah and his family). This device even

31. Gerhard von Rad, *Genesis*, Old Testament Library, rev. ed. (London: SCM, 1972), 34–35.
32. Ibid., 35.
33. David L. Petersen, "Genesis and Family Values," *Journal of Biblical Literature* 124 (2005): 5–23. This was his 2004 SBL presidential address, perhaps rightly underlining the significance of this topic for contemporary theological reflection.

extends to the book's genealogical interludes.[34] The notion that family life contains frequent reversals, surprises, or shifts in the balance of relationships, which is tied inextricably with reflection on God's freedom to elect whomever God pleases, may also contribute to reflection on the kinds of issues in family life that Petersen's study considers.

There is no space to reflect comparably on the ways in which Genesis resources our theological reflection on broader questions of male and female, and of gender in general. In a celebrated tour de force, Phyllis Trible rereads the Eden story to suggest that the text does not push the reader to patriarchal conclusions, but rather envisages a male and female created to be in a relationship of appropriate mutuality.[35] In contrast, many have suggested that Genesis simply reflects its patriarchal assumptions back to the reader without particular subtlety or the promise of surprising insights. A recent thorough study of all the actions attributed to women in Genesis, and all the descriptions applied to them, tends toward a conclusion that "the focus in Genesis is whether they can bear [children], who provides their fertility, and what circumstances allow them to become pregnant. The physical act of bearing, not motherhood, is the issue."[36] Refocused within the prominent theme of family in Genesis, this remains a significant if circumscribed role, and much could still be learned about the complex practices of family life, for both men and women, by continuing to attend to the perspective of Genesis on these matters.

Genesis and Blessing

It is sometimes said that Genesis 12:1–3 is not just a significant text in Genesis but even a programmatic text for the whole of the Old Testament, and indeed Christian Scripture. Christopher Wright places great emphasis on this "pivotal text" in his "missiological reading" of the whole Bible, seeing it as the turning point from the "bleak narratives" of Genesis 1–11 toward the story of God's mission, which will unfold in the rest of the whole canon.[37] The logic is clear: the calling out of Abraham sets in motion the specific story of Israel, whose divinely ordained job is to be "a light to the gentiles," leading the way in showing how a people might live for the glory of God. Taken up into the New Testament,

34. See, e.g., Gordon J. Wenham, *Genesis 16–50*, Word Biblical Commentary 2 (Waco: Word, 1994), 162, writing in this instance on 25:12–18.

35. Phyllis Trible, "A Love Story Gone Awry," in *God and the Rhetoric of Sexuality*, Overtures to Biblical Theology (Philadelphia: Fortress, 1978), 72–143.

36. Tammi J. Schneider, *Mothers of Promise: Women in the Book of Genesis* (Grand Rapids: Baker Academic, 2008), 218.

37. Christopher J. H. Wright, *The Mission of God: Unlocking the Bible's Grand Narrative* (Nottingham, UK: Inter-Varsity, 2006), 191–221, esp. 194–95. Interestingly, this perspective requires a very bleak reading indeed of the Babel narrative (ibid., 198), which we shall have cause to question at the end of the present chapter.

the calling of Abraham (and then Israel) is seen to be a key instrument in the unfolding plan of a God whose overall desire is always to bless everyone. Jewish scholars in particular, though also several Christian ones, have responded that such a reading sees God's election of Israel in *instrumental* terms, as a means to an end, and rather neglects the blessing in itself, which was uniquely Israel's, as God's elect people.[38] The "missiological" (or at least Christian) readings that want to see 12:1–3 leading directly on to its Christian fulfillment can sometimes be concerned with tracing how that promise to Abraham is in frequent jeopardy through the book and remains largely unfulfilled by the end. This offers a helpful way of following the narrative through its different twists and turns, in the familial saga that then plays out, either leading toward or pulling away from the resolution of the "plot" set in motion by the promise to Abraham. Ironically, one of the elements that can become lost in such perspectives is the present reality of blessing as it is experienced (in Genesis, yet also more generally).[39]

Blessing is a major theme in Genesis. Not only is Abraham blessed in 12:2 in terms of becoming "a great nation," such that in him "all the families of the earth shall be blessed" (12:2–3),[40] but there also are many other instances of specific divine and familial blessing in the narratives. Notable points of focus on blessing include the wrestling encounter where Jacob is named Israel (32:26, 29), and climactically in two full chapters where Jacob is engaged in blessing his sons (chs. 48–49, noting esp. 49:28).

Yet *blessing* remains one of those words more easily understood than defined.[41] To bless is to convey some kind of benefit, but the focus is perhaps less on the benefit and more on the life or relationship thus benefited. Indeed, blessing can sometimes be the enriching of a life by the very act of stating or emphasizing a relationship. In their dynamic celebration of "theology as praise," Hardy and Ford write movingly of what it means to bless God: "Blessing is the comprehensive praise and thanks that returns all reality to God, and so lets all be taken up into the spiral of mutual appreciation and delight which is the fulfilment of creation. For the rabbis of Jesus' time, to use anything of creation without blessing God was to rob God. Only the person receiving with thanks really received from God."[42] Several aspects of blessing are in the foreground here: mutuality

38. For a full discussion and review of the options, see Moberly, *Theology of the Book of Genesis*, 141–61.

39. A succinct overview of "blessing" (and some of the secondary literature) is offered by Keith Grüneberg, *Blessing: Biblical Meaning and Pastoral Practice*, Grove Biblical Books B27 (Cambridge: Grove Books, 2003).

40. Or "bless themselves." All commentaries rehearse this translation crux, which need not detain us here.

41. The next four paragraphs draw on my "Speech-Act Theory," in *Words and the Word: Explorations in Biblical Interpretation and Literary Theory*, ed. David G. Firth and Jamie A. Grant (Nottingham, UK: Apollos, 2008), 75–110, here esp. 82–85.

42. Daniel W. Hardy and David F. Ford, *Praising and Knowing God* (Philadelphia: Westminster, 1985), 81.

and receptivity among them. To receive a blessing may involve material things or offspring, but even these would be a blessing only if accompanied by the transformation of spirit and attitude that allows them to be received with thanks. In general, we may say that whether something or some event is a blessing depends significantly (though not exclusively) on how it is perceived. This is even true of those archetypal elements of Old Testament blessing: land and offspring.

This notion of blessing helps to make sense of the story of Isaac's blessing of his sons in Genesis 27. Isaac offers to bless Esau (v. 4), but Rebekah contrives to have Jacob appear before him under the pretense of being Esau in order to acquire this paternal blessing for himself. Isaac, thereby fooled, duly gives his blessing to Jacob, including the declarative "Let peoples serve you, and nations bow down to you. Be lord over your brothers" (v. 29). At that point Esau enters, and Jacob's deception is uncovered. "Bless me, me also, father!" cries Esau (v. 34). But in a move that easily puzzles many interpreters, Isaac replies, "Your brother came deceitfully, and he has taken away your blessing" (v. 35). Many modern readers then quickly side with Esau: given that this seems so unfair of Jacob, why can his father not simply reverse or restore the blessing to its intended recipient? Failing that, can he at least have another blessing in any case? It is this last, less satisfactory, option that Isaac feels able to bestow.

The reason for this "resolution" is to be found in the performative nature of blessing rather than in any supposedly primitive view of "word-magic."[43] Blessing is more like an aspect of a relationship than the awarding of a medal. In the Olympics, awards can be given and taken away, as Job might have said. But in Genesis 27, no convention was apparently in place for the withdrawal of the blessing; one reason for this is that with Jacob's having fled the scene, it is not actually possible for him to be recalled to account in order to be told that he has acted deceitfully. As Thiselton observes, "To give the same blessing to Esau would be like saying 'I do' to a second bride," an example that happens to make it very clear that such an impossibility is socially constructed rather than logically impossible, given the existence of polygamous practice in Genesis, as indeed seen in Esau's subsequent action in Genesis 28:9![44]

Jacob, however, has escaped with an ill-gotten blessing: rather like stolen cash, it is not useless but is difficult to deploy as part of a life of praise and thanksgiving to God, with all the self-involving implications that has for him. One implication that the narrator surely intends for us to notice is that when Jacob finds himself in the east, at his uncle Laban's house, he works seven years to wed the attractive Rachel, only to wake the next morning and find that he has wed Leah instead (29:25). But just as the performative act of blessing cannot be undone, neither can the performative act of entering into

43. This contrast was first and programmatically made by Anthony C. Thiselton, "The Supposed Power of Words in the Biblical Writings," *Journal of Theological Studies* 25 (1974): 282–99.
44. Ibid., 294.

a marriage covenant, at least not then, or even today on the morning after the vows. Commentators have tended to find this less puzzling than the incident in chapter 27. This is surely because the conventions of saying "I do" (or its ancient equivalent) are better understood than the conventions of blessing.

In due course in the Old Testament, blessing becomes the priestly prerogative, most famously in the Aaronic blessing of Numbers 6:24–26. The familial focus of Genesis, as we saw above, means that it is the head of the house who tends to bless in Genesis. Arguably one of the valuable features of these narratives for today's world is the significance they attach to blessing, or perhaps to the priestly dimension of human existence as shown in the interactions between these characters.

Genesis and Torah: "The Old Testament of the Old Testament"

On a straightforward surface-level reading of Genesis in the context of the ongoing scriptural narrative that proceeds on through Exodus, the Pentateuch, and beyond, one cannot help but notice that the kinds of practices and faith commitments embodied by the lead characters of Genesis are notably different from those found elsewhere in the Old Testament (or indeed in the New Testament). Of course, the framework of life with YHWH is not set forth in terms of the torah or the requirement of torah obedience, since the story has not reached that point yet.[45] But even more so, the ancestors build local altars and worship at sacred trees (and go on their relaxed way); they meet God in person for afternoon tea or indeed wrestle with him; and apparently there are even some household gods among the family baggage at times, although the texts want to make it clear that these are not directly the possession of the patriarchal figure himself.[46] Such characteristics of the text have inspired the rather engaging label "ecumenical bonhomie" to describe this apparently relaxed notion of the life of faith as it is found in Genesis.[47] One cannot imagine such an attitude accompanying later descriptions of major figures trying to pass off their wives as their sisters, for example.

Walter Moberly has offered one compelling way of accounting for this phenomenon, characterizing Genesis as "the Old Testament of the Old Testament."[48] In essence, Genesis is to the rest of the Old Testament as the Old

---

45. Though note that one of the points of Levenson, "Conversion of Abraham," is that torah obedience is there for those with eyes to see it.

46. See, e.g., the mysterious *terafim* mentioned in Gen. 31:19, 34, 35.

47. This oft-cited phrase was coined by Gordon J. Wenham in his article "The Religion of the Patriarchs," in *Essays on the Patriarchal Narratives*, ed. Alan R. Millard and Donald J. Wiseman (Leicester, UK: Inter-Varsity, 1980), 157–88, here 184.

48. R. W. L. Moberly, *The Old Testament of the Old Testament: Patriarchal Narratives and Mosaic Yahwism*, Overtures to Biblical Theology (Minneapolis: Fortress, 1992; repr., Eugene, OR: Wipf & Stock, 2002).

Testament is to the New Testament in later Christian thinking. Thus one finds a mix of discontinuity and continuity, between the "old" text and the later one. The first text remains part of the one sacred narrative of God's people but is not straightforwardly determinative of contemporary faith and practice. Moberly offers an account of how the classic pentateuchal issues of the name of God, in key texts such as Exodus 3 and 6, as well as several other features of the book of Genesis, can all be understood within the framework of Genesis being an earlier period in the divine economy. It is a stimulating account of both Genesis and of the theological construction of Scripture (both Jewish and Christian). The result is to let Genesis speak in its own voice yet also as a coherent part of the whole of Scripture.

Genesis 1–11 as an Introduction to Scripture

So far our discussion of theological elements of Genesis has proceeded mainly with reference to aspects of the ancestral narratives. Yet it would not be difficult to fill a whole book with a discussion entirely focused on chapters 1–11. However, as we have seen, the main themes and concerns of these chapters, including, most obviously, creation itself, are not straightforwardly present in the rest of the book (or the rest of the Old Testament) in anything like the same way. Here I suggest that this may be deliberate, and that one helpful way to make sense of this strangeness of Genesis 1–11 is as a "prologue" or introduction to canonical Scripture.

Andreas Schüle has offered a fine study of Genesis 1–11 titled "the prologue of the Hebrew Bible."[49] His frame of reference is that Genesis 1–11 is inextricably tied to the Scripture that follows it and exhibits what can be called a "canonical consciousness." In historical terms, he sees the work of the final Priestly redactor (P) crafting chapters 1–11 as an introduction to the forthcoming story, meaning the rest of the Hebrew Bible. The role of P in bringing together the final Pentateuch does lend a certain historical plausibility to this proposal. It offers a resolution to the most basic conundrum about Genesis 1–11: that its main points of reference do not recur through the rest of the Old Testament. Further, it is no surprise that the "introduction" should be written last, as any essay writer can attest. More particularly, it fits historically to suggest that the context shaping Genesis 1–11 is Babylon.[50] Schüle explores Genesis 1–11 in a theological vein, alert to the dialogues it sets up with the rest of Jewish Scripture. He works with a notion of P's drawing together prior traditions, which results in his talking of "theologies" of the text, those of

---

49. Andreas Schüle, *Der Prolog der hebräischen Bibel: Der literar- und theologiegeschichtliche Diskurs der Urgeschichte (Genesis 1–11)*, Abhandlungen zur Theologie des Alten und Neuen Testaments 86 (Zurich: Theologischer Verlag Zurich, 2006).

50. We return to this point below in studying the Babel story in Gen. 11.

the P and the non-P material, and he does suggest that there are limits to the topics on which the resulting canonical "introduction" is willing to enter into dialogue (such as eschatology and nationalism, for example, two key scriptural themes that are more or less absent from Gen. 1–11).[51]

I suggest that Schüle's essentially historical and literary-critical "canonical" thesis might be adapted into a general hermeneutical claim about Genesis's role in the two-Testament Christian Bible as a whole. The hermeneutical function served by Genesis 1–11 for the Christian reader is also that of "prologue," but it need not be because the author of any part of the text (e.g., P) thought in those terms. Rather, it is a result of the final location of these chapters at the entrance to the Christian Bible. The result of this placement is that one reads the stories of chapters 1–11 with (at least) a double reference: they describe characters moving in the narrative world of Genesis, in the strange time before Abraham and the beginnings of Israel, yet they also refer forward, as it were, to highlight themes and questions that the reader knows well from later developments. Schüle's argument is in effect a particular version of this idea: the original readers of P would have had these later developments in mind as they read Genesis 1–11. Arguably, though, the hermeneutical effect is the same with regard to today's reader who brings her or his own experience to the text, along with the experiences of readers down through the centuries.

The questions engaged by chapters 1–11 range over such topics as what it means to be made in the image of God; what sin is, or why we sin or hate or murder; how God will respond to this; and what one needs to do or be to escape such judgment. It is worth suggesting that on the whole it is precisely part of the function of Genesis 1–11 to *raise* these questions and provoke the reader to reflect on them, rather than to *answer* them. Forewarned, or at least foreprovoked, the reader then comes to the rest of the Bible with certain key questions in place as hermeneutical guides for the subsequent reading. In some cases, such as with "the image of God," it will not be until the New Testament that the Christian reader is encouraged to move toward a more direct resolution of the question of what this actually means.[52]

Conclusion

We have considered a range of theological interests that are relevant to any reading of the book of Genesis as the first book of Scripture. Some of these interests are straightforward themes found in the text. Others arise as we

51. Schüle, *Der Prolog der hebräischen Bibel*, e.g., 425–30.

52. I consider this specific example and point toward the above general understanding of Gen. 1–11 in my "Humans in the Image of God and Other Things Genesis Does Not Make Clear," *Journal of Theological Interpretation* 4 (2010): 111–26.

reflect on the role of Genesis in wider contexts. All of them are theological: both in the sense of relating to the theological concerns of Genesis itself, and in impinging upon the theological horizons of readers ancient and modern. What then might a theological interpretation of a particular passage in Genesis look like? We turn now to a story that is situated at a key juncture of the book, allowing us to consider issues relevant to both Genesis 1–11 and the book as a whole: the Babel story in Genesis 11.

A Theological Reading of the Babel Story: Genesis 11:1–9

A First Reading

We begin with a more or less "surface level" reading based on the NRSV translation, with minor modifications (indicated by underlined text and explained in the notes). This will tend toward a literarily oriented reading, though we shall deliberately incorporate historical and other data as seems appropriate.

> [1]Now all the earth[a] had one language and the same words. [2]And as they migrated from the east, they came upon a plain in the land of Shinar and settled there.
>
> ---
> [a]The NRSV's "the whole earth" loses the repetition of "all the earth" throughout the passage.

Although the passage immediately follows the "table of nations" in Genesis 10, the opening "Now" simply moves us to the next story rather than tying the text in chronologically. In fact, readers of Genesis 10 are fresh from reading about the descendants of Japheth, Ham, and Shem being described as each "with their own language(s)" in 10:5, 20, and 31, using the more common word *lashon* for tongue or language. Here in verse 1 there is literally "one lip" (*safah*) and the odd expression "one words," with a strange plural form of the word *one*. The NIV helpfully suggests "common speech" as a paraphrase.

Shinar is Babylonia. Already in 10:9–10 readers have encountered Nimrod, of whose kingdom Babel was included as the "beginning" (*reshit*, possibly "head" or "most significant [city]"). Shinar appears a handful of times in the biblical texts, including Daniel 1:2 as the name of the land to which the Babylonians took the temple vessels at the fall of Jerusalem.

An NRSV footnote to verse 2 indicates that the direction of travel is relative. Since we do not know where "they" have come from, *miqqedem* could be rendered "from the east" or "eastward." Either way, maybe the reader hears an echo of Cain settling "east of Eden" in 4:16, and recalls that the narrative is located away from the original place of God's presence.

³And they said to one another, "Come, let us <u>bake</u>ᵇ bricks, and burn them thoroughly." And they had brick for stone, and bitumen for mortar. ⁴Then they said, "Come, let us build ourselves a city, and a tower with its <u>head</u>ᶜ in the heavens, and let us make a name for ourselves; otherwise we shall be <u>scattered</u>ᵈ upon the face of the whole earth."

ᵇIt is impossible to capture the startling assonance of the Hebrew text in translation, which is particularly marked in this verse, but "bake bricks" at least attempts to point in this direction.

ᶜ*Ro'sh*—"head" can be translated "top" (so NRSV), but the NIV's "that reaches to the heavens" is probably more helpfully vague about how this actually works in terms of dimensions.

ᵈThe NRSV adds "abroad" on each of the three occasions the verb "scatter" occurs (here, v. 8, and v. 9), which is elegant though not necessary. I have omitted all three.

The settlers decide to build, and the work takes on a beautifully emphasized repetitive quality as like-sounding words are piled up in quick array. The Hebraic style might be hinted at with a rough translation such as "let us brick bricks, and burn them for burning." Brick, stone, tar, clay, and a city with a mighty tower emerging out of the plain: it may be hard to hear this description today without thinking of the Orcs laboring to build Saruman's kingdom in and around Orthanc, his tower in the plains of Isengard, with all that is symbolized by that in the world of *The Lord of the Rings*.⁵³ Closer to the world of the text, the "baking of bricks" phrase is also found in Exodus 5:7, perhaps suggesting connotations of slavery and hard labor.

Then, acting as one—with the strikingly repeated cohortative verbs "let us"—they decide to construct the city and the tower. "With its head in the heavens" suggests its prominence and self-proclaimed significance, perhaps, rather than a literally minded notion of building so high that they would reach the heavens. This self-proclamation is explicit in the next phrase, "make for ourselves a name." And then crucially, the final clause indicates their goal in terms of not "scattering" over the earth. This word, *scatter (puts)*, has already occurred in Genesis 9:19 (where the whole earth was "peopled" from the sons of Noah) and 10:18. Regardless of how positively or negatively such a scattering is to be understood, it is clear that the central desire, to stay in one place, sits uneasily in Genesis 1–11, where humankind's mandate is to "fill the earth" (1:28). Our passage is, we may note, as much about the building of the city as the tower, which is perhaps to be understood simply as the most extreme manifestation of the desire to stay in one city rather than spread outward.

Thus far the perspective is that of the settlers themselves. Now it is time for YHWH to see what is going on. In a rather nice touch, for all that the city

---

53. Though Tolkien's description is sparing compared to the intense film depiction; see J. R. R. Tolkien, *The Lord of the Rings*, part 1, *The Fellowship of the Ring* (1954; repr., London: HarperCollins, 1992), 278 (in book 2, ch. 2).

was built to reach the heavens, he is presented as having to "come down" to see what all the fuss is about:

> ⁵The Lᴏʀᴅ came down to see the city and the tower, which mortals had built. ⁶And the Lᴏʀᴅ said, "<u>Look, one people!</u>ᵉ And they have all one language; and this is only the beginning of what they will do; nothing that they <u>plot</u>ᶠ to do will now be impossible for them. ⁷Come, let us go down, and confuse their language there, so that they will not understand one another's speech."

> ᵉThe typically laconic Hebrew seems worth capturing here, as if the result of Yʜᴡʜ's descent to see what is happening is a slightly bemused and altogether unhurried divine reflection.
> ᶠYazmu, from zamam, "to plan" (so NIV), but probably with a slightly negative edge, hence NRSV's "propose" seems unduly relaxed.

Yʜᴡʜ is unimpressed, and the narrator rather enjoys telling us about it. "Mortals," the NRSV's leaden gender-inclusive term of preference, translates "the sons of Adam," which perhaps has diminutive connotations in the face of these sons' visions of grandeur in the preceding verses. It also allows the narrator to say *banu bene ha'adam*, skipping over the consonants with barely disguised enjoyment.

The resultant exclamation, "one people," is the first time the word *'am* (people) has been used in Genesis. A word that will come to do plenty of work representing the *'am* of God, in various ways, through long sections of the Scripture to come, seems almost to have been smuggled in by these nondescript settlers, who are referred to in this narrative (and only sparingly) as "they" or "each one." The status as God's people has been preempted by the people's working out how to be "a people" without reference to God, for which the key seems to be the city (with accompanying tower) as a form of self-organization and self-government.

Unhindered by problems of communication, the people will be able to plot as they will and thus do as they will. The solution, therefore, is to undo what appears to be the central point about the city-and-tower project, that it represents a kind of collective will to power on the part of "the people." Verse 7 begins, "Come, let us go down . . . ," and theologians have long pondered the plural voice here, so obviously reminiscent of Genesis 1:26, with all the musing upon the Trinity that this has brought forth.⁵⁴ However, here in the Babel story it seems most likely to be simply a divine riposte to the repeated cohortative "let us" refrain of vv. 3–4. In what is perhaps a mimicry of the humans' speech, Yʜᴡʜ says, "Let us go down." One might imagine this as a formulation of a plan, to be executed in verse 8, or a piece of commentary

---

54. Most OT scholars find the plural "Let us . . ." language of Gen. 1 and 11 to refer to Yʜᴡʜ's addressing his divine council, which, while plausible, may not illuminate Gen. 11 all that much. Arguably the plural "like one of us" in 3:22, the most recent divine plural usage in Genesis, might offer a more helpful comparison, with the shared theme of a threat to a human-divine boundary.

on YHWH's actions supplied by the narrator for the benefit of telling the story. There is little need to suggest that there is a "problem" here with regard to a deity who has already come down (v. 5) now speaking of the need to "go down" (v. 7)—though the tradition is not short of those who would find evidence here of two sources poorly edited together.[55]

The key, though, is language (or again, literally, "lip," as in v. 1), and this YHWH will confuse. Fox offers the translation "Let us baffle their language" in a typically creative way of anticipating the forthcoming wordplay with "Babel" in verse 9.[56] The result, as YHWH imagines it, is that no one will "hear" (*yishm'u*, from *shema'*, "hear") or "understand" anyone else's speech. It is debatable how far this is to say that each person will have a new language or tongue. Brueggemann addresses the heart of the matter by suggesting instead that the point is that "no one will listen to their neighbor." This, as he puts it, switches the issue at hand from "a verbal, semantic problem" to "a covenantal, theological issue."[57]

The text does not explain the link between the confounding of language in verse 7 and the scattering about to occur in verse 8: it simply puts the two together (and does so again in the recap in v. 9). Are they to be understood as two ways of talking about the same thing?

> [8]So the LORD scattered them from there over the face of all the earth, and they left off building the city. [9]Therefore it was called Babel, because there the LORD confused the language of all the earth; and from there the LORD scattered them over the face of all the earth.

The very thing the settler-builders feared, that they would be scattered over the face of all the earth (v. 4), now occurs, and is attributed to the direct action of YHWH. Perhaps that action was the confusing of the language, and perhaps that in turn is to be understood, with Brueggemann, in more general terms as the breakdown of communication. In any case, the building project ceases. It is unclear how much significance should be attributed to the oddity that this third mention of the city, in verse 8 (after vv. 4 and 5), is uniquely not paired with "and a/the tower." Without a doubt the story has passed into tradition as the story of "the tower of Babel," but probably the emphasis on the tower as something separate from the city misses an important aspect of the story, that the gathering in a city is one key element of the problem.

The city is called Babel. As befits a tale about a tower built to the heavens, this revelation effects a vertiginous shift of perspective. The story—which has,

55. With regard to the previous note, it may be helpful to read v. 6 as YHWH's "report" to the divine council, in between visits.

56. Everett Fox, *The Five Books of Moses: A New Translation with Introductions, Commentary, and Notes*, The Schocken Bible, vol. 1 (Dallas: Word, 1995), 49.

57. Brueggemann, *Genesis*, 103.

albeit awkwardly in the light of Genesis 10, narrated events in the time of "all the people" wandering the land east of Eden with a common language—is shifted into a frame that clearly invites its city-tower building project to be understood as Babylon, Israel's great sixth-century oppressor. The word *Babel* (*babel*) brings out the wordplay with the verb *balal* (vv. 7, 9)—confuse, confound, or "baffle" (Fox); thus one might have suggested that the name of the city in verse 9 is "Confusion," except that names are not normally translated. The NRSV retains "Babel" in Genesis 10:10 (though the NIV does not), but elsewhere, on more than two hundred occasions, all translations are impressively uniform: *babel* = Babylon. So at the level of trying to read the story in a historical context, the presenting question is clear: Is this a story about Babylon? Is Babylon its referent? Concomitantly, when and why was it written? And what role does it play now in the eleventh chapter of the book of Genesis?

Finally, the story ends with a recap of the two-sided key to the action of the whole narrative: YHWH's confusing of language and scattering of "them," the generally underdefined settler-builders of the story. There will be no more unanimity of purpose and plotting, yet also there will be no more hiding away in a city when they should be settling the whole earth. This scattering looks like both a punishment and a push that will enable the fulfillment of the commission to fill the earth. The resultant interplay of positive and negative evaluations of this plot development is key to any theological interpretation of the Babel story.

A first reading of the text has already led us to many questions of historical, philological, and theological significance, and in general it has proceeded without reference to the extraordinary mass of secondary literature that has attached itself to this concise text. There are now several points to take up in more detail. First, though, a brief word about how we shall navigate that voluminous secondary literature.

The Shadow of Babel

Perhaps it is fitting that a tower built to the heavens should beget a text that casts its shadow to the ends of the earth. The reception history of Genesis 11:1–9 could fill a very large volume (and go back a very long way, through *3 Baruch*, Josephus, and many others), without even stretching to include all those instances where "Babel" is simply alluded to for its symbolic value. This is a text with extraordinary cultural resonance. On matters of language, culture, and civilization Babel offers an irresistible focal point. From George Steiner's celebrated study of translation (*After Babel*), to Jeffrey Stout's well-known discussion of contemporary ethics (*Ethics after Babel*), and at more or less all stations in between, one can find Babel imagery in many places. And how much more in biblical studies, at every level, from John Collins's *The Bible after Babel*, a survey of "historical criticism in a postmodern age,"[58] through to a delightful pop-up book for children. And so the familiar question arises of how much a writer on a text such as this should advertise his or her awareness of other discussions. I have chosen to take a minimalist route here, focusing on the text itself and referring to other sources only where they have offered particularly helpful or representative views. A recent monograph by André LaCocque runs to nearly two hundred pages of informed analysis from a variety of angles, and includes fifteen pages of small-print bibliography.[59] It is a fine study, even if its detours into psychology and deconstruction seem to me to engage fairly minimally with the work of the Yahwist and treat the text more as a freestanding entity. Maybe there is an irony in the standard biblical studies' mode of referencing secondary literature that an attentive reader of the Babel narrative might ponder. Unlike in some academic disciplines (e.g., much philosophy), writers in biblical studies have traditionally demonstrated their right to add their voices to the tradition by way of exhaustive citation of all who have gone before. The result is an ever-taller tower of footnotes, building one upon the other, yet to what end? The demonstration that all voices have been considered and now an opinion can be offered that commands attention? Meanwhile the text has long since been scattered abroad and is preached on, read meditatively, studied in small groups, and so forth, by many who will never encounter a single such footnote. It may be an uncomfortable question for the scholar to ponder how much interpretive work contributes more to the building of the tower than to the scattering abroad of the wisdom and insight that might allow readers across the whole earth to be blessed.

Locating Babel: Historical and Literary Frames for Reading the Text

Returning to the text, one central theological issue raised in our reading is how one is to construe the theme of "scattering," a question we put in shorthand form as whether the scattering is to be understood positively or negatively. In order to address this inherently theological matter in appropriate engagement with the Genesis text, we shall first explore some of the historical and literary frameworks that may contribute to a wise reading.

We have alluded (above) to the two general directions in which literary readings tend to go, and these are very much the topic of recent scholarly attention. They are helpfully characterized by Ellen van Wolde in her wide-ranging

---

58. The subtitle of a book by John J. Collins, *The Bible after Babel* (Grand Rapids: Eerdmans, 2005).

59. André LaCocque, *The Captivity of Innocence: Babel and the Yahwist* (Eugene, OR: Cascade Books, 2010).

summary of synchronic perspectives on the story.[60] Van Wolde sees the standard "Christian" view as focused on human pride in the wake of the fall; a human "vertical" aspiration to storm the heavens, as it were. This results in a "negative" interpretation, whereby the scattering is (or at least is indicative of) YHWH's displeasure and judgment.[61] She contrasts this with a more Jewish tradition of emphasizing Genesis 11 as a tale of the dispersing of humans over the earth, in response to their predominantly "horizontal" aspiration to stay together in one place.[62] This leads instead to a more "positive" reading whereby the scattering becomes a means to a divinely intended end. She herself has a third rubric under which she wants to read the text: with an emphasis on the face of the earth as the major reference point, rather than any anthropocentric orientation. For van Wolde, indeed, the earth with its oft-mentioned "face" is one of the central "characters" in the primeval history,[63] and her reading imagines the story of Genesis 1–11 as unfolding *toward* the vantage point afforded by the tower, which thus serves as a "lookout" over both Genesis 1–11 and the plains of Shinar. It is the preservation of the earth that is secured by the scattering, in van Wolde's reading.[64]

On a formal, literary level (which is self-consciously her own perspective) this is a striking observation and offers an interesting reading. Clearly, in the text, the earth is a major character. Despite various repetitions of key terms throughout this short piece, there are three subjects that appear more than any other, five times each: YHWH, who appears only at the midpoint of the narrative in a delayed entrance; and then the earth and "language" (in fact, "lip"), which occur in collocation at the beginning and end of the story: verse 1 beginning "the earth was one language," and verse 9 recapping with "YHWH confused all the language of the earth." Van Wolde's perspective offers the thought that it really is "the earth" that "was one language" in verse 1, rather than this being simply a way of referring to the people of Babel (who are undercharacterized in this text and only rarely indicated directly). The result is an ecologically oriented reading that resists anthropocentric categories. In the present time it is not hard to see the theological resonance in this and the potential it offers for a theologically engaged perspective on Genesis 1–11 (and in turn the whole book). Certainly one trend in biblical scholarship is to focus on just these elements of the biblical text and to foreground

60. Ellen van Wolde, "The Tower of Babel as Lookout over Genesis 1–11," in *Words Become Worlds: Semantic Studies of Genesis 1–11*, Biblical Interpretation Series 6 (Leiden: Brill, 1994), 84–109.

61. Ibid., 91–94.

62. Ibid., 100–101.

63. In particular, compare Ellen van Wolde, "Facing the Earth: Primaeval History in a New Perspective," in *The World of Genesis: Persons, Places, Perspectives*, ed. Philip R. Davies and David J. A. Clines, Journal for the Study of the Old Testament: Supplement Series 257 (Sheffield: Sheffield Academic Press, 1998), 22–47.

64. Van Wolde, "Tower of Babel," 104–9.

the questions they raise about humanity's currently problematic relationship with the environment.[65]

There is perhaps a tendency on these issues to polarize the options: some will claim that an earth-focused reading is correct, essential, disastrously overlooked, and so forth; while others will insist that it is a distraction from the core scriptural narrative regarding humanity before God. Doubtless the path of wisdom is precisely to recognize that humanity is created into a complex ecosystem of many variables and many "faces" (to borrow van Wolde's felicitous terminology). Care of the earth is part of care of the human race, and vice versa. It would therefore be no surprise to notice that Genesis neither overestimates nor underestimates the significance of the earth as a "character." In this particular case, though, it may be significant that the middle three of the five references to the earth are in fact all in the context of some form of the phrase "scattered over the face of the whole earth." If the earth is rightly understood as the recipient of this "scattering," then it is humankind that is duly scattered. To summarize: van Wolde helpfully moves the discussion of the positive/negative spectrum of evaluations of the scattering on to a third topic, the earth upon which the scattering takes place, but this is not the same as addressing the scattering directly as a matter of enduring anthropocentric theological significance. In other words, the question remains: as human readers of this text, do we see here the humans as punished or as helpfully pushed out?

Most writers on the Babel narrative address this topic, but from our perspective it is interesting to ask how far they get in addressing it theologically. For some it sets up a binary opposition of options, which inherently invites a postmodern destabilization. Any text that leans two ways invites a deconstruction, and the coincidence of the topics of language and a large construction site (the tower) render this narrative almost irresistible for postmodern biblical scholars as a trigger to talk about deconstruction.[66] Meanwhile the selfsame data, for others, invites a rehabilitation of a source analysis, based on the classic logic that where two perspectives coexist in a text, they come from different sources.

This is not the place to review source-critical options for the Babel narrative, though there is a long tradition of reading its (somewhat elusive) narrative doublets and supposedly varying perspectives as evidence of an amalgamation

---

65. In addition to van Wolde's own work, note the five-volume *Earth Bible* project, including Norman C. Habel and Shirley Wurst, eds., *The Earth Story in Genesis*, Earth Bible 2 (Sheffield: Sheffield Academic Press, 2000); also Ellen F. Davis, *Scripture, Culture, and Agriculture: An Agrarian Reading of the Bible* (Cambridge: Cambridge University Press, 2009).

66. It was the final topic of the Bible and Culture Collective project in the 1990s; cf. Danna Nolan Fewell, "Building Babel," in *Postmodern Interpretations of the Bible: A Reader*, ed. A. K. M. Adam (St. Louis: Chalice, 2001), 1–15. It was also famously one of the few biblical texts discussed by Jacques Derrida, in "Des Tours de Babel," trans. J. F. Graham, *Semeia* 54 (1991): 3–34, though examining Derrida's reading would take us too far afield.

of two or more separate tales, paradigmatically in Gunkel's significant commentary on Genesis.[67] As Baden has shown, such a view is not necessarily invalidated by the success of alternative attempts to read the narrative as a literary whole (such as van Wolde's, for instance); it is not in principle impossible, but just seems rather unlikely in this case. In Baden's perspective, "The more effective argument against Gunkel's theory is a simple source-critical one. Genesis 11:1–9 shows none of the hallmarks of a composite text: contradictions, doublets of other narrative inconsistencies."[68]

A more subtle approach to reading Babel in the context of a source-critical perspective is to recognize that although the Babel narrative itself may be a unity, it is now placed in a conspicuous position in the composite narrative of Genesis 1–11 and beyond, which is at minimum a combination of P and J. This is considered in Harland's reading of "horizontal" and "vertical" perspectives, which allocates the emphasis on sin and punishment (as per van Wolde's typically Christian view) to J, and the perspective on scattering and filling the earth (the more traditionally Jewish option) to P. Harland observes that the former has had some prominence as a result of the predilection of significant Christian commentators (Gunkel, von Rad, and others) to want to read J narratives without reference to P, meaning that 1:28 has not featured strongly as an intertext for 11:1–9. His own view is that the canonical compilation of P and J is to be taken more seriously, with the result that "particular ways of reading the text can lead to different interpretations; . . . method affects how the sin of the tower of Babel is interpreted."[69] Although he describes this approach as moving in a canonical direction, it seems that at the key point, regarding a theological analysis of the narrative as we have it in the canon, it still stops short of asking what is at stake theologically in having these two perspectives together.

These literary-critical perspectives bring us also to ask the more straightforwardly historical question raised above: when might the Babel narrative have been written, and for what purpose? More obviously than with any other Genesis text, 11:1–9 invites us to consider Babylon as the context for its

---

67. See the survey in Claus Westermann, *Genesis 1–11: A Commentary*, trans. John J. Scullion (Minneapolis: Fortress, 1984), 536–39; and Gunkel, *Genesis*, 94–95. This tradition culminates in a four-layer theory propounded in the epic study of Christoph Uehlinger, *Weltreich und "eine Rede": Eine neue Deutung der sogenannten Turmbauerzählung (Gen 11, 1–9)*, Orbis biblicus et orientalis 101 (Freiburg: Universitätsverlag, 1990).

68. Joel S. Baden, "The Tower of Babel: A Case-Study in the Competing Methods of Historical and Modern Literary Criticism," *Journal of Biblical Literature* 128 (2009): 217. For literary elegance in the passage, note especially the chiastic proposals of Jan P. Fokkelman, *Narrative Art in Genesis: Specimens of Stylistic and Structural Analysis*, 2nd ed. (Sheffield: JSOT Press, 1991), 11–45; and Gordon J. Wenham, *Genesis 1–15*, Word Biblical Commentary 1 (Waco: Word, 1987), 235.

69. Peter J. Harland, "Vertical or Horizontal: The Sin of Babel," *Vetus Testamentum* 48 (1998): 532–33. A similar perspective is offered by Schüle, *Der Prolog der hebräischen Bibel*, 394–405.

composition. Indeed, it is commonly argued that what is in view is Babylon experienced as a sixth-century oppressor and locus of exile. The data, however, is somewhat more elusive. The tower construction is regularly compared by commentators to the Babylonian ziggurat construction, with occasional attention drawn to the imperial pretensions of such "gates of the gods," but in itself this does not provide much of a clue to the dating of the text, since these Babylonian "towers" date back even to the late third millennium BCE. More telling, perhaps, is the absence of significant inner-biblical reflection on the tale, as per most of Genesis 1–11. There are prophetic passages where one can discern echoes of a Babylon figured in terms of a tower that reaches to the heavens: in the poetic assaults of Isaiah 13–14 or Jeremiah 51, for instance, or perhaps most pointedly in the anticipation of a recovery of the "pure speech" lost at Babel (Zeph. 3:9–10). This fits easily with a theory that the Babel narrative takes shape in the exile and therefore leaves no interpretive trace in the rest of the Old Testament, but it is not conclusive in the way that such an observation is, say, for Cain and Abel, or Noah and the flood, if only precisely because Babylon remains such a strong presence in the Old Testament. One can explain the significance of the story along a range of possible datings.

It is often observed that one need not date the text in order to make sense of it. In line with our earlier discussion of Genesis 1–11 as a prologue to the Bible, it is therefore worth pointing out that here is a clear example where the text works powerfully as part of an initial framing device for subsequent reading. Whether or not the Babel narrative was written in exile, it speaks powerfully to the exiled Israelites. Whether or not it historically reflects a context of Babylonian oppression, it sets the reader of the Old Testament looking for ways in which the actions of God may be anticipated in subsequent contexts of oppression. Indeed, by leaving the reference to Babylon relatively low-key in verse 9, Genesis 11 invites readers to see the dynamic of judgment as applicable to more than just the Babylonian empire of the sixth century. The mythic dimensions of the text cast their illuminating light over the rise and fall of empires down through the whole Old Testament, and for the Christian reader at least, on into the New and toward the present day. Part of its canonical function, in other words, is symbolic, encouraging the reader to ask how far its analysis of human aspiration and divine judgment may be discerned in other situations.

The text's reticence in defining the sin of the city's architects and tower builders, a sin regularly parsed as "hubris" in the literature, might offer a further theological angle of reflection, for this kind of underdetermination of detail is a frequent feature of Old Testament narrative, not just in Genesis. The hermeneutical result, though, is interesting. If we cannot recover the sin "behind" the text, as it were, whether that be in terms of historical reference or literary intention, we might consider that this leaves the reader in a position where a variety of possibilities exist for thinking about what the sin might be. And thus readers are led to self-examination: in what ways, such readers may ask, are we engaged in activities that might be construed as akin to building the tower of Babel? This lacuna of the text becomes the occasion for the reader's self-examination.

Discerning Divine Action: Scattering as Blessing?

Taking into account all the various literary and historical hypotheses regarding our text, then, we come directly to the theological question, over the threshold of which it does seem that biblical scholars are strikingly keen not to cross. But a canonical reading presses the question: insofar as this text weaves together elements of punishment and blessing, how should one rightly understand such a dual emphasis as a theological whole?

Babel represents the human intuition that coordinated effort and the concentration of resources are basically good and important ingredients in the securing of human welfare. This controlling narrative is embedded deep in the human psyche and seems so self-evident in some ways that it finds its way into large parts of the Christian tradition. For "Babel" read: city, security, might, self-determination, autonomy, and so forth—or indeed any variation on "Let us make a name for ourselves" (v. 4). Likewise, improved communication, increased coordination, and speed and ease of access to information are all held to be self-evident values in today's world, in the face of which God's intervention in Genesis 11 seems like the imposition of a barrier that, with effort, we might overcome and indeed do well to overcome. This perspective is found not just in modern (or postmodern) culture, but is alive and well in the church, and—let it be said—in the academy too, including the theological academy, where scholarly endeavor can give the impression of making its own effort to overcome Babel.

But if the scattering that is effected in the narrative is directed toward the end of allowing humanity to fulfill its potential blessing in Genesis 1, then our perspective on all these characteristics of our world is challenged. It is in slowing down, stumbling over local detail, and attending to the particularities of how each person speaks from each place that the blessing of 1:28 can be fulfilled. In the context of Genesis 1–11, this "positive" implication of "scattering" has been given resonance already in the use of the same Hebrew verb, *puts*, in 10:18 ("The families of the Canaanites spread abroad"), and possibly in 9:19 ("The whole earth was peopled" from the sons of Noah).[70] Diverted from building projects, the people spread out to fulfill their real calling.

70. In 10:18, *nafotsu* is the plural Niphal form of *puts*. Commentators divide on how to read *naftsah* in 9:19, either as a third-person feminine singular Qal of *nfts*, "disperse," hence "populated" (or "peopled," so NRSV); or a third-person feminine singular Niphal of *puts*, hence "was scattered" (or, by supplying a subject, "the people were scattered," so NIV); see

This approach to the Babel narrative has been emphasized in recent years in terms of culture: Babel understood not as the loss of a much-desired uniformity of humankind, but rather as the release of a divinely intended cultural diversity. It becomes possible to "read from the margins"—to articulate Latin American, African, and Asian readings of Genesis 11:1–9, for instance, which celebrate the view from the dispersion.[71] But rather than abandon the theme of judgment in order to make way for blessing, the theological dynamic of the text as we have it appears to propose the altogether more demanding route of finding blessing precisely through the acceptance of, if not punishment, then at least limitation.

If this is indeed a theologically fruitful idea, then it clearly functions well as part of (and possibly a climax to) the prologue to the canon. Readers would be alerted to look for ways in which the narratives to follow challenge notions of improvement, advance, and increase, and look for divine blessing occurring in all sorts of ways that allow for limitation, locality, and the struggle with a life that does not work the way one might wish. In theological terms, there is a divine grace to be found in limitation. Readers of Genesis 11:1–9 are invited to see a God who removes from their shoulders the impossible burden of organizing the human race and its environment in a way that can be made successful.

It seems likely that echoes of this theme are to be found in many places throughout Genesis, though perhaps not marked as clearly as they are here in the Babel story. Thus at least one aspect of the multifaceted Eden story of Genesis 2–3 must surely be that the man and the woman are sent forth to populate the earth, in accordance with the purpose of their creation, and not to rest in the haven of Eden all their days. Some have suggested that death is to be seen at least in part as a divine release from the toil of the post-Eden life, again offering the possibility of seeing this ultimate form of limitation as a blessing in some perspectives. Likewise the narratives of Genesis 6 can also be seen in this way: divine limitation on the activities of "the sons of God," for the sake of the "daughters of humans," as well as the sending of the flood, to bring a judgment that in turn will bless. Many of the later narratives of Abraham and his family are also much engaged with questions of limitation, whether in terms of limiting the chosen people to one family, or such turning points as the limp with which Jacob/Israel walks after being struck by his assailant (32:25, 31). In so many of these

---

Wenham, *Genesis 1–15*, 155. A resonance between 9:19 and the Babel story thus must be left as a possibility rather than a certainty.

71. See the essays gathered in (the significantly titled) *Return to Babel: Global Perspectives on the Bible*, ed. John R. Levison and Priscilla Pope-Levison (Louisville: Westminster John Knox, 1999), 1–33. See also Theodore Hiebert, "The Tower of Babel and the Origin of the World's Cultures," *Journal of Biblical Literature* 126 (2007): 29–58, for whom the text "is exclusively about the origins of cultural difference" (31).

stories one has the temptation to say "if only it had been done better," or "if only these human frailties had not intervened and left things worse." Yet throughout Genesis and beyond, the hope is not for a utopia, where all is well and all shall be well in the best (and most organized) of all possible worlds; instead, the hope is for a world where blessing can actually be enjoyed, in this particular world.

It is important to see the ways in which grace both is and is not disruptive of human effort in the Babel text. God clearly steps in and disrupts the building of the city and tower. But this should not be understood in terms of a straightforward opposition between divine action and human initiative. Rather, it is a blocking of one kind of human activity in order to channel it (via the scattering) into another. In this sense, grace operates in the creating of a life and context within which human endeavor can flourish toward God. To be able to see the Babel story as a vehicle of blessing, as "good news," to use a traditional Christian label, is one key aspect of any Christian theological reading of the text. In contrast, many readings that see the key to the primeval narrative as "the increase of sin" (or some such) tend to emphasize that the Babel narrative offers no hope for humanity at all.

It is the "good news" aspect that is picked up in an interesting way in Acts 2 with the tale of the Holy Spirit's coming upon the gathered faithful: "All of them were filled with the Holy Spirit and began to speak in other languages. . . . 'We hear, each of us, in our own native language'" (2:4, 8). Sometimes read as a "reversal of Babel" in anticipation of the new creation, it is better to read Acts 2 rather as a "fulfilling" of the promise of human scattering. It is not that the church will represent a new humanity where all finally get to speak the one language profitably for humankind before God, but rather that the church will enact the new reality so that the ways of God can indeed be lived and shared in every local tribe and tongue. Only a handful of chapters later, in Acts 8:1, we read that "a severe persecution began against the church in Jerusalem, and all except the apostles were scattered [*diesparēsan*] throughout the countryside of Judea and Samaria." Again, what seems like the dark workings of judgment turns out to "people the earth," not in this instance with the human race but with the beginnings of the global church. The goal is not to return to the way things were before the persecution, but to learn to discern the ways of God in the new reality that results. One suspects that much of what happens in the life of the church needs to be seen in this way.

On such a reading, Pentecost represents a rare moment where participants are privileged to see this big-picture perspective, which by definition is normally inaccessible to all its participants who remain rooted in their own local situations. In this sense Pentecost is a foretaste of a kingdom to come. In the meantime, from the viewpoint of humanity's mission on God's earth, it is the fulfillment of the strange promise inherent in the Babel narrative.

FURTHER READING

Genesis

Barton, Stephen C., and David Wilkinson, eds. *Reading Genesis after Darwin*. New York: Oxford University Press, 2009.

Hendel, Ronald, ed. *Reading Genesis: Ten Methods*. Cambridge: Cambridge University Press, 2010.

Levenson, Jon D. "The Conversion of Abraham to Judaism, Christianity, and Islam." In *The Idea of Biblical Interpretation: Essays in Honor of James L. Kugel*, edited by Hindy Najman and Judith Newman, 3–40. Leiden: Brill, 2004.

Moberly, R. W. L. *The Theology of the Book of Genesis*. Old Testament Theology. Cambridge: Cambridge University Press, 2009.

Petersen, David L. "Genesis and Family Values." *Journal of Biblical Literature* 124 (2005): 5–23.

Van Wolde, Ellen. *Stories of the Beginning: Genesis 1–11 and Other Creation Stories*. London: SCM, 1996.

The Babel Narrative (Genesis 11:1–9)

Hiebert, Theodore. "The Tower of Babel and the Origin of the World's Cultures." *Journal of Biblical Literature* 126 (2007): 29–58.

LaCocque, André. *The Captivity of Innocence: Babel and the Yahwist*. Eugene, OR: Cascade Books, 2010.

Van Wolde, Ellen. "The Tower of Babel as Lookout over Genesis 1–11." In *Words Become Worlds: Semantic Studies of Genesis 1–11*, 84–109. Biblical Interpretation Series 6. Leiden: Brill, 1994.

2

∞

The Book of Exodus

Jo Bailey Wells

Exodus has come to refer to a theme as much as a book or an event. Popularly, the theme has to do with the emancipation of a people, from slavery to freedom—a theme that surely is founded on the archetypal emancipation of Israel from Egypt, as described in the book of Exodus. But the release of Israel from oppression under Pharaoh occupies only chapters 1–15 of a book that continues through to chapter 40. Our introduction to the book and its theme or themes will not be confined to the escape from Egypt, for, as we shall see, if there is one theme to the book of Exodus, it must surely be "God." The book expounds the sovereign nature of God—with respect to creation and history, over despotic rulers and human need, declaring a covenant of commitment and a shape for living, all with a particular people in view: the Israelites. The consequence of the nature of God is the people of God.

In Exodus we meet a God who is attentive to pain and active against oppression. We meet a God who is awesome, even frightening, and not to be taken lightly. We meet a God who is devoted to a particular people through thick and thin. We meet a God who is more merciful than judgmental, but also a God who is jealous, whose very name may indeed be understood to make this point: "Yhwh, whose name is Jealous, is a jealous God" (Exod. 34:14).[1] The words of the self-revelation of Yhwh in chapters 32–34 provide

---

This chapter is dedicated to Walter Moberly in gratitude for the way he taught me *how* to read the Old Testament as well as showing me, through scholarship, ministry, and friendship, *why* it matters.

1. This is a literal statement in the MT: *qanna' shemo*, "jealous [one] is his name."

the fullest statement about the name and character of God in the whole of the canon. According to Jewish tradition, thirteen attributes are revealed here, on the lips of God himself.[2] Associated with the *name* of God, YHWH— and encompassed by his glory and holiness—is the full range of Hebrew vocabulary for mercy and forgiveness, amid an awareness (and experience) of the gravity of sin.

At the same time, it would be entirely possible to fill our discussion with reflection upon the exodus as an event of social and political liberation. We will say a little more about this below. In my own judgment, however, it is equally significant, if not more significant, that the book of Exodus challenges readers to ponder what ways of living are appropriate responses to the character of YHWH as revealed in the text. For this reason I am going to focus on two fundamental aspects of the theological vision of the book, both properly understood in relation to this area: holiness and priesthood. These have not always loomed large in (Protestant) accounts of the book, but perhaps it is time to allow them to become more central again in our understanding. These two aspects are necessarily to be understood in the light of this book's central event: God's invitation to covenant and the election of Israel "to be a special possession." The second half of this chapter will therefore focus on the crucial verses containing this idea, Exodus 19:1–8, in more detail.[3]

Exodus in the Canon

From its beginning, the book of Exodus reads as a sequel to the book of Genesis. It is not without significance that the opening verses of Exodus begin with a genealogy.[4] The particular focus on the Israelite people stems from the promise of blessing made to Abraham and Abraham's descendants (Gen. 12), according to which a nation and a land will ensue. Genesis has focused on the fortunes and failings of particular individuals descended from Abraham; now Exodus is concerned with Jacob's offspring as a whole. In particular Exodus focuses on God's promise to them of becoming a people and a nation. The

2. Yet the precise distribution of the thirteen attributes is disputed. For a helpful discussion, see Benno Jacob, *The Second Book of the Bible: Exodus* (New York: Ktav, 1992), 984–85.

3. My account in this chapter is partly drawn from a longer discussion of these themes in my *God's Holy People: A Theme in Biblical Theology*, Journal for the Study of the Old Testament: Supplement Series 305 (Sheffield: Sheffield Academic Press, 2000), esp. 27–57, with other sections noted in what follows. Original text is from *God's Holy People*, by Jo Bailey Wells, © 2000; edited and revised with permission from the Continuum International Publishing Group. I am grateful to Continuum for permission to adapt this material, and to the editors of this volume for assisting me in shaping this chapter to its present form.

4. Jon D. Levenson, *The Hebrew Bible, the Old Testament, and Historical Criticism: Jews and Christians in Biblical Studies* (Louisville: Westminster John Knox, 1993), 153.

opening verses of the book refer to the original seventy pioneers who have migrated to Egypt, with clear reference to the list given in Genesis 46:8–27. God's call to Moses at the burning bush underlines the continuity in introducing himself as "I am the God of Abraham, the God of Isaac, and the God of Jacob" (Exod. 3:6). Likewise, the phrase "I have given heed to you and to what has been done to you in Egypt" (3:16) echoes precisely the dying words of Joseph in Genesis 50:24: "God will surely come to you [or literally, "take heed of you"] and bring you up out of this land."[5] When Joseph is referred to in the opening verses of Exodus, it is taken for granted that the reader understands who he is.

Exodus offers the second installment of a journey that began with Abraham and will continue on through the books of Leviticus and Numbers. The books of Exodus to Numbers stand apart from the rest of the Pentateuch in the way that they focus on the life of Moses and on the work of founding a new people.

With regard to the rest of the Old Testament, the motifs of the book—of the exodus, of the wilderness, of Sinai—are repeatedly echoed. In particular the escape from Egypt is viewed as the event of supreme religious significance. Even elsewhere in the Pentateuch it is no mere historical event of the past,[6] but a permanent symbol that constantly imposes itself afresh on the collective memory. In the Psalms, in the historical books, and in the Prophets, the experience of the exodus is declared again and again[7]—so that Amos, for example, can voice God as saying to a generation at least five hundred years later, "I brought you up out of the land of Egypt" (Amos 2:10).

This kind of understanding also continues in later Jewish tradition. As the rabbis would say, "There is no earlier and no later in the Torah,"[8] and to this day the Passover meal includes the strong theological claim that every generation should consider itself as the generation that was brought out of Egypt. One would expect the first ritual reenactment of Passover to occur in the future, that is, after the event. But in Exodus 12, the very Israelites about to leave Egypt are also the first participants celebrating the *remembrance* of leaving Egypt by following a prescribed ritual. Thus time is collapsed in both directions in this ritual, in that those Israelites leaving Egypt act like later Jews celebrating Passover, and later Jews celebrating Passover act as if they are ancient Israelites leaving slavery in Egypt.

---

5. The Hebrew in Exod. 3:16 is *paqod paqadti* ("I have given heed" to you), following Gen. 50:24, *paqod yifqod* (God "will surely heed" you). Joseph's words in Gen. 50:24–25 are repeated again in Exod. 13:19.

6. See, e.g., the chapter on Deuteronomy in this volume.

7. Hoffman finds the exodus theme referred to about 120 times. See Ya'ir Hoffman, *The Doctrine of the Exodus in the Bible* [in Hebrew, with English summary] (Tel Aviv: Tel Aviv University, 1983), 11.

8. Babylonian Talmud, *Pesahim* 6b.

An Outline of the Book

The book of Exodus reads like a self-contained continuous sequential account. The narrative is not comprehensive but proceeds by episodes. These episodes have clearly been highlighted to serve the narrator's larger goals. Sarna puts it best: "This discriminating selectivity is undoubtedly conditioned by didactic considerations."[9]

Based on the dominant narrative, which follows Israel's foundational journey, it is common to divide the book into four broad sections. Yet such sections are not so much neat or clear as convenient for practical purposes, and many other analyses of the book are possible. Strikingly, the most recent full-scale commentary on Exodus offers a twofold division of the book, around the themes of the power and the presence of Yhwh. This is certainly helpful in discerning that the nature or character of Israel's God is at the heart of the book.[10] Nevertheless, there is merit in retaining the fourfold way of looking at the book.

First, in chapters 1:1–15:21, we find a narrative of oppression, struggle, and liberation from Egypt. Chapter 15, operating as a lyric poem or song, is a transitional passage that "celebrates" what has occurred but looks forward to what is ahead.[11] Second, from 15:22–18:27 the story sets off into the wilderness, recounting the wanderings of the Israelites from the Red Sea to Sinai. Third, and most obviously a discrete section at the center of the book (containing what scholars call the "covenant code"), chapters 19–24 narrate the Sinai covenant and the receiving of the law. Finally, chapters 25–40 describe the tabernacle instructions and construction, although with a profound narrative interlude concerning the golden calf and other key matters in chapters 32–34.

Perhaps more than with any other book of the Pentateuch, the material in Exodus is diverse in form and content. Narrative provides the framework, within which are interwoven sections of law and instruction, especially Exodus 25–31 and 35–40, relating to the sanctuary and the priesthood. Then within the mixture of narrative and law is also found some liturgical material, which might have served as the early worship texts by which God's people responded to their creator and redeemer. The clearest examples are chapters 12–13, which celebrate the Passover and festival of unleavened bread, and chapters 14–15, which celebrate the sea crossing, culminating in the Song of the Sea (15:1–21).

---

9. Nahum M. Sarna, *Exploring Exodus: The Origins of Biblical Israel* (New York: Schocken Books, 1996), 6.

10. Thomas B. Dozeman, *Exodus*, Eerdmans Critical Commentary (Grand Rapids: Eerdmans, 2009), 44–47, taking 1:1–15:21 as concerning "the power of Yhwh" and 15:22–40:38 as about the "presence of Yhwh."

11. See the thorough analysis of this chapter as the pivotal section in Mark S. Smith's *The Pilgrimage Pattern in Exodus*, Journal for the Study of the Old Testament: Supplement Series 239 (Sheffield: Sheffield Academic Press, 1997), 205–26.

Christian interpretation of the book has tended to underemphasize the fact that the book concludes with lengthy passages concerned with the tabernacle. Clearly, on its own terms, this material is highly significant; what is more, it is largely repeated. Israel has been warned to tear down the altars and break the pillars of foreign peoples in their land, lest they "make a covenant with the inhabitants of the land to which [they] are going" (34:11–16). Now, because of their covenant with YHWH, they are to build pillars and altars according to his careful directions (chs. 35–39). Israel's worship is to be entirely separate and distinct from that of other peoples. The tabernacle passages are followed by narrative describing the completion of the tabernacle (39:32–43; 40:16–33), the consecration of the space and articles within in varying grades of holiness (40:1–11), and the anointing of the priests (40:12–15). The book ends with a description of the glory of YHWH as descending visibly in a cloud and filling the tent of meeting and the tabernacle, in the sight of all Israel. The presence of God travels with Israel, and his holiness is evident to and understood by all.

Overall, the content is commonly understood to originate from a variety of sources and periods. There has been broad agreement that the epic traditions (J and E) likely lie behind chapters 1–24 and 32–34, while later priestly tradition (P) shapes chapters 25–31 and 35–40. If so, this suggests that the book we now call Exodus evolved over a very long period and likely exhibits as much editing, integrating, and reworking as perhaps any other book in the Old Testament. This makes the narrative all the more remarkable for the way it witnesses to Israel's accumulated retelling of its origins. The predominant image is that of journeying, at the behest of a God who is alive and active and calls his people to follow. Like much of the Pentateuch, that the genre of storytelling predominates has significance for how readers receive the text as well as the theology we may find there.

Some Key Theological Themes in the Book

God: The Central Character

A *theo*logical introduction to Exodus focuses our present interest in the second book of the Pentateuch on, primarily, the subject of *theos*, of God. As a gripping narrative that recounts God's freeing and forming of his own people, Exodus stands out with relative clarity as a *theological* text. Thus, following the events of the book in narrative order, it is *God* who calls Moses to lead his people, *God* who rescues the Hebrews from a cruel pharaoh, *God* who sustains them in the wilderness, *God* who invites his people into covenant relationship, *God* who gives them the law, and *God* who promises an ongoing presence. In other words, Exodus presents "history" in such a way as to offer some memorable answers to the questions of who God is and how God works. This is not to suggest that there are no other important players in the story—Moses in particular is key—but God is the central character and the chief actor. The book begins by describing the (partial) fulfillment of God's promises to Israel's forebears (1:1–7) and ends with the assurance of God's guiding presence for future travel (40:34–38). That is to say, God sets the story in motion and God sustains it. Exodus *invites* a theological reading—one assuming that God is integral to the reader's attention, even as other interests may be pursued at the same time.

Starting with the text itself and reading it theologically does not preclude matters of interest that lie behind the text, such as the possible origins of the writings or the historical realities to which they might refer.[12] Nor does it rule out matters of interest that lie in front of the text, such as the way it interacts with the situations of contemporary readers, their worldviews and concerns. The book may be read in many different ways, depending on one's interests and circumstances, and this chapter will seek to consider some of these. But the starting point is the book itself, the text as we have received it. Moreover, as I urge, the narrative that the book presents demands, first and foremost, a *theological* reading of the text simply because its focus has to do with how God has delivered Israel from Egypt (chs. 1–18) and how God has related to Israel at Mount Sinai (chs. 19–40). This theological horizon of the text should appropriately be brought into interaction with whatever historical or ideological interests the reader may bring.

It is significant for a theological reading of Exodus that the genre of narrative forms the framework within which the other kinds of literature find their place.[13] We suggest that through reflection on the account of what God has done, we come to understand what God is like. On the whole there are no evaluative comments or explanatory sidebars to fill us in. There are no subtitles within the book to mark new sections (unlike the "generation" headings in Genesis). Rather, we are drawn in to observe the action—to follow the content—and then work out for ourselves what the actors are like and why the narrative is shaped as it is. John Goldingay helpfully likens this hermeneutical effect to the way films (rather than books) build characterization: "In films . . . only when directors are desperate do they have characters talking to camera. Films have to *show* rather than *tell*. They show people acting in certain ways and leave us to work out what this says about their character."[14] Thus we are

---

12. See below on the relation of the book to historical events.

13. Terence E. Fretheim observes this especially with regard to law and narrative in his commentary *Exodus*, Interpretation (Louisville: John Knox Press, 1991), especially with regard to chs. 12–15 and 19–40. See his convenient chartlike presentations of various sections of the book (134, 202).

14. John Goldingay, "Introduction to Genesis and Exodus," in *Genesis and Exodus*, by John W. Rogerson, R. W. L. Moberly, and William Johnstone (Sheffield: Sheffield Academic Press, 2001), 9–34, here 11.

required to pay careful attention to the emphases and nuances of the text itself. It necessarily demands our *interpretation* and thus opens the door to a plurality of views. The text itself does not tell us what we should conclude even though it offers hints and direction.

Exodus represents perhaps the strongest and clearest narrative within the Pentateuch. Thomas Mann describes Exodus as an epic: "What the *Aeneid* was to ancient Rome, Exodus is to ancient Israel."[15] At the same time, it provides an unusual emphasis on moments of direct theological revelation, where the name and nature of God are reported and revealed in a strikingly direct manner. There are three notable theophanies in Exodus: first with Moses at the burning bush (Exod. 3), then with all the people at Sinai (Exod. 19–20), and finally with Moses again at Sinai (Exod. 33–34). In each case, direct and personal conversation between Moses and God takes place. We shall return to Exodus 19–20 more fully later in this chapter, given its climactic place for Exodus and for the Old Testament more generally. On the two occasions when Moses is alone with God—chapters 3 and 33–34—Moses boldly asks God who God is and what God is like, and God answers. The answers that Moses receives bear great weight theologically and warrant our close attention. Indeed, our theological reading of Exodus here is appropriately shaped around these moments of direct encounter—not least in the revelation of the divine name "Yhwh" and its significance.[16] In the climactic moment of divine self-revelation at 34:6–7, we find a double self-naming, "Yhwh, Yhwh," that is unique in Scripture, as part of a self-description of God that in turn becomes central to Israel's understanding throughout the canon.[17]

God's interactions with Moses amply bear out the portrayal of God as a relational, confrontational, collaborative, dynamic being. The relationship between Yhwh and Moses in particular is highlighted.[18] The result is a book that demonstrates what is possible between God and the exceptional person on the one hand, and what is intended for all Israel on the other hand. We may call this the theocentric relationship. At the start of the book (1:9), Israel

15. Thomas W. Mann, *The Book of the Torah: The Narrative Integrity of the Pentateuch* (Atlanta: John Knox, 1988), 79.

16. The divine name in Hebrew consists of four consonants (Y + H + W + H) and no vowels, hence the use of the term "Tetragrammaton" (four letters) to describe it. The name is not pronounced in Jewish tradition out of the concern not to treat it in an unworthy way. In this book we thus adopt the increasingly common scholarly convention of rendering it in English without vowels, therefore "Yhwh."

17. For a helpful "canonical" study of how this passage about Yhwh's being "compassionate, gracious, and slow to anger" reappears at key moments in the canon, see Nathan C. Lane, *The Compassionate but Punishing God: A Canonical Analysis of Exodus 34:6–7* (Eugene, OR: Pickwick Publications, 2010).

18. Out of 770 references to Moses in the OT, approximately a third occur in the book of Exodus.

is declared a "people" ('am) by none other than the pharaoh, suggesting for the first time a common ethnic identity among those descended from Jacob. But much more significantly, Israel is then declared "my people" by YHWH in 3:7. With this first-person pronoun, God asserts a possessive relationship with Israel, in conflict with the way in which the pharaoh is prompted to assert his authority and ownership. Just as God appears to and calls Moses at the mountain of God (Horeb, Exod. 3:1), so God appears to Israel and calls Israel at the mountain of God (Sinai, Exod. 19:11). God offers the covenant, gives the law, and guides the building of the tabernacle—so that all Israel may live theocentrically.

Liberation

Liberation, as we have already recognized, is a key theme in Exodus. We might usefully locate liberation in the text under several categories.

First, and most obviously, are the political dimensions of the text. In some ways Exodus has come to be regarded as the model for understanding God's dealings with oppressed people as well as God's critique of exploitative power; that is, a model of salvation that necessarily involves political liberation. Yet the term "liberation" is not prominent in the text; more dominant is the nexus of terms derived from the Hebrew verb 'abad (to serve): serve, service, servants, slavery, worship.[19] The Hebrews are freed from enforced service to the pharaoh in order that they may choose freely to serve God. Thus Jon Levenson has described the exodus not so much as an instance of liberation (as that term is generally understood) but as a change of ownership; from a tyrannical slave master (the pharaoh) to a loving God, under whom Israel will now serve and flourish in a loving relationship. "The point of the exodus," he states, "is not freedom in the sense of self-determination, but *service*, the service of the loving, redeeming, and delivering God of Israel, rather than the state and its proud king."[20] In other words, any discussion of liberation needs to be balanced with an appreciation for the Jewish specificity of this text.[21]

A second aspect of the liberating emphases of the text has to do with the place of women. The early chapters of Exodus offer a profile of five lowly women who take on strategic significance for the fulfillment of the divine promises of creation and history. Two are Hebrew midwives, Shiphrah and Puah, who disobey the pharaoh's orders with charm and creative determination;

19. See Goldingay, "Introduction to Genesis and Exodus," 15.
20. Jon D. Levenson, "Exodus and Liberation," in *Hebrew Bible*, 126–59, here 144.
21. For some of the discussion provoked by Levenson's proposal, see the exchange of essays in Alice Ogden Bellis and Joel S. Kaminsky, eds., *Jews, Christians, and the Theology of the Hebrew Scriptures*, SBL Symposium Series 8 (Atlanta: Society of Biblical Literature, 2000), 215–75.

another is the biological mother of Moses, who hides her fine baby; a fourth is Moses' sister, who patiently keeps watch on the riverbank; and the fifth is Pharaoh's daughter who, despite realizing the baby's origins, decides to protect and raise the child as her own (Exod. 1:15–2:10). As Fretheim has put it, her actions toward Moses anticipate those of God toward Israel.[22] The actions of all these women demonstrate active resistance and creative disobedience. But it is subtle: their combination of wisdom, patience, and courage permits a defiance that is rewarded not with any public recognition or heroism, but with the raising of a leader who becomes a hero through his acts of public defiance. It is these seemingly minor female characters who enable the survival of Moses, and through him the liberation of Israel. Though God appears absent in the first two chapters of Exodus,[23] we find evidence of his work through the liberating actions of these strong women.

As a final point, in recent times scholars have begun to take seriously that there might also be ecological aspects to the central dynamic of liberation in Exodus. As Fretheim suggests with respect to the plagues, "Although common parlance refers to these events as plagues, the narrative uses the language of sign and wonder (7:3); as such, they are ecological signs of historical disasters (Passover, the Red Sea crossing). . . . The stylized form of the plague accounts may reflect a ritual that dramatized an experience of ecological disaster."[24] In such a model God's rescue relates to more than bringing Israel out of a foreign land; it also demonstrates his ability and willingness to harness the powers of the natural environment, for the sake of liberation. Ellen Davis contrasts the power-driven industrial economics of Egypt with the more communitarian culture of agrarianism, seen most clearly in the counternarrative of the giving of the manna in chapter 16. "Against this social background [of a conspicuously wealthy elite], the wilderness narrative in Exodus traces the emergence of a people charged to cultivate a radically different way of living in community on the land."[25] Such a way involves memory, restraint, and trust—habits that are cultivated through the practices of Sabbath. Indeed, there is much to be said for understanding Exodus as a whole as setting up a theologically significant contrast between slavery and Sabbath-keeping, which may still speak strongly to the world in which we live today.[26]

22. Terence E. Fretheim, *The Pentateuch*, Interpreting Biblical Texts (Nashville: Abingdon, 1996), 103; cf. also Fretheim, *Exodus*, 31–41.

23. It is often noted that only with the Israelites' cry to God at 2:23 does God become significantly present in the narrative (2:24–25), although there are less decisive references earlier, in 1:20–21.

24. Fretheim, *Pentateuch*, 103.

25. Ellen F. Davis, *Scripture, Culture, and Agriculture: An Agrarian Reading of the Bible* (Cambridge: Cambridge University Press, 2009), 69.

26. On this see further Ellen F. Davis, "Slaves or Sabbath-Keepers? A Biblical Perspective on Human Work," *Anglican Theological Review* 83 (2001): 25–40.

Holiness

The first reference to holiness in the story of Israel lies with Moses' encountering of God as YHWH at Horeb.[27] Moses sees a thornbush that is on fire but not burning up (3:2). He then hears a voice demanding that he take off his shoes, because the ground on which he is standing is holy (v. 5). As Gilbert points out, it seems that this ground is not holy before the revelation of YHWH. It is his presence that makes it holy.[28] What follows from YHWH is an expression of concern for the sufferings of God's people in slavery, a promise of deliverance, and a call to Moses to lead his people out of Egypt, to a land flowing with milk and honey (vv. 7–10). This is followed by a self-disclosure of the divine name YHWH (3:15).

This story is the foundation for all that ensues. As Rendtorff describes it: "Chapter 3 begins like an aetiological saga about a holy place (vv. 1–6), but then becomes a divine discourse with a wider scope."[29] The rest of the book of Exodus (and indeed, the whole story of Israel) flows out of this theophany. Not only the revelation of the divine name (YHWH) and the divine nature (holiness) but also aspects of the style of the narrative suggest that an important new beginning is depicted here.[30] That God has not revealed himself until this point in the story suggests that his climactic entrance will now dramatically shape the rest of the story.

Later in the book of Exodus, the incidences of the vocabulary of holiness confirm this understanding of the holiness of Sinai due to God's presence. Out of a total of ninety-three occurrences of the root *qdsh* in the book of Exodus, at least seventy-eight concern the sanctuary of YHWH. Four of these relate to the restrictions concerning access to Mount Sinai itself in chapter 19.[31] Virtually all the rest occur in chapters 26–40 and relate to the tabernacle, which is built at Sinai and eventually carried to Zion. Because it is the holy place where God is present, its furnishings, its ministers, and its offerings must all be protected, restricted, and made holy.

The first thing that Moses is told at the burning bush is "Come no closer!" (literally, "Do not approach," 3:5). There is need for caution, respect, and an "access permit" where God is so intensely present; he is not to be encountered lightly. In each incident relating to God's presence, rules are laid down. In this

27. The *qdsh* root is used in Gen. 2:3, when God "hallows" the seventh day, but this lies outside Israel's particular story, which begins with Abraham. Other uses of the root in Genesis do not bear directly on our discussion.

28. Maurice Gilbert, "Le sacré dans l'Ancien Testament," in *L'expression du sacré dans les grandes religions*, vol. 1, *Proche-Orient ancien et traditions bibliques*, ed. Julien Ries et al. (Louvain-la-Neuve: Centre d'Histoire des Religions, 1978), 209.

29. Rolf Rendtorff, *The Old Testament: An Introduction* (London: SCM, 1985), 140.

30. Compare R. W. L. Moberly, *The Old Testament of the Old Testament: Patriarchal Narratives and Mosaic Yahwism*, Overtures to Biblical Theology (Minneapolis: Fortress, 1992), 5–26.

31. See Exod. 19:10, 14, 22, 23.

instance, Moses' "permit" involves taking off his shoes. In chapter 19 the rules concerning who has access, and how, are carefully spelled out and even repeated (19:12–13, 21–24). As the narrative continues, YHWH's holy presence with Israel on Sinai becomes focused in the tabernacle (25:8; 29:38–46; 40:34–38), where the rules and regulations are detailed even further, until the point where YHWH will choose another mountain on which to make his sanctuary.[32]

One further occurrence of *qdsh* in Exodus is undoubtedly the most significant and most surprising of all. In the book of Exodus the usage is unique: as an adjective, *qadosh* is used to describe not a mountain or tabernacle or institution, but Israel. At the outset of the second recorded theophany in Exodus, the encounter in which the covenant is presented to Moses, YHWH speaks directly to the people of Israel and promises that "you shall be for me a priestly kingdom and a holy nation" (Exod. 19:6a).[33]

At the outset of the Sinai narrative, the focus is thus placed very firmly upon Israel. YHWH promises them that they will be a nation with the characteristic of holiness. According to the biblical narrative that comes before this revelation in the Pentateuch, holiness as a characteristic is associated with the presence of YHWH, is revealed to special people (such as Moses, their leader), requires caution and commands fear, and belongs to the place where YHWH dwells (Sinai/Horeb). If the words here were not on the lips of YHWH himself, they might sound blasphemous. For this is a statement suggesting that people can, in some way, become like God.

The whole of chapter 19 acts as preparation for the main event: YHWH's delivering the law. In 19:5–8 the people have expressed themselves ready, only to learn that more is required. Preparations of the whole people of God are then executed over a period of two days (vv. 10–15), followed by further instructions and preparation on the third day, chiefly regarding the priests (vv. 20–25). Those who draw nearer to the presence of YHWH must prepare more. The point of this preparation emerges from the repetition of certain phrases: "Warn the people not to break through," "Do not let either the priests or the people break through" (vv. 21, 24), and the resultant "Otherwise . . . he [YHWH] will break out against them" (vv. 22, 24). These warnings introduce the dimensions of fear and danger involved with the presence of the holy God: "The issue at stake is not whether God is a stuffy monarch, who does not think enough honor has been shown to him. [Such a] picture is a total misunderstanding. Rather, the warning is given for the sake of the people, who have no experience as yet of the dimensions of divine holiness, and lest warned destroy themselves."[34] We shall return to this key text and theme in the second half of the present chapter.

---

32. That is, Mount Zion (1 Kings 8:1–13).
33. Details of this text and its translation are considered further below.
34. Brevard S. Childs, *Exodus*, Old Testament Library (London: SCM, 1974), 370.

Priesthood[35]

In Exodus 28–29 God specifically directs Moses concerning the institution of priests. These instructions are set within a wider concern for the establishment of the tabernacle (Exod. 25–31), the means by which God's presence will "go forth" with Israel after they leave the holy mountain.

God commands Moses to "bring near to you your brother Aaron, and his sons with him, from among the Israelites, to serve me as priests" (28:1). This is followed by details of the holy garments that they should wear (28:2–43) and of the sacrifices and other activities that Moses should perform for their ordination (29:1–37). Throughout, the concern is for Aaron and his sons, and the altar at which they serve, to be made holy (29:21, 33, 37). Priests and tabernacle serve the same end: Israel's holiness and YHWH's indwelling among them. Exodus 28–29 culminates in one of the key theological passages of the "priestly" material: "I will meet with the people of Israel there [at the entrance of the tent of meeting], and it shall be sanctified by my glory; I will consecrate the tent of meeting and the altar; Aaron also and his sons I will consecrate, to serve me as priests. I will dwell among the people of Israel, and I will be their God. And they shall know that I am YHWH their God, who brought them out of the land of Egypt that I might dwell among them; I am YHWH their God" (29:43–46). Aaron and his sons are those who are consecrated to be priestly to YHWH (28:3, 41; 29:1, 44; 30:30): in the passage both "consecrated" and "priestly" are terms derived from the *qdsh* root. The frequent word pair implies that their consecration has this particular purpose: priests are those who are *li*, "to me" (i.e., "mine"), in an especially focused, wholehearted way, just as the consecration "to me" of the firstborn, whether human or animal, indicates their belonging to God (Exod. 13:2), and just as the consecration of the seventh day makes it a Sabbath "*to* YHWH" (20:10). As such, the priests wear sacred garments (28:3–4), eat sacred food (29:33), and perform sacred acts that are not of their own design or making; they are specified in every detail by God, something they will pass down to their descendants (28:43; 29:29, 42). It is, quite literally, as if Aaron and his sons are no longer "their own people" with any individual identity: they belong to God.

Inextricably linked with the notion of the consecration of priests (and of the tent of meeting and the altar) is the idea of God's meeting and dwelling with his people; this is the wider concern of chapters 25–31, as clearly stated at their outset. Priests are those who, by virtue of their identity as belonging to God, enable YHWH to be fully present to his people, so enabling the people to recognize him fully as YHWH their God, and thus themselves as his people, with the same understanding of belonging. The holiness of the priesthood is connected to the special status of the entire nation. God's meeting with priests

---

35. This section is revised from, and summarizes, my *God's Holy People*, 107–11.

at the tabernacle is representative of his meeting with all Israel. The priests act on behalf of all. In large measure YHWH's presence actually depends on what *priests* do: they act on behalf of Israel, representing how Israel, as a people, may be holy before God and providing a model to which others aspire.

This subject is supremely addressed in Exodus 32–34, the account of Israel's failure to worship YHWH appropriately and of God's withdrawal of his presence. It is simultaneously an account of Aaron's failure and Moses' success in acting on behalf of God's people. The story of the failure of a priest—particularly of Aaron, the father of all Israelite priests—follows soon after the story of his institution; this juxtaposition is no accident. Rather, the narrative fills out the picture of priesthood given in the earlier legislation, especially reinforcing the identity and role of the priest on behalf of the entire nation.

Read this way, Exodus 32 serves as a commentary on the priesthood; it is not without significance that the chapter closes with a record of Moses' making atonement for the sin of the Israelites in worshiping the golden god they have made. This provides a supreme picture of a priest as one who acts on behalf of the whole people, an emphasis that is developed even further in the succeeding chapter. As Childs states: "All [the themes of this chapter] circle about the role of the faithful mediator, Moses, who wrestles with God for the sake of Israel."[36] Moses asks for God's forgiveness for a crime in which he has had absolutely no involvement: he goes so far as to offer his own life for the sake of God's mercy on the people. The essence of Aaron's mistake lies in the way he distances himself from the problem (Exod. 32:22–24), suggesting concern for himself above that of the people before whom he is appointed priest.

Exodus and Its Relation to History

Matters pertaining to history in relation to the book of Exodus have tended to dominate scholarly discussion over the past century. Yet the book of Exodus does not concern itself with when and where it was written. Nor is it concerned with who wrote it: the text itself does not claim Mosaic authorship, and Moses is described in the third person throughout. Clearly it is written with hindsight: chapter 6 sets the time when God is revealed as YHWH in contrast with the former time of the patriarchs, when he was not so known. And the regulations presuppose the settled life of Israel—likely in the period of the monarchy, sometime between Solomon and the exile. Implicitly, then, there is an invitation to study the narrative against that background. Given how Ezra–Nehemiah tell us of the way the story in Genesis–Exodus and the rules of life in Exodus are applied to the community back in Judah in the fifth century, then most obviously we are invited to read Genesis–Exodus as

36. Childs, *Exodus*, 599.

stories of the nation's origins in such a way that their continuing relevance is assumed and freely embraced. The concern with worship and the presence of some liturgical material within the narrative underlines this understanding of the book's function.

This challenges some of the scientific assumptions that have accompanied the modern instinct to reconstruct the history of the period, based on the account given here. The text was not written for such a purpose: if it were, it might, for example, have included the name of the relevant pharaoh, who plays such a major role in the narrative. Israel's story can sometimes be dated from the exodus,[37] yet it is notoriously difficult to establish a chronology for the exodus events themselves. In arguing for the primacy of a theological interpretation of Exodus, we are suggesting that the attempt to treat the biblical material on the exodus as history writing (in the modern sense of that idea) is misguided.[38]

Other ancient Near Eastern sources have not produced significant corroborating evidence for Israel's descent to, sojourn in, or exodus from Egypt—a period (sometime during the second millennium BCE) that spanned at least 430 years, according to Exodus 12:40. Archaeological records have shown that contact between Egyptians and their Semitic neighbors was far from unusual. It is generally agreed that Egypt was the dominant military and cultural force through this period, extracting forced labor regularly from surrounding nations, including from Canaan.[39] The lack of evidence for particular conflict between Israel and Egypt does not disprove the events of Exodus, even as it underlines the importance of the theological nuances embedded in Israel's account of their origins.[40] Israel's telling of their tradition emphasizes God's sovereignty over both human and natural forces, as well as God's call to Israel to cultivate a radically different way of living and relating.

Reading the book on its own terms does tend to suggest that chronology is not a particular concern of the text. The phenomenon of historical anachronism in storytelling is well illustrated by Exodus 19. Moses is told to "consecrate" the people (v. 10; cf. v. 14), and the "priests" are told to "consecrate" themselves (v. 22). This involves the people's washing their

37. As, for example, in 1 Kings 6:1, "In the four hundred eightieth year after the people of Israel came out of the land of Egypt, in the fourth year of Solomon's reign over Israel."

38. As, for example, in Roland de Vaux, *The Early History of Israel*, vol. 1, *To the Exodus and Covenant of Sinai* (London: Darton, Longman & Todd, 1978).

39. Donald B. Redford, *Egypt, Canaan, and Israel in Ancient Times* (Princeton, NJ: Princeton University Press, 1992), 209.

40. For recent debate on the historical circumstances of Israel's emergence as a distinct political entity, see Mark S. Smith, *The Early History of God: Yahweh and the Other Deities in Ancient Israel* (Grand Rapids: Eerdmans, 2002); and Stephen L. Cook, *The Social Roots of Biblical Yahwism*, Society of Biblical Literature Studies in Biblical Literature 8 (Atlanta: Society of Biblical Literature, 2004).

clothes (v. 10) and abstaining from sexual relations (v. 15) as if this were an established procedure for consecration. No further comments or clarifications are offered. Likewise, the text seems to assume that the sons of Aaron have been assigned to the priestly office (v. 22). Yet as we have seen, the institution of the Aaronide priesthood is not recorded until Exodus 29. Only on the basis of the narrative of Exodus 19 do we learn that God's purpose is to bring about his holiness among his people, to which end the procedures for consecration, including that of the priesthood, are laid down. We might say that the book as a whole is written from a particular (Priestly, P) theological perspective, and the narrative cannot be unpacked into its constituent parts as it was before the intense reworking that we noted earlier. All of this complicates the task of relating the text of Exodus to particular historical moments—a task that is at best a distraction from the purpose of the received text.

A Theological Reading of Exodus 19:1–8

Having covered some basics regarding Exodus and its major themes, it is time to look at the book itself by examining a specific text. To exemplify a way of interpreting Exodus theologically, I will focus on a text that stands at the very center of the book, both literarily and theologically:

> [1]On the third new moon after the Israelites had gone out of the land of Egypt, on that very day, they came into the wilderness of Sinai. [2]They had journeyed from Rephidim, entered the wilderness of Sinai, and camped in the wilderness; Israel camped there in front of the mountain. [3]Then Moses went up to God; YHWH called to him from the mountain, saying, "Thus you shall say to the house of Jacob, and tell the Israelites: [4]You have seen what I did to the Egyptians, and how I bore you on eagles' wings and brought you to myself. [5]Now therefore, if you obey my voice and keep my covenant, you shall be my treasured possession out of all the peoples. Indeed, the whole earth is mine, [6]but you shall be for me a priestly kingdom and a holy nation. These are the words that you shall speak to the Israelites."
>
> [7]So Moses came, summoned the elders of the people, and set before them all these words that YHWH had commanded him. [8]The people all answered as one: "Everything that YHWH has spoken we will do." Moses reported the words of the people to YHWH. (Exod. 19:1–8)

We have already seen some of the important points that will help us to approach Exodus 19 in an appropriate context. God's appearance in Exodus 3 sets up an association with God's special presence at the mountain, his name as YHWH, and the character of holiness. The words of YHWH in the theophany recorded in Exodus 19 introduce the whole of the Sinai narrative and summarize the salient features of the covenant: God's history of faithfulness (v. 4), Israel's call to obedience (v. 5), and God's promise of privilege (vv. 5b–6). The remainder of the chapter then suggests the terms on which Israel may meet with its God at Sinai, incorporating restrictions that develop the significance of a relationship with a God who is holy. All these features provide background for our focus on Exodus 19:1–8.

The Structure and Form of Exodus 19:1–8

The whole Sinai pericope has presented many challenges to scholars on account of numerous literary difficulties within the text. There are many tensions that arise out of chapter 19 alone. Consider, for example, the frequency of Moses' journeys up and down the mountain (vv. 3, 14, 20, 25); the repetition of the warning for the people not to overstep their bounds on the mountain (vv. 12, 21) despite the report that they are fearful and fixed at the foot of the mountain (v. 16); the alternate descriptions of God, as dwelling on the mountain (v. 3), yet also descending periodically (vv. 11, 18); the dual imagery of God's presence, in smoke and fire (v. 18), and in rainstorm and thunderclouds (vv. 9, 16, 19); and the variation concerning whether Moses is with the people (vv. 10–19) or alone (vv. 20–25) when he meets God. These examples illustrate well the extreme complexity of exact source division in the book of Exodus, a problem that has evoked the widest possible disagreement among scholars.[41] Durham goes so far as to suggest that Exodus 19 may be "the one most reworked passage in the whole Bible."[42] This point has an important theological implication: the repeated attention received by this account of Yhwh's revealing himself to Israel and calling them to a special identity and role serves to underline its centrality for Old Testament theology and faith.

These historical uncertainties have frequently led to a fragmentary analysis of the narratives and an implicit denial of their unity. Furthermore, the scholars who have tried to demonstrate the homogeneity of the literary work have been accused of "generally failing to explain the literary difficulties which have been discussed by source and tradition critics."[43] Far more fruitful, for this portion of the Sinai pericope at least, have been the approaches that consider the poetics of the text, that is, literary aspects such as the structure and development of the plot and the characterization, which is the approach I adopt below. In view of the poetic, metric character of 19:3b–6, a literary study of the divine discourse seems particularly appropriate.

---

41. So Brevard S. Childs, *Introduction to the Old Testament as Scripture* (Philadelphia: Fortress, 1979), 165.

42. John I. Durham, *Exodus*, Word Biblical Commentary 3 (Waco: Word, 1987), 259.

43. Gregory C. Chirichigno, "The Narrative Structure of Exod 19–24," *Biblica* 68 (1987): 457–79, here 457.

A Literary Reading

The first two verses of the chapter, in a strikingly poetic style, tell the reader that Israel has arrived at Mount Sinai in the third month after they have escaped from Egypt. It is emphasized as a special day ("on that very day") because it marks the completion of an itinerary and the reaching of a goal: Israel has reached the special mountain where God is present. There is a careful specificity and precision with respect to the past and the present. What follows clearly stands in contrast to this journey from Egypt; the scene is being set as a prelude. It is as if everything that has gone before, since YHWH called Moses to take his people out of Egypt (in ch. 3), has been leading toward this moment.

The clause in 19:3—"And Moses went up"—marks the beginning of a new episode that is then characteristically followed by a string of dependent verbal clauses. Moses' action carries an urgency and an eagerness: the narrative strains forward to a significant event. Without any delay, the purpose of God's bringing Israel to Sinai is announced to Moses through a voice out of the mountain (vv. 3b–6).

A careful study of the rhetorical pattern of communication between YHWH as one party, and Moses and the people as another party (so characteristic of the Sinai narratives), suggests two points of significance. First, both YHWH's speech and the people's reply are presented in direct discourse. Alter regards the primacy of direct discourse to be a characteristic feature of biblical narrative, serving to "bring . . . the speech-act into the foreground"[44] and focus attention on the main content of the speech, here contained in verses 4–6a. Indeed, the reference to "my voice" in YHWH's own speech and "all that YHWH has spoken" in the people's response serves to emphasize this direct speech of YHWH. Muilenburg describes the language of this direct address as that "of proclamation and urgent call to hearing, of stress upon the first and second persons, the *I* and the *Thou*."[45] This emphasis is made even more evident by the presence of two similar clauses at the opening (v. 3) and closing (v. 6) of YHWH's speech, forming an *inclusio*:[46]

> Thus you shall say to the house of Jacob and tell *the sons of Israel*. (v. 3b)
> . . .
> These are the words that you shall speak to *the sons of Israel*. (v. 6b)

The text twice suggests an anxious concern to communicate something to "the sons of Israel" and indeed to any subsequent reader of the text. We are

---

44. Robert Alter, *The Art of Biblical Narrative* (Berkeley: Basic Books, 1981), 67; cf. more broadly 67–69.

45. James Muilenburg, "The Form and Structure of the Covenantal Formulations," *Vetus Testamentum* 9 (1959): 347–65, here 352.

46. As a chiasmus it is incomplete; in an *inclusio* only the extremes correspond.

drawn in to discover the content of this message. Further, the pronounced "I-Thou" style makes it clear that the message concerns the nature of the YHWH–Israel relationship. There is a repeat of "you" in verse 4 and "to me" in verse 5, which Muilenburg describes as "producing a remarkable climactic effect in the *I-Thou* relation, enhanced by the assonance of the whole unit."[47] The climax occurs at verse 6a: "You shall be to me a priestly kingdom and a holy nation."

The second point is the democratic nature of this theophany.[48] The address is in the second-person plural; everyone is being addressed in a manner that is socially inclusive and corporately empowering. In comparison to the pattern of message and oracle communication found earlier in the story of the plagues (chs. 7–11), there is less emphasis on the privileged communication between God and Moses, and more on that between God and his whole people. Later in the Sinai narrative, the commandments are given in the second-person singular (20:2–17; 34:11, 14, 17). But here in Exodus 19, the oracle belongs equally to the people as to Moses, and in due course they all will encounter YHWH for themselves at Mount Sinai (19:17; 20:18–20).

Several times the narrative stresses that Moses' role is simply as go-between, or as point person on the ground: he is to relate YHWH's exact words to the people and their response back to YHWH (19:3c, 6c, 7b, 8c–d). At this point, Moses is not privileged in being given personal communication. The conversation is essentially between YHWH and the people. The direct discourse is that of YHWH and the people, not Moses. Whereas the appearance of God in Exodus 3 and the communication that followed it represent an encounter between God and Moses, the appearance of God in Exodus 19 and the conversation that follows it are essentially between God and the whole people of Israel.

In the conviction that YHWH's words are carefully crafted and that their literary form adds significance to the message, I now turn in more detail to their composition. Although there is general agreement that these are poetic lines, containing rhythm and symmetry, there is little consensus among scholars concerning the exact parallels and the envelope structure that may be identified.

James Muilenburg suggests that the verses are "so closely woven and the structure so apparent that the excision of any line of verse actually mars its unity and destroys its literary character."[49] He represents the structure of verses 3b–6b in a fashion similar to the following:

3b Thus you shall say to the house of Jacob, and tell *the sons of Israel*:

4a   You have seen what I did to the Egyptians,
4b   and how I bore you on eagles' wings,
4c   and brought you to myself.

---

47. Muilenburg, "Form and Structure," 353.

48. Compare Martin Noth, *Gesammelte Studien zum Alten Testament*, 3rd ed., part 1 (Munich: Kaiser, 1966), 331–32.

49. Muilenburg, "Form and Structure," 351–52.

5a   *And now* if you will obey my voice

5ab   and keep my covenant,

5b   you shall be my own possession among all peoples;

5c   for all the earth is mine,

6a   and <u>you</u> shall be to me a kingdom of priests

6ab   and a holy nation.

6b These are the words that you shall speak to *the sons of Israel*.

Within the envelope formed by the instructions to Moses concerning "the sons of Israel" (vv. 3b, 6b), Muilenburg identifies a further envelope formed by the lines beginning with the emphatic second-person pronoun "you" (underlined above), which encloses the main message. These pronouns combined with the emphatic "and now" (italicized), he suggests, bring about three divisions in the message, as separated in the schema above. The first forms a parallel with the second, since both contain three lines, or clauses.

Since each division culminates in the last of its three lines, the words being stressed are "and brought you to me," "you will become to me a (treasured) possession" and "holy nation." Given that the message as a whole builds to a crescendo, the climax of the whole message lies in its last line, "and a holy nation" (v. 6ab). Muilenburg makes this especially clear: "It is precisely this final line which contains the burden to the whole message, as is shown by the introductory pronoun [you], the preceding *for all the earth is mine*, which serves to set it apart and yet to relate it to the whole, and by placing the *goy qadosh* [holy nation] in the crucial position it requires. Indeed the whole message culminates in these words."[50] The focal point of Yhwh's speech is a new description of Israel's function and character. The call to obedience is aimed at realizing this special identity; it emphasizes not the call to obedience but the identity that obedience creates.[51]

Muilenburg's analysis is valuable. There is little with which I wish to argue, and there is much to commend. Yet there appears to be one significant omission. Muilenburg seems to skip over the small phrase of verse 5c, "for all the earth is mine." In his model, this dangles uneasily between the second line, beginning with the emphatic "and now," and the final section, a line opening with "and you," while belonging to neither. I suggest that it be linked with verse 6a, thus turning the final two-part line into three parts and increasing the symmetry of the message. Muilenburg simply writes that it sets apart the final and most important line and yet relates it to the whole. This seems to contradict his earlier statement that every line is crucial, for it does not strike

50. Ibid., 353.

51. Daniel C. Van Zyl, "Exodus 19:3–6 and the Kerygmatic Perspective of the Pentateuch," *Old Testament Essays* 5 (1992): 264–71, here 268.

me that, according to his analysis, the excision of this line would "destroy" the literary character of the composition.

My own view is that we should indeed associate the phrase "for all the earth is mine" with verse 6a. Rudolf Mosis has carried out a detailed grammatical study of these verses, on the basis of which he challenges the punctuation of the MT.[52] He suggests that the *soph pasuq* (the end of sentence/verse marker [:]) belongs after "among all peoples" rather than after "for all the earth is mine." This implies that this phrase belongs with verse 6a, giving to the presentation of the promise a chiastic structure (A B B' A'), as follows:

A   You will become my own possession
   B   among all peoples.
   B' Indeed, all the earth is mine.
A' But you, you shall become to me a priestly kingdom and a holy nation.

This analysis has significant implications for the interpretation of these verses. First, it makes clear that the text is concerned to establish not only the nature of YHWH's relation to Israel but also Israel's relation to others. It explains what *segullah* (possession) means in the wider context of God's world: why and how Israel is special. It is not difficult to see the statement as affirming YHWH's relation to the whole earth, all peoples, as well as to Israel. Even as God makes a declaration of unique devotion to Israel, Israel is reminded that God is devoted to all peoples. That is, God's commitment in this particular situation does not diminish God's commitment to all people; indeed, at the poignant moment of invitation into special commitment—a "marriage"—the wider commitment to all people is reiterated. As we shall see, the election of Israel actually is God's means of granting blessing to all the earth.

Aware of the tension, the speech continues with an explication of the promise to be a *segullah*, a special possession. The repeated use of the expression "to be for me" or "to become" forcefully underlines the dimension of election, while making a contrast clear. The second half of this section (B' and A') is a restatement and development of the first. It begins with an affirmation that the whole world is YHWH's possession, yet Israel has a particular place at the heart of it. Further, Israel's privilege and responsibility within this world is emphasized: "But you, you shall be to me a kingdom of priests and a holy nation." We may understand these two titles, therefore, not only as explanation and intensification but also as qualification of *segullah* (special possession), specifying Israel's place at the heart of God's earth.

In summary, a poetic analysis of YHWH's speech in 19:3b–6b suggests that its internal parallels and patterns point to the last of the three phrases—that

52. Rudolf Mosis, "Exod 19, 5b–6a: Syntaktische Aufbau und lexicalische Semantik," *Biblische Zeitschrift* 22 (1978): 1–25.

God has brought Israel to Godself as a possession—to serve as the climax to which the whole speech progressively builds. As a parallel, "priestly kingdom" progresses to "holy nation," and the phrases use a chiastic structure to develop the notion of "treasured possession" in verse 5b. The notion of belonging to YHWH—as a jewel in God's crown—is the overarching message. This is expressed in some way through Israel's becoming a priestly kingdom and a holy nation.

19:3–8—Further Considerations

With regard to specific details of the text, some further points may be made. In verse 4, YHWH refers to Israel's experience of what he has done and thus urges the people to recall who he is and what he is like—his power, his protection, and his presence. Buber suggests that the image is one of Israel's utter dependence on YHWH's care.[53] As mentioned above, the stress lies on the last of the three phrases, that God has brought Israel to himself. Literally, this may be taken as a reference to the mountain, where his presence may be encountered dramatically and intensely. It seems reasonable also to understand it in terms of Exodus 3, in which God has revealed himself to Israel in a new and more intimate way, by the name of YHWH. As suggested above, this would not be a surprising allusion, given the subject of holiness, which follows.

In verse 5, YHWH explains to Israel the manner of the relationship with him in which they are invited to participate. It seems that on the condition of their being obedient and faithful to his covenant, certain blessings will ensue. Here is the core of the passage, which Muilenburg suggests exemplifies the covenant *Gattung* (larger theme or genre), consisting of a conditional statement promising divine favor for obeying YHWH's will or threatening punishment for disobeying. Muilenburg cites many examples of this type of speech.[54] However, verses 5–6 appear to differ from his model in the aspect of "conditional promise," in that the relationship of protasis (the statement of condition) to apodosis (the result of meeting the condition) is not consequential. The connection is far more subtle. Rather, as Patrick puts it, "the protasis is a *definition* of the requirements of the position or vocation designated by the titles of the apodosis."[55] Obedience is the *basis* for the identity of the covenant people.[56] In other words, to be YHWH's own possession, his priestly kingdom and holy nation, entails submitting to his will. Israel is invited to accept this offer. Thus the "if" is not a conditional, suggesting cause and effect, but almost the

53. Martin Buber, *Moses* (Oxford: Phaidon, 1946), 102.

54. Muilenburg, "Form and Structure," 355n2.

55. Dale Patrick, "The Covenant Code Source," *Vetus Testamentum* 27 (1977): 145–57, here 149.

56. Van Zyl, "Exodus 19:3–6," 267.

reverse. It describes a logical relation between responsibilities and privileges, in which Israel is invited to participate.

The statement that Israel will be a people treasured by YHWH, therefore, is not to be seen as a reward for obedience; rather, it is a consequence of the covenant that YHWH is making here. At some point in the future they will become a *segullah*, a *"treasured possession"*; exactly *when* (under what circumstances) this happens, and what it involves, remains an open question. Clearly it describes Israel's relation to YHWH in comparison to that of other nations.

Verse 6 begins with an emphatic "you yourselves." This does not merely underscore Israel's uniqueness as described in the preceding verse; it also underscores the choice of these particular descriptions for *Israel*, however surprising they may sound. Both descriptions present interpretive difficulties, which are examined in more detail below. It suffices to say here that all three titles in verses 5b–6a (*segullah, mamleket kohanim,* and *goy qadosh,* defined below) are assumed to be closely related and to develop progressively—from the first to the second to the third—in the intensity of their meaning. Each is a referent for the same subject: the communal house of Jacob, the collective sons of Israel (relative to all of YHWH's other peoples), to whom the whole discourse is addressed and who reply to the promise in unison.

Although Moses transmits the message to *the elders*, it is reported in verses 7–8 that "*all* the people answered *together*," stressing again the socially equalizing character of God's appearance and the communal unity of purpose and desire. Their response to *do* all that YHWH has spoken presupposes verse 5a ("if you [plural] obey . . .") and can be understood only as a commitment to obey the covenant law. Dale Patrick suggests: "If our passage is an offer, then we would expect a response of acceptance or rejection, and the pledge of obedience constitutes an acceptance."[57] This launches the relationship into effect: at the moment the people make this pledge, they become YHWH's own possession, his kingdom of priests, his holy nation. Following Buber's existentialist interpretation of Sinai, the covenant is "not a contract but an assumption into a life relationship."[58] If they had refused to pledge obedience, there would have been no story to tell; the fact of the telling presupposes Israel as YHWH's people.

The Key Terms in Exodus 19:5–6

On the basis of the poetic structure of Exodus 19:3b–6b, we have identified the thrust of YHWH's speech as designating the new position and vocation of the people of Israel, relative to all of YHWH's other peoples. This is a result of

57. Patrick, "Covenant Code," 149.
58. Buber, *Moses,* 103.

the gift of a covenant and a corresponding special status, and it is described in verses 5b–6a:

> You shall be to me a *segullah*
>   among all peoples.
>   For all the earth is mine,
> but you, you shall be to me a *mamleket kohanim* and a *goy qadosh*.

Given the parallels that have been identified, it is clear that the meaning of each of the three (underlined) titles expands and intensifies the one before it. I shall turn now to examine the implications of each, as well as the phrase in between.

First, *segullah* (special possession) has royal associations in Akkadian as well as Hebrew literature.[59] As far as other biblical references are concerned, it is found in 1 Chronicles 29:3 and Ecclesiastes 2:8 to signify treasure, such as gold and silver or the jewel in a crown belonging to a king. Equally it is a term used metaphorically, especially in Deuteronomy, applied to God and speaking of his elect, although in each of these situations it is used in connection with *'am* (people).[60]

All of these texts are considered to be written at a late date; thus historically as well as canonically, we may suggest that they depend upon the theological usage in Exodus for their meaning. The reverse argument has little strength. Nevertheless, later connotations do provide clues to suggest that here in Exodus 19 the term signifies a royal treasure and is used metaphorically to describe the special status of the people of Israel. They belong to God in a special way, and this special way has royal associations.

Given the context, the referent of the term can be taken for granted, particularly since there follows a phrase referring to all other "people." At the same time, by its royal resonance, the term preserves a divine transcendence: as the possession of YHWH's crown, Israel depends on him (as described in v. 4) and recognizes him as King and Lord (by the obedience described in v. 5a). Precisely in the statement that follows, "for all the earth is mine," God claims this lordship, which also stretches over all peoples. Exactly *how* Israel's special place works out in this earth full of other peoples is not yet clear; rather, verse 5b is a statement of affairs, albeit one that begs for an explanation.

Next we turn to the phrase *ki-li kol-ha'arets* (for all the earth is mine). It is significant that the titles used to describe Israel as a covenant people are interspersed with two references to others (in 5b and 5c). What the reader is given is not a description of Israel in isolation, but in relation to the whole of God's earth. Because of the covenant, Israel is a *special* possession among

---

59. Moshe Greenberg, "Hebrew *segullah*: Akkadian *sikiltu*," *Journal of the American Oriental Society* 71 (1951): 172–74; see also William J. Dumbrell, *Covenant and Creation: An Old Testament Covenantal Theology* (Exeter, UK: Paternoster, 1984), 80–105.

60. See Deut. 7:6; 14:2; 26:18; Ps. 135:4; Mal. 3:17.

all peoples. Does this not leave a mystery? How can this be, given that YHWH considers all people as belonging to him? I suggest that the succeeding lines hint at an explanation and underline the importance of the relationship with covenant outsiders.

Our phrase here is not simply a tautological repetition of the preceding clause. Rather, as a parallel, it develops and intensifies it. The preceding promise, "my special possession among all peoples," demands an explanation concerning the place of Israel *and* the place of the nations in YHWH's world. With a small adjustment to the punctuation, we may see how verses 5c and 6a might offer that explanation:[61]

> You will be to me a treasured possession
>   among all peoples.
>   In fact, all peoples are my possession,
> but you, you . . .

On the basis of this expression, then, the reader may conclude that the succeeding two titles describe how Israel is *special* or *treasured* in a manner that distinguishes them from other peoples. It is not feasible for the expression to denote that Israel is any *more* "possessed" by YHWH than any other peoples, for all are his possession. Rather, it must therefore be that this people are special in the sense of some distinguishing characteristic or role. The reader is led to expect verse 6a to elucidate this.

Given this conclusion concerning the relation of the clauses from verse 5 to verse 6, the conjunction with which verse 6 begins could be understood to imply a causal link. Thus:

> Because all of the earth is mine,
>   *therefore* you yourselves will be to me . . .

This is an option to which we should remain open.

The preceding and succeeding phrases are concerned with defining the status of *Israel* with respect to YHWH, relative to (yet distinct from) "all the earth." The context of theophany—of God's appearing—is sufficient to designate the status of YHWH as Lord of all. It therefore seems that this phrase is concerned with the status of "*all the earth*" with respect to both YHWH and Israel, in order that Israel understands itself and its God *in relation to others*. The concerns could be represented as a triangular set of relationships among God, Israel, and others. This phrase about "all the earth" precludes a narrow-mindedness

---

61. I propose adjusting the MT punctuation: if the *soph pasuq* sentence marker were placed so as to precede rather than follow the phrase of v. 5c (as argued above), then it is easy to see how v. 5c could serve as preface for v. 6a, delineating for the reader the aspect of v. 5b that v. 6a is explaining.

or egocentrism as a result of Israel's election. Israel is necessarily related to all God's people, though this relationship is different from that which ordinarily exists between other people groups.

The exact nature of Israel's special relationship with other peoples, and what this means, is not spelled out here. The silence on this subject leaves room for interpretation on the basis of later developments. All we can conclude is that this relationship matters; verse 5 cannot be allowed to imply absolute exclusivism or to encourage a ghetto mentality. Although the relationship does not imply a situation in which Israel is defined in terms of a hierarchy alongside other peoples, or in terms of a specific *mission*, such interpretations are possible. The succeeding titles that describe Israel must be examined before any further conclusions are drawn.

The third phrase that demands attention is *mamleket kohanim* ("a priestly kingdom," v. 6a). This title not only presents a unique juxtaposition of two (otherwise common) terms in the Old Testament, but also the grammatical construction is uncertain. It is therefore not surprising to find ancient translations of the text paraphrasing it differently. There are at least four variations: the LXX renders it *basileion heirateuma* (a royal priesthood); the Vulgate reads *regnum sacerdotale* (a priestly kingdom); the Syriac Peshitta, "kingdom and priests"; and the Targums read "kings (and) priests." Likewise, the title has been rendered in a wide variety of ways by modern interpreters.

The great variety of interpretations may be attributed to the fact that the Hebrew construction is ambiguous. Does *mamleket* describe *kohanim*, or are the two terms to be taken in parallel (each as absolutes)? If the latter, then *mamleket* stands in apposition to the noun *kohanim*, which follows it, as in the Syriac translation "kingdom and priests" (although there is no "and" in the MT). Taken as a construct, which is the most natural reading of *mamleket*, it is still possible to read it in either of two ways. The first noun can express an attribute of the second, resulting in the LXX's rendering "royal priesthood." Alternatively, the second may describe the first, which is more common, as in the Vulgate translation "priestly kingdom."

Overall, it is my view that this last approach seems the most likely: taking the title as two nouns in which the second complements the first. Thus, for the most literal translation, and that which I prefer, we have "kingdom of priests."

The term "kingdom" carries over the notions of royalty, which are already implied in *segullah*. If YHWH is king, then it follows that the people over whom he exercises his kingship will be his kingdom. Because of YHWH, Israel has royal associations. God's kingdom is made up of people who submit to his kingship, who "listen to his voice and keep his covenant" (v. 5a). This kingdom is qualified by the term "priests." The most obvious interpretation of this is to suggest that the people over whom YHWH exercises his kingship will be priestly.

What does it mean for Israel, God's kingdom, to have a priestly character? The immediate context of Exodus 18 and 19 provides some clues concerning this identity. On a minimal understanding, it suggests those who are concerned with approaching God, who are "consecrated" to him and his service, and who specialize in things sacred. Priesthood is a special expression of separation and devotion.

In contrast with the individuals who are described as priests,[62] the use of the term here describes the totality of God's people. The whole of YHWH's speech is addressed to corporate Israel, and the people as a whole reply to it. The concern here is with the priesthood of *all* believers (the community of faith) and not, as much Protestant interpretation has traditionally taken it to mean in the light of 1 Peter 2, the priesthood of *every* believer (each individual within the community).[63]

The fourth and final phrase to be explored is *goy qadosh* ("holy nation," v. 6a). This title is also a unique expression in the Old Testament. Because of this, it has been common to interpret it with reference to its nearest parallel, *'am qadosh*, which occurs several times in the book of Deuteronomy.[64] On three occasions, this is accompanied by a description of Israel as YHWH's *segullah* (treasured possession) also.[65] It seems reasonable to assume, on a historical as well as a literary-canonical reading, that these texts take their lead from the material in Exodus 19.

The translation of the vocabulary contained in this title is relatively straightforward, but more interesting is the *choice* of terminology used. The use of *goy* rather than *'am* bears significance; these terms are not used interchangeably in the Bible. Speiser offers an instructive analysis. First, unlike *'am*, the word *goy* never occurs as "YHWH's *goy*," either as a phrase or as a single word with the possessive suffix. And *'am* is found hundreds of times with pronominal endings, suggesting that it is something subjective and personal.[66] *Goy*, rather, is something objective and impersonal: there is not the least hint of personal ties in the notion of a *goy*. The term is almost always used to denote foreign nations, *hagoyim* (the nations), that is, those from which the subject (usually Israel) commonly distances itself.[67]

A second major distinction is that, in effect, an *'am* is a discrete group of persons (composed of individuals, each an *ish*, "man"),[68] whereas a *goy* is a

62. For example, Jethro (Exod. 18:1) and the priests associated with Aaron (19:22, 24).

63. For the classic discussions, see Luther (*De instituendis ministris ecclesiae* and *On Christian Liberty*) and Calvin (*Institutes* 4.4.9).

64. See Deut. 7:6; 14:2, 21; 26:18–19; 28:9.

65. See Deut. 7:6; 14:2; 26:18–19.

66. See, e.g., E. A. Speiser, "'People' and 'Nation' of Israel," *Journal of Biblical Literature* 79 (1960): 157–63.

67. Aelred Cody, "When Is the Chosen People Called a Gôy?" *Vetus Testamentum* 14 (1964): 1–6, here 5.

68. Compare 2 Sam. 15:30; 16:18.

collective, regimented body whose indivisible unit is the *'adam*, the mortal who is merely one of a crowd, a statistic.[69] This difference is illustrated in texts where *'am* and *goy* are juxtaposed (Exod. 33:13; Deut. 4:6b).

What may we infer from the promise that Israel be a "holy nation" rather than a "holy people"? The use of *goy* suggests that Israel is not necessarily a group made up of kinship ties in the sense of close family connections and blood ties. It is something different that brings these people together as a *nation*. And as a nation, the people have a structural unity with which they have political relations with other nations.[70]

What is more, a nation is a body that is *formed*, *founded*, and *established*;[71] the term "nation" assumes a maker and sustainer. The context here is already stressing that Israel is constituted by YHWH alone (Israel has done nothing to effect its own existence or status), and it is perpetuated by means of obedience to YHWH. In other respects, Israel is no different from *hagoyim* (the nations). If anything, the use of the term *goy* identifies Israel with them. Only through their relationship with YHWH are they unique. It is this tie that brings them together and holds them together. This uniqueness is expressed completely and concisely in the one adjective *qadosh*.

For Israel to function as a nation, a deep unity of spirit and purpose is suggested that brings it to behave collectively. The terminology leaves little room for individual action that does not foster this communal experience and purpose of nationhood. Such collective action is already expressed in *mamlaket kohanim*, as discussed above.

Finally, more may be invested in the term *goy*, based on the context in which this word forms the final climax. Recalling the other themes of the divine discourse, it develops the notions of utter dependence on YHWH (v. 4), complete obedience to him (v. 5a), and acknowledgment of his kingly rule over the whole earth (v. 5b). Moreover, it forms the climax of two parallels: together with the other terms of verse 6a, it develops the implications of *segullah*, and it also intensifies the parallel that immediately precedes it, "priestly kingdom."

The first of these parallels provides a straightforward and primary interpretation for *qadosh*. The term "treasured possession" is intensified jointly by "priestly kingdom" and "holy nation." If, as we have suggested, the first develops the notions of royalty, then equally we should recognize how the second develops the aspect of belonging to God. Fundamentally, I suggest, the adjective "holy" describes that with which God's presence abides, or that which belongs to YHWH. For Israel to be a holy nation, founded by YHWH, it must live in his presence and be his.[72] Whereas all the earth is "to me" (*li*,

69. Compare Job 34:29; Ezek. 36:13.
70. Gilbert, "Le sacré dans l'Ancien Testament," 238.
71. Compare Speiser, "'People' and 'Nation,'" 160.
72. Compare Num. 16:3–5; Jer. 2:3.

v. 5c), Israel belongs to God in a particular kind of way, denoted by the term "holy." Israel lives in his presence; Israel is particularly close to him.

The second parallel, within verse 6a, suggests that Israel as a holy nation progresses to the idea of Israel as a priestly kingdom. Likely "holy" corresponds to "priestly" as "nation" corresponds to "kingdom." It is not uncommon for *goy* (nation) to be used in some way alongside *mamlakah* (kingdom). Although the two terms are not synonymous (since parallel expressions rarely are), we have seen how "nation" can be understood to develop the notion of related-ness to a sovereign, which is expressed by "kingdom"—not merely of Israel as subject to royalty but also of creation as subject to the Creator and depen-dent on the Sustainer. In this case a similar relationship between "priestly" and "holy" may also be assumed. The use of *qadosh*, therefore, indicates not only a sense of belonging to Yhwh but also a quality of relationship with him that denotes a religious dimension, in the manner of priests.

As the climax of the whole speech, therefore, I conclude that the term *qa-dosh* expresses the goal of Israel's calling. It encompasses the various dimen-sions of relating and belonging to God: according to sheer necessity in utter dependence (as in v. 4), legally and morally in obeying and keeping laws (as in v. 5a), personally and emotionally as a treasured possession (as in v. 5b), and religiously and loyally as priestly royal subjects (as in v. 6a). Furthermore, the text makes it clear that the depth and breadth of this special relationship in no way precludes God's or Israel's relating to other peoples of the earth. On the contrary, we may surmise that this is necessary.

The Call to Holiness

This analysis of the speech that inaugurates and summarizes the event of Israel's election at Sinai has identified a climax in the words *holy nation*. This title expresses Israel's uniqueness, in the eyes of Yhwh, among all other peoples of the earth. It describes an identity that is to become both a reality when the covenant is made and a priority according to which Israel is required to live. This rather ambivalent state, whereby Israel is *declared* holy yet equally called *to be* holy, I describe as "the call to holiness." "Holy" describes a status, a standard, and a function.

The distinctiveness of Israel in regard to other nations, as expressed by the terminology of *qdsh*, may be understood to include several dimensions. "Holy" carries a richness and depth of meaning that is not readily conveyed by any single word in English. Based on this passage, I offer four ways of understanding Israel's distinctiveness.

First, Israel is unique. Although it is one nation among others, it is marked out in a special way. Yhwh stresses those to whom he is talking: "you" is em-phatic in verse 4 and repeated twice, and also emphatic ("you yourselves") in verse 6a. The implication is that Yhwh does not speak like this to others also.

Above all other descriptors, Israel is unique because it is a *holy* nation; Israel is associated with God. God's presence resides with and is invested in Israel.

Second, Israel belongs to God. The term *segullah* (v. 5b) denotes possession, and the terms "kingdom" and "nation" in verse 6a imply belonging, the belonging of a subject to a king. Thus the relationship is not one of equals, but of the subjects' dependence. Because a royal sovereign has founded them as a group of people, he will protect and sustain them as his, so they are to live in utter dependence on the one who is the Creator and Sustainer of all (v. 5c).

Third, Israel must live for God. Israel as a people has a common purpose in its relationship with YHWH. Thus it is united in its priorities to obey God fully and to keep his covenant (v. 5a). The relationship demands submission and obedience in order that association with the presence of God brings alignment with the will of God. This alignment has moral-ethical dimensions and religious priestly ones (v. 6a).

Finally, Israel must relate to others. YHWH's special relationship with Israel does not preclude God's relating with other peoples. Similarly, it does not preclude Israel's relations with other nations. Being "holy" does not infer a separation in terms of isolation; rather, it allows for a broadness and a generosity of outlook. Indeed, we may suggest that it even *demands* a relationship with others, for if Israel is invested with God's presence and is said to be priestly in nature, then Israel must not only represent that presence but must also mediate it to others.

The New Testament

The concerns of holiness in the Torah emerge in association with the revelation of the name of God as YHWH. In Exodus this occurs at the point where God calls Israel out of Egypt and brings them to Sinai. At Sinai he initiates the covenant with them, calling them to obey his commandments and so to live according to the special relationship he is establishing. Among all people, they will belong to him in a special way and be a priestly kingdom and a holy nation.

The Torah, from Exodus to Deuteronomy, spells out in great detail the commandments they should follow, in both cultic and ethical terms, to live in a manner appropriate to their new status. These may be summarized by the requirement to "be holy, because I [YHWH] am holy." They include the institution of priests, who are "holy to YHWH" in a particular way, required to be guardians of holiness in Israel, and enabled to draw close to YHWH in a special way. As "holy" individuals, they focus the holiness of all Israel, belonging to God in a particular way, living faithfully according to particular commandments, and especially in Deuteronomy, modeling a close dependence on YHWH on behalf of all Israel.

There is a trajectory from the Torah that then runs on through the whole of the rest of the canon, although there is not space here to explore all the ways in which this occurs. However, a brief conclusion is appropriate regarding the reuse of Exodus 19:6, and in particular its notion of "belonging to God," in 1 Peter 2:9–10, which begins with the claim that "you are a chosen race, a royal priesthood, a holy nation, God's own people."[73]

We have understood Exodus 19:6 to be seminal for understanding the "journey toward holiness" of Israelite life. Its reuse in the New Testament is made central for this understanding within the new framework of Christian faith. The appropriation of Exodus 19:6 in 1 Peter 2 involves a shift in its interpretation. Though in the context of torah we have understood the titles "priestly kingdom" and "holy nation" to develop the understanding of Israel as a special possession of God, in the 1 Peter context the priority is reversed. "Royal priesthood" and "holy nation" build toward understanding more fully the church as "God's own people." The priority for messianic believers is to understand themselves in terms of belonging. This is the goal of holiness as presented in 1 Peter: that believers should comprehend the way in which they are marked out from other people, in terms of belonging. They are absolutely distinct from others because they are God's. Once they fully realize this belonging, then they will live accordingly. This, in turn, serves another priority: that of demonstrating God's deeds of salvation publicly. If others identify their holiness through their worship and lifestyle, then it will follow that others will be drawn in to God's holiness themselves.

The relation of the Old to the New is not simply one of the latter superseding the former; nor is it a simple (typological) relation of "just as then . . . , so now . . ." Elements of both relations are involved here, intertwined. As far as there is a shift, we may notice how the new meaning is found from within the old meaning. There is a consistency, whereby the earlier language and imagery prove flexible and open to a subsequent context. What is more, this rereading becomes valuable for understanding the depth and riches within the first reading. Within the language and context of Exodus 19:5–6, we have identified an openness that has allowed for the possibility of this refocusing in a different context. Although the use of Exodus 19:6 in 1 Peter 2:9 underlines a shift in meaning—reversing the priority of the terms and describing an initiative for missionary activity—this is a shift that the language of Exodus 19:6 itself has left open.

Thus, first and foremost, we noticed that the descriptions given to the nation of Israel when the covenant is first established are made with a reference to all the nations of the world. Israel's election, like Abraham's election, is made in the context of an awareness of all people—as if to stress the pointedness of God's particular choice. He has not chosen any other people or nation, though he could have; among all of them, he has chosen "*you.*" The reference

---

73. For the trajectory throughout the canon, see my *God's Holy People*, chs. 4–7; this section summarizes my argument in *God's Holy People*, 208–40.

to other peoples receives no further attention in the Torah, except negatively. The concern is, rather, for Israel's uniqueness: because of its election, it must not be like other peoples. In the New Testament the focus of the plan of holiness is shifted in the direction of the gentiles. Those who are included in God's people are no longer defined by race, but by Israel's messiah. Second, God's people are to be seen to live such holy lives that the gentiles may notice and come to glorify God for themselves (1 Pet. 2:12).

Our interpretation of Exodus 19:6 plays its part in understanding the Old Testament emphasis on being "priestly" as involving primarily a mode of being before God. But the fact that the priest acts both on behalf of the *people* and of *God* again leaves the whole concept open for a shift in meaning from the Hebrew context to the Christian context. There is a richness and openness to the imagery of the priest as looking both ways—to God and to people—that allows for the shift in the people's direction, which we find in the New Testament. The priestly role of the New Testament people of God involves their mediating God's blessings in the world.

Conclusion

A theological exploration of Exodus has led us to a theocentric reading, whereby we follow God as the chief actor in an unfolding narrative. The narrative begins with attentiveness to suffering, follows with liberation and formation, and culminates in Israel's invitation into covenant at Exodus 19. Our close study of Exodus 19:3–8 reveals that the covenant at Sinai has relevance even beyond Israel and its dealings with its God. The covenant also stands as a pointer to a wider goal, "for all the earth is mine." That wider goal invites an even more radical theocentricity, expressed in the language of holiness. The revelation of the holiness at the heart of YHWH (Exod. 3) becomes an invitation for all Israel to share in that holiness (Exod. 19). Israel is invested with the character of YHWH for the world. The structures of Israel's life—determined by and described in the commandments and instructions that follow throughout the second half of the book of Exodus—establish the habits and practices of holiness. These include priestly ministry, the practice of Sabbath, and the dedication of a tabernacle—all of which are given to express the foundational reality of God, God's holiness, and God's investment in every people.

FURTHER READING

Brueggemann, Walter. "The Book of Exodus." In *The New Interpreter's Bible*, edited by Leander E. Keck, 1:677–981. Nashville: Abingdon, 1990.

Croatto, J. Severino. *Exodus: A Hermeneutics of Freedom*. Maryknoll, NY: Orbis Books, 1991.

Dozeman, Thomas B., ed. *Methods for Exodus*. Methods in Biblical Interpretation. Cambridge: Cambridge University Press, 2010.

Gammie, John G. *Holiness in Israel*. Overtures to Biblical Theology. Minneapolis: Fortress, 1989.

Langston, Scott M. *Exodus through the Centuries*. Blackwell Bible Commentaries. Oxford: Blackwell, 2006.

Larsson, Goran. *Bound for Freedom: The Book of Exodus in Jewish and Christian Traditions*. Peabody, MA: Hendrickson, 1999.

Miller, Patrick D. *The Ten Commandments*. Interpretation: Resources for the Use of Scripture in the Church. Louisville: Westminster John Knox, 2009.

Sarna, Nahum M. *Exploring Exodus: The Origins of Biblical Israel*. New York: Schocken Books, 1996.

3

—∞∞∞—

The Book of Leviticus

JOEL N. LOHR

If you read people passages from the divine books that are good and clear, they will hear them with great joy. . . . But provide someone a reading from Leviticus, and at once the listener will gag and push it away as if it were some bizarre food. He came, after all, to learn how to honor God, to take in the teachings that concern justice and piety. But instead he is now hearing about the ritual of burnt sacrifices!

Origen, 185–254 CE[1]

Difficulties in reading the book of Leviticus are long-standing. Since its inception, the church has wrestled with how to read this book, and one might argue that most of the New Testament law-and-gospel debates pertain not to larger so-called moral laws of the Pentateuch, but rather to those that are more ritually and "religiously" oriented, that is, to laws like those found in Leviticus. Sacrifices, rituals, taboos, defilement: what are we to make of this "bizarre food" that causes us to "gag and push it away," to use the words of Origen? What are we to do with all of Leviticus's minute, intricate, and at times obscure laws? Though Origen speaks of Leviticus as

---

I dedicate this chapter to Walter Moberly, who, to my knowledge, has not written on the book of Leviticus. I hope that my attempts to make sense of this book honor his now long-standing custom of illuminating the Bible for both the church and academy.

1. Origen, *Homily 27: Numbers 33:1–49*, quoted in Ephraim Radner, *Leviticus*, Brazos Theological Commentary on the Bible (Grand Rapids: Brazos, 2008), 17.

83

he does above, the book was in fact the subject of one of his greatest commentaries.[2] Like other church fathers, he believed that the things apparently
most obscure can actually be our best teachers. How might this apply to us
as Christian readers today?

As we will see, part of the problem in reading Leviticus relates to scholarship's largely Protestant makeup and its general lack of interest in, or even
disparagement of, priests and ritual. But there is so much more to Leviticus
than dry and dull laws related to Israel's priests. Recall that when Jesus
was asked, "What is the greatest commandment?" he turned not only to
Deuteronomy but also to Leviticus. The second-greatest commandment,
according to Jesus, is to love our neighbors as ourselves, a teaching found in
Leviticus 19. In this chapter I hope to show that the location of the Second
Commandment according to Jesus is not out of place in Leviticus, though
we will not look at that passage directly. I also bring out something of why
Origen was so interested in Leviticus, though I will not deal with him directly either. My approach to the book is to work through some of the issues
involved in reading Leviticus well: understanding its communal nature, the
interrelatedness of ritual, "list," life, death, and purgation (or purification),
as well as exploring how Leviticus might have functioned in ancient Israel,
in particular by looking at the Yom Kippur (Day of Atonement) ritual in
Leviticus 16. Leviticus is a well-crafted book, with layers of sophistication,
nuance, and theological insight, especially when we keep in mind the overall rhetoric of the Pentateuch and how this literature was read—or better
heard—in the ancient world.

We will also think through how Leviticus complements the rest of the Pentateuch and its various genres, and how, if most scholars are correct, the book
(and other priestly material) has been integrated into the rest of the Pentateuch.
It seems very probable that the priestly writers had the final say regarding the
shape of these five seminal books. Although we will not explore the specifics
of the source-critical theories in detail, it is important to recognize that even
if they were working with older traditions, the priests and priestly writers are
likely responsible for the final shape and overall rhetoric of the Torah itself,
and thus for its larger ideas about being made in God's image, loving one's
neighbor, the importance of corporate responsibility, loyalty to YHWH alone,
treating the poor and disadvantaged rightly, and other ethical teachings that
continue to shape modern ethics and inform the lives of contemporary Jews
and Christians. In short, the priests who wrote and compiled Leviticus might
be credited with the enduring value of the Pentateuch. We owe it to them to
pay close attention to the book they put at its center.

---

2. Some of Origen's exegetical work on Leviticus has been lost; however, his homilies are
preserved. See *Homélies sur le lévitique: Texte latin, introduction, traduction et notes*, ed.
Marcel Borret, 2 vols., Sources chrétiennes 286–87 (Paris: Cerf, 1981). For more on Origen and
Leviticus, see Radner, *Leviticus*, 17–28.

Leviticus in the Pentateuch and Canon

Leviticus stands at the heart of the Torah and must be understood as an integral part of that larger whole. Perhaps no one has done more in recent scholarship to demonstrate the important role that Leviticus has in the Pentateuch (and Hebrew Scripture) than the pentateuchal scholar James Watts. Although the effects of this work have not yet, in my opinion, been felt in theological interpretation and pentateuchal scholarship more generally, they are significant and will inform various aspects of our reading in this chapter.[3] For now we begin by noting Watts's seminal, albeit simple, insight that the Torah is a collection that was not meant to be *read* as a book (say, by an individual), but was meant to be *heard*, almost always in a corporate or communal setting. Watts builds this case from internal and external evidence, and his point is easily overlooked, especially by readers who take for granted the invention of the printing press in the late Middle Ages.[4] That the Torah was heard publicly may seem to be a simple-enough claim until we begin to ponder the fact that reading large books publicly requires a certain type of literature, with structures conducive to that task. For instance, what might be thought of as unexciting or dull repetition to the average modern reader could take on new significance when one recognizes that repetition is necessary for mental retention, at times functions as a powerful tool of rhetoric, and can be used to convey key ideas carefully and emphatically. In such a case, repetition does not bore, *it persuades*.

Persuasion is key to the discussion here, and this is why we begin with Watts in our investigation of the placement of Leviticus in the canon. To put it simply, the Torah as a whole and Leviticus in particular are intended to persuade their listeners to do something—to act or live in a certain way. For Watts, this relates to listeners' accepting the authority of the Aaronide priesthood. His proposal has merit.[5] For our purposes, however, I wish to draw attention to the more basic idea of Watts that artful, public persuasion employs various modes of speech and well-integrated genres. A good public speaker knows

---

3. James W. Watts's work in this area is extensive. I draw from a number of his key pieces, most notably *Reading Law: The Rhetorical Shaping of the Pentateuch*, The Biblical Seminar 59 (Sheffield: Sheffield Academic Press, 1999); *Ritual and Rhetoric in Leviticus* (Cambridge: Cambridge University Press, 2007); as well as the helpful chapter "The Torah as the Rhetoric of Priesthood," in *The Pentateuch as Torah: New Models for Understanding Its Promulgation and Acceptance*, ed. Gary N. Knoppers and Bernard M. Levinson (Winona Lake, IN: Eisenbrauns, 2007), 319–31 (some of which appears in ch. 7 of his *Ritual and Rhetoric*). In what follows I do not reference his work in detail (to keep this introductory discussion from becoming bogged down) but instead encourage the reader to consult the above-mentioned works to learn more. My indebtedness to his work will be readily apparent.

4. For more on the internal and external evidence for this, see Watts, *Reading Law*, ch. 1.

5. Watts suggests that Leviticus and the Pentateuch more generally were carefully constructed in order to bolster the Aaronide priesthood of 5th–4th-century BCE Yehud.

that the use of different speech forms can be effective for engaging an audience and that using asides—well-crafted stories, personal reflections, or even humor—can be key not only for keeping an audience's interest but also in helping the listener to "take on board" the message being spoken. As we shall see, so it is with the Pentateuch.

How does this relate specifically to Leviticus and its place within the canon? Watts argues that three main genres of the Pentateuch are closely related and depend on one another: *narrative*, *list*, and *divine sanction*. Leviticus, probably more than any other book in the Bible, can be largely classified as list—ritual observances; taboos; civil, moral, and social commandments; instruction on food; and so on—with two short narratives occupying important places within it (Lev. 8–10; 24:10–23). For Watts, divine sanction generally refers to the promises and threats ("blessings and curses") contained in Leviticus and the Torah more generally (e.g., Lev. 26 and Deut. 27–30), but it might also be said that much of Leviticus is in some sense presented as being divinely sanctioned, especially given the regular, in places chapter-by-chapter, indicators that "the LORD spoke to Moses, saying . . ." For the purposes of our discussion in this section, we notice Watts's important idea that divine sanction has little power without a compelling backstory to support the lawgiver, or in the case of Leviticus, to support the God of Israel, who speaks through Moses. Further, readers, or *listeners*, will not likely assent to a list and its commands (or really tolerate such lists, in terms of giving them ear) unless they have been convinced of the importance of the list giver and the fundamental teachings contained therein. So the story of God as creator, the one who called Abraham, rescued Israel, and then gave the torah at Sinai through Moses, comes to be of central importance for any giving of instruction in Leviticus, especially as this literature is primarily listlike in nature. Also important, however, is that the *content* of the list must be compelling, something worthy of obeying. To put this another way, Leviticus cannot be read apart from the larger Pentateuch because it was not meant to be a law code like those a modern-day lawyer might consult when in need of direction for a particular case. Leviticus is part of a larger story. It belongs to a particular people. Leviticus affects and is addressed to the people Israel, not simply priests, despite the seemingly priestly orientation of Leviticus as a whole.

Leviticus's placement at the heart of the Pentateuch—the very center of the Torah—is therefore key. Leviticus might be thought of as "list," but it can really be understood only in light of the books and other types of literature that surround it.[6] In some ways Leviticus is not so much the buried law code found in the middle of the Pentateuch (and generally ignored today) as it is

---

6. For more on this, see the helpful article by Rolf Rendtorff, "Is It Possible to Read Leviticus as a Separate Book?" in *Reading Leviticus: A Conversation with Mary Douglas*, ed. John F. A. Sawyer, Journal for the Study of the Old Testament: Supplement Series 227 (Sheffield: Sheffield Academic Press, 1996), 22–35.

the very climax or even driving force of the Torah, the very teaching of God given at Sinai. This is a point we may not fully appreciate if we read it apart from the other books of the Pentateuch or if we read it through eyes that discount priesthood and ritual—the eyes of traditional Protestantism. When it comes to theological interpretation of the book or even specific chapters of Leviticus, interpretation is best done in the light of the Pentateuch's literary context and the larger book itself, even while we can accept that the Torah was not necessarily composed as one unit, and that Leviticus was not written as a single book itself. Reading Leviticus as a book that cannot be separated from the rest of the Pentateuch is a key feature of the present chapter.

Outline of Leviticus

The first chapters of the book (1–7) are striking in their immediate and narrow focus on laws related to offerings (burnt, cereal, well-being, purification, and reparation).[7] No time is wasted introducing these instructions, thus highlighting that the book assumes the readers (or hearers) are people familiar with sacrifices in general, as well as with the all-important backstory provided by the narratives of Exodus. Chapters 8–10 contain instructions for installing priests and anointing Aaron and his sons, and included here is narrative material that describes offerings made and the cost involved in not administering these properly (the very lives of priests are at stake). Chapter 11 begins with teachings on clean and unclean food, and then continues into laws on sexuality, childbirth, leprosy and sickness, and other bodily ailments that cause uncleanness. In some ways chapters 11–15 function as a list of occasions that make offerings to Yhwh necessary. Chapter 16 might be considered the very center of Leviticus, with its teachings on Yom Kippur (or Day of Atonement/ Purgation). If the work of Wilfried Warning is correct, the narrative markers of Leviticus point to chapter 16, not 19, as the literary center of the book, an idea to which we will return.[8] Warning's suggestion needs to be taken seriously, if for no other reason than that this solemn day has remained at the very center of Jewish life, both in the past and into the present.

Chapter 17 begins what scholars call the Holiness Code (more below); here, through specific laws on maintaining purity mainly through social action, Israel is able to live a life that is "Holy to Yhwh." From a literary and rhetorical perspective, we observe that in addition to the common literary marker of chapters 1–16 ("The Lord spoke to Moses"), added into this section is the recurring divine refrain "I am Yhwh your God." The effect this has is to

---

7. To keep them vivid, I follow Milgrom in naming these offerings. They are traditionally rendered: burnt, grain, peace, sin, and guilt offerings.

8. See Wilfried Warning, *Literary Artistry in Leviticus*, Biblical Interpretation Series 35 (Leiden: Brill, 1999), 178.

elevate even further the sense of divine authorization already present in the book, something particularly potent when we recall that the book was heard, not read. Within these chapters we find teachings on food (ch. 17), sexual relations (18), practical living as a community (19), grave offenses (20), rules for the Aaronide priesthood (21–22), festivals and other laws (23–24), and teachings on Sabbath and Jubilee years (25). Chapter 26 concludes the book with its divine sanctions, a set of self-contained exhortations to obey the teachings just given. These blessing-and-curse formulas are clearly intended to underline the importance and seriousness of what has been said. Chapter 27 then starts a new section, especially after chapter 26 so ably concluded the book in content, form, and thrust. Chapter 27 ends the book with a verse containing phraseology close in form and content to the previous ending of chapter 26. This last chapter of the book reads like an appendix, inserted to clarify a matter important to the ancient world. It stipulates the particular values that are to be assigned to various persons, animals, or other items promised in vows, in case a vow is broken and payment is required.

Generally speaking, scholars understand the block of literature beginning in Exodus 25 and ending at Numbers 36 to be priestly material (P). There are many and clear exceptions within this literature (not every verse or section is considered to be P material) and this is not to say that the material is unified or understood to be written at one time by one author (or school); it is, rather, a statement about the orientation and genre of this block of literature. The P material in this block is distinctive for its emphasis on instruction (or list) and matters relating to holiness, worship, and purity. If for no other reason, this idea is important for outlining the book of Leviticus because any outline will only be partial insofar as it does not outline this larger priestly unit (Exod. 25–Num. 36) as well.[9]

As discussed above, Leviticus contains twenty-seven chapters, and there is a high level of scholarly agreement that the book is best divided into two main sections: chapters 1–16 and 17–26 (with ch. 27 functioning as an appendix). As mentioned, the first section is primarily concerned with offerings and matters of ritual cleanliness (and returning to a state of purity if unclean) while the second section is often called the Holiness Code (or *Heiligkeitsgesetz*, abbreviated as H). This second section has earned its title due to its strong emphasis on practical, holy living and its repeated use of holiness language (Israel must be *qadosh*, "holy"). In these chapters holiness seems to become more closely connected to morality and is extended to the entire people and land in ways that are not envisioned in chapters 1–16 (where some aspects of holiness seem reserved for the priests and the sanctuary).[10] The usefulness of

9. For more on matters of the composition of this larger section, as well as of the Pentateuch more generally, see the introduction to this book (above) and Nathan MacDonald's discussion in ch. 4 (below).

10. I here draw from Jacob Milgrom, *Leviticus: A Book of Ritual and Ethics*, Continental Commentary (Minneapolis: Fortress, 2004).

this division for our purposes is questionable, though it is clear in reading the text of Leviticus itself that the theological focus and vocabulary do shift in noticeable ways. Furthermore, the H section starts in chapter 17 similarly to Leviticus 1, using the same sacrificial vocabulary to begin it as if it were a new section.[11] This likely indicates a compositional development (i.e., the hand of a new scribe), yet it is clear that great care was taken to link the two sections.

As a book, Leviticus begins and ends in the same way. It indicates that the words contained within it are given to Moses by YHWH, within a geographical and historical context: "the tent of meeting" (1:1) and "Mount Sinai" (27:34). The point made in these verses—that the words of Leviticus are given directly by YHWH to Moses—is in some ways a controlling feature of the book: it resurfaces over and over, with each new set of laws, with similar words being reiterated to form a regular refrain: "The LORD spoke/said to Moses, saying . . ." These literary markers, identifying a series of divine speeches in the book (thirty-seven in all), are usually highlighted in Leviticus manuscripts by a blank line (as in Codex Leningradensis) and were rightly recognized by the medieval scribes responsible for modern chapter divisions of the Bible (they quite often begin a new chapter of Leviticus); they have also been the subject of a recent monograph by Warning, mentioned above. Warning argues that these markers and the divine speeches they contain should be used to determine the structure of the book. Warning then suggests that Leviticus is a unified book, written by one author. Although his authorship thesis is certainly open to question (a later editor could equally have been responsible for introducing these markers),[12] the main point for our purposes is that Leviticus, *in its final form*, has been carefully structured—beginning, end, and every point in between—to emphasize the divine sanctioning of its teachings, presented as the very words of God, given to Moses at Sinai.

Scholarly, Historical, and Hermeneutical Issues

In this section, I discuss a number of hermeneutical issues related to Leviticus, to assist the reader in gaining a perspective with which to interpret the book. We will do this in an overview fashion. Such an approach runs the risk of

11. This point is made by Mary Douglas and supported by Jacob Milgrom, *Leviticus 17–22: A New Translation with Introduction and Commentary*, Anchor Bible 3A (New York: Doubleday, 2000), 1332. For a helpful description of the Holiness Code, see Jan Joosten, *People and Land in the Holiness Code: An Exegetical Study of the Ideational Framework of the Law in Leviticus 17–26*, Supplements to Vetus Testamentum 67 (Leiden: Brill, 1996), ch. 2.

12. For precisely this critique, see Jan Joosten's review of Warning's book in *Revue d'histoire et de philosophie religieuses* 81 (2001): 214. Another attempt to argue for the compositional unity of the book is Nobuyoshi Kiuchi, *Leviticus*, Apollos Old Testament Commentary 3 (Downers Grove, IL: InterVarsity, 2007), esp. 16–18.

becoming superficial and cursory in nature, but I hope that covering a range of subjects will be of use to the reader, especially since many of the ideas encountered here will be of relevance for our exegesis of Leviticus 16 below. We will consider five key topics:

- Corporate responsibility
- Protestant biases against ritual and priests
- Anthropological readings of Leviticus
- Death and life in Leviticus
- Leviticus and the New Testament

Corporate Responsibility

Although it may not be immediately apparent, a central emphasis of the book of Leviticus is corporate responsibility. Probably no other study has explored this topic more ably than Joel Kaminsky's *Corporate Responsibility in the Hebrew Bible*.[13] The matter is particularly important for our biblical book because most of its laws seem concerned, in one way or another, with how the actions of some (or someone) affect the whole. That is, Leviticus is concerned with how both right living and transgression affect the communal life of Israel under God. To highlight this idea, consider the rabbinic midrash with which Kaminsky opens his study: "Rabbi Simeon bar Yohai taught: There is a story about men who were sitting on a ship, one of them lifted up a borer and began boring a hole beneath his seat. His companions said to him: 'What are you sitting and doing?' He replied to them: 'What concern is it of yours, am I not drilling under my seat?' They said to him: 'But the water will come up and flood the ship for all of us'" (*Leviticus Rabbah* 4.6).[14]

Although Kaminsky does not explicitly treat Leviticus in his monograph, his work overall certainly applies to Leviticus in important ways. His conclusion that "being human means that we are linked to other people through the consequences of their actions" seems particularly relevant when we come to understand that Leviticus's emphasis on *tahor* and *tame'* (clean and unclean) is not simply due to antiquated ideas regarding taboos or superstition, but is intricately related to how sin and other actions or conditions can pollute a wider community (and God's sanctuary) if they are not dealt with swiftly, correctly, and completely.[15] We will return to this in a moment. For now, note how even positively stated laws in Leviticus, those foundational for Jewish, Christian, as well as modern Western life, are given a particular emphasis in

13. Joel S. Kaminsky, *Corporate Responsibility in the Hebrew Bible*, Journal for the Study of the Old Testament: Supplement Series 196 (Sheffield: Sheffield Academic Press, 1995).
14. Cited in ibid., 11.
15. Ibid., 188.

the book to highlight life in a *community* as opposed to life as an *individual*. One might think, for example, of the above-mentioned Second Commandment of Jesus: "Love your neighbor as yourself" (Lev. 19:18). This commandment seems simple enough; yet for Leviticus, it can be understood only in light of larger questions regarding communal life. In the context of Leviticus, to love one's neighbor is to turn a neighbor from sin, thereby keeping guilt from damaging the larger community: "You shall not hate in your heart anyone of your kin; *you shall reprove your neighbor, or you will incur guilt yourself. You shall not take vengeance or bear a grudge against any of your people, but you shall love your neighbor as yourself: I am the* LORD" (Leviticus 19:17–18).

In a separate article, Kaminsky explores this teaching as it has come to be understood in the modern West.[16] He rightly concludes that Westerners who think that the biblical idea of loving one's neighbor is to "live and let live" misunderstand it; such a way of thinking is completely foreign to the traditional teachings of Judaism and Christianity, and most certainly to the book of Leviticus. To *love* a neighbor is to *reprove* a neighbor, to correct a neighbor, to turn him or her from sin.

The laws of Leviticus thus cannot be separated from the larger communal context in which they are given and meant to be kept. Disobeying God's teaching has deep implications for the larger community, but so does obeying them. The blessings and curses of chapter 26 make this clear, as do numerous other parts of the Pentateuch, especially Deuteronomy. Particularly easy to overlook here, however, is how Leviticus understands certain transgressions as being too grievous or damaging to be atoned for (or purged) from the community. It is tempting to think that these laws simply have to do with penal retribution, or even with a lack of power or willingness on the part of the Deity to forgive, yet the text is ultimately not interested in these ideas. The biblical record overall is clear that God *can* forgive sins like murder and adultery, as seen in the stories of David, Moses, and possibly Cain. The issue here, however, relates to how certain sins taint the community or sanctuary so much that atonement (or purgation) is not to be sought; rather, the offender or offenders are simply to be removed from society by exclusion or execution. Such seemingly extreme action keeps the larger community and sanctuary from being defiled; it also makes clear just how serious communal purity is. Sins in this category include "sexual sins ([Lev.] 18:20, 23–25, 27–30), idolatry (20:2–5), murder (Num. 35:16–21, 31) and profaning the sacred (e.g., [Lev.] 7:19–21; 22:3, 9)."[17] In each instance, maintaining the purity of the community is fundamental to the law itself.

---

16. Joel S. Kaminsky, "Loving One's (Israelite) Neighbor: Election and Commandment in Leviticus 19," *Interpretation* 62 (2008): 123–32.

17. T. Desmond Alexander, *From Paradise to the Promised Land: An Introduction to the Pentateuch*, 2nd ed. (Grand Rapids: Baker Academic, 2002), 209. He (inadvertently?) omits cursing one's parents (Lev. 20:9).

Rituals such as purification offerings, the Day of Atonement (or Purgation), and removing grievous sins all have the effect of keeping the sanctuary from becoming tainted, as well as ensuring that a holiness balance is kept within the community. Throughout this chapter I have been referring to the sanctuary in relation to defilement, not simply to the people Israel. I do this because of Milgrom's argument that acts of purification purify not so much (or only) the offerer, but especially the sanctuary since it (too) has become tainted because of sin (hence blood is placed on the altar, not on the person who is bringing the offering).[18] Purification offerings keep inadvertent sins from tainting the sanctuary, and the yearly Yom Kippur ritual cleanses the sanctuary of the remaining sins and those of the brazen, intentional sinner. Maintaining a holy people and sanctuary secures a balanced world order, and in some ways the earthly community with its sanctuary represents a larger, balanced cosmic order. Samuel Balentine develops this idea in light of the Day of Purgation in which the balance of society is restored. Following Milgrom, he highlights the idea that this is needed so that God will not leave the sanctuary due to its becoming too polluted. As Balentine states, "When the sanctuary is holy, God is present, *and the world is secure*, because heaven and earth are joined in common pursuit of God's creational intentions."[19] This cannot be achieved unless the larger people of God pursue a common end of keeping things holy by living in holy ways, rectifying impurities, and removing grievous impurities altogether. Underlying Leviticus is a larger order that modern-day, autonomous Westerners may have difficulty understanding. The sin of a neighbor does more than affect that one person; it may indeed pollute the entire community. And God's very presence with his people is therefore in danger.

For some Christians it may not be difficult to see parallels in resetting the world's rightful order through celebration of the Eucharist, an act that rebalances the world through the forgiveness found in the body and blood of Jesus. For others, such an idea will seem foreign. This naturally leads us to our next section.

Protestant Biases against Ritual and Priests

Perhaps no Old Testament scholar sums up a modern Protestant bias against priests and rituals better than Julius Wellhausen. His highly influential theory

18. For an overview, see Milgrom, *Leviticus: A Book of Ritual and Ethics*, 30–33. My parentheses indicate that I prefer to see both the sanctuary and the people as needing purification, rather than Milgrom's more restrictive idea that only the sanctuary is in view. For reasons why, see Roy E. Gane, "Privative Preposition מן in Purification Offering Pericopes and the Changing Face of 'Dorian Gray,'" *Journal of Biblical Literature* 127 (2008): 209–22.

19. See Samuel E. Balentine, *The Torah's Vision of Worship*, Overtures to Biblical Theology (Minneapolis: Fortress, 1999), 164. He works from Jacob Milgrom, *Leviticus 1–16: A New Translation with Introduction and Commentary*, Anchor Bible 3 (New York: Doubleday, 1991), 258–61.

regarding the composition of the Pentateuch, the Documentary Hypothesis, was built upon the premise that P was late, that is, the last section added to the Pentateuch (J, E, D, and *then* P). Such an idea is not untenable (I assume a comparable premise in this chapter), but his reasons for this conclusion are part of his larger argument about the development of religions more generally, and of Israelite religion in particular. For Wellhausen, P is late because it represents the highly regulated, stilted, and bureaucratic religion of a later period, which squelched the earlier, freer, "heart religion" found in the JE material of the Pentateuch. He arrived at this conclusion through examining five areas of Israel's life: place of worship, sacrifices, festivals, priesthood, and priestly income. Wenham conveniently summarizes Wellhausen's findings in tabular form (see table 3.1).

Table 3.1 Wellhausen's Documentary Hypothesis

	Early Monarchy/J E	Late Monarchy/D	Postexilic/P
Place of worship	Any holy place	Attempt to centralize all worship in Jerusalem	Jerusalem the only sanctuary
Sacrifice	Voluntary, joyful family occasions	Sacrifices only in Jerusalem; secular slaughter elsewhere	Sacrifices highly regulated and expiatory
Festivals	Local harvest celebrations	Pilgrimage to Jerusalem required	Festivals fixed by calendar; linked to history, not to harvest
Priesthood	Anyone can act as priest and sacrifice	Tribe of Levitical priests becoming important	Highly organized priesthood with great authority; descended from Levi and Aaron
Priestly income	Parts of sacrifice voluntarily given by offerer	Shoulder, cheeks, and stomach of sacrifices	Many sacrificial animals, tithes, firstlings

Adapted from Gordon J. Wenham, *Exploring the Old Testament: A Guide to the Pentateuch* (Downers Grove, IL: InterVarsity, 2003), 170.

For Wellhausen, the minute priestly laws of Leviticus are a late, constricting development, and his preference for the earlier, "heart" religion of the patriarchs, in which people worship God freely and directly, is readily apparent. It is no surprise to recognize that Wellhausen was a Lutheran, and that he conducted his research in a late nineteenth-century German Lutheran context. Luther's preference for "grace" over "law," and his fundamental idea of "the priesthood of all believers," is hardly veiled in Wellhausen's work, and Wellhausen's disparagement of priestly regulation and minute legal codes is not out of keeping with much of the biblical scholarship of his day, or that which followed. It is no secret that modern biblical scholarship was given birth by German Protestantism and was subsequently nurtured and developed by the larger Protestant world. The trend to treat ritual and priesthood negatively, and to pit law against gospel (or grace), continued with particular force in biblical scholarship in the years leading up to the Holocaust. That a regulated, ritualistic form of worship might indeed be a deeply participatory and profoundly meaningful way to worship God is something that was regularly underemphasized in mainstream biblical scholarship until Catholics and Jews joined in academic study of the Bible, in the years following Vatican II and with the advent of modern Jewish biblical scholarship.[20] Increasingly, scholars are much more careful with how they describe priestly material; however, the residual effects of Wellhausen's work (and modern Protestant scholarship more generally) can still be felt, especially in the tendency to tame and spiritualize ritual, or at times to shun and disparage it.[21]

But perhaps a continued reluctance toward ritual is not surprising. Not only is the Western world in which we live (and in which scholarship thrives) much less formal and less inclined toward ceremony than it was a few generations ago but also how one worships in a religious setting each week, or how one worships God daily, will undoubtedly contribute—even if subconsciously—to how one reads religious texts. If a scholar is part of a religious tradition that tends to minimize ritual, liturgy, and formulized prayers, or one that sees its religious leader not so much as a priest (one who represents the people to God) but rather as a "prophet" (one who speaks for God to the people), that person will likely read texts like Leviticus in a particular way. If one views Christian worship services primarily as a time in which to "hear the word," and less as a time in which, through the Eucharist, Christ's atoning sacrifice is in some way re-presented to mediate the sins of the world, that person may well be less interested in texts that present ritual and repeated sacrifice positively, as things that may have real power. To be sure, this is not to suggest that such a person is incapable of coming to a deeper understanding of ritual and repeated sacrifice. However, it may not come naturally, and there may be subconscious barriers to reading a book like Leviticus appreciatively or even well. In the same way that the Christian tradition understands faith and obedience to be prerequisites for proper reading of its Scriptures, so too might one argue that Leviticus is best read through eyes that value ritual.

20. For a helpful overview that traces the beginnings of modern Jewish biblical scholarship, see S. David Sperling, "Modern Jewish Interpretation," in *The Jewish Study Bible*, ed. Adele Berlin and Marc Zvi Brettler (New York: Oxford University Press, 2004), 1908–19. On the rise of Catholic biblical scholarship, see Luke T. Johnson, "What's Catholic about Catholic Biblical Scholarship? An Opening Statement," in *The Future of Catholic Biblical Scholarship: A Constructive Conversation*, ed. Luke T. Johnson and William S. Kurz (Grand Rapids: Eerdmans, 2002), 3–34.

21. Examples of such work are not hard to find. For example, the recent commentary of Kiuchi, *Leviticus*, puts heavy emphasis on OT ritual as symbol. Though there is much value in his work, in places ritual becomes little more than something that needs to be overcome in order to see its "true" meaning; see esp. 30–49.

However, in some sense a Christian will always be removed from Leviticus in ways that an observant Jew will not. This is because the application of its laws will never be for Christians what it is for those who seek to live by them day to day.[22] To be sure, for both groups there is a host of ways in which Leviticus is interpreted figuratively, the most significant for Jews being that there no longer are centralized worship or physical sacrifices made through the priests of Aaron. However, the problems for Christians are still greater, and as others have suggested, in some ways Christians will always be "reading other people's mail" even if they claim this mail as their own.[23] For this reason a person's encounters with observant Jews who take the commandments of Leviticus seriously (in ways that gentile Christians never can) are likely to help facilitate a deeper appreciation of this book. Further, as I can attest, sympathies for formalized worship and high eucharistic theology can also help in gaining a deeper appreciation and understanding of Leviticus. No longer is it a book weighed down with bureaucracy and ritual that need to be overcome, but one that holds deeply meaningful tradition and rituals pointing to the profound shaping of lives lived under God and with others, and which point to order and significance in every sphere of life.[24]

Anthropological Readings of Leviticus

The past fifty years have brought about great changes in the study of the Bible, due in no small part to the contributions the discipline received from anthropology. In particular, the work of British anthropologist Mary Douglas has significantly affected the study of Leviticus, even while her original work has been much modified and in places abandoned altogether. Originally, Douglas included a chapter on the abominable foods in Leviticus (particularly Lev. 11) in her landmark book *Purity and Danger*.[25] In that study, Douglas

22. That those with a practical sympathy for the *mitzvot* (commandments) of the Torah are its best interpreters is a key point of Gershom M. H. Ratheiser, *Mitzvoth Ethics and the Jewish Bible: The End of Old Testament Theology* (London: T&T Clark, 2007). See my review of this work in *Reviews in Religion and Theology* 15, no. 2 (2008): 237–41.

23. This now-common phraseology stems from Paul van Buren, "On Reading Someone Else's Mail: The Church and Israel's Scriptures," in *Die hebräische Bibel und ihre zweifache Nachgeschichte: Festschrift für Rolf Rendtorff zum 65. Geburtstag*, ed. Erhard Blum, Christian Machholz, and Ekkehard W. Stegemann (Neukirchen-Vluyn: Neukirchener Verlag, 1990), 595–606.

24. For more on how Jews and Christians might learn from each other in reading the Hebrew Scriptures together, even while there will always be fundamental differences between them, consult my work in Joel S. Kaminsky and Joel N. Lohr, *The Torah: A Beginner's Guide* (Oxford: Oneworld, 2011). See also R. W. L. Moberly, *The Old Testament of the Old Testament: Patriarchal Narratives and Mosaic Yahwism*, Overtures to Biblical Theology (Minneapolis: Fortress, 1992), 147–75.

25. Mary Douglas, *Purity and Danger: An Analysis of Concepts of Pollution and Taboo* (London: Routledge, 1966), ch. 3.

argued that distinctions in Leviticus regarding purity and pollution are not primitive superstitions but rather reveal a complex, ordered system. Douglas rejected the widespread idea that the distinctions between clean and unclean animals in Leviticus are arbitrary. Rather, these distinctions reinforce the created order as reflected in Genesis 1, a text that scholars attribute to the same priestly authors who produced Leviticus 1–16. In her view, the priestly material (P) shows that only animals that fully conform to each of the three realms of creation—sky, land, and sea—are fit for Israelite consumption. As Douglas makes clear, this is because there is a direct correlation between P's conception of holiness and the idea of wholeness. To maintain holiness, not only must one avoid unethical behaviors, one also must not consume things that are viewed as unwholesome or outside regular classification. Thus one avoids eating animals like pigs because pigs do not exhibit all the characteristics one finds in the exemplary idea of a four-footed domestic land animal: unlike cows and sheep, they do not chew their cud. As Douglas declares, "The dietary laws would have been like signs which at every turn inspired meditation on the oneness, purity and completeness of God. By rules of avoidance holiness was given a physical expression in every encounter with the animal kingdom and at every meal."[26]

Not all scholars were convinced by her work, and in later publications Douglas came to acknowledge that aspects of her model were inadequate. Though she continued to maintain her basic premise that distinctions of purity and pollution are not arbitrary (i.e., they are still part of a complex, ordered system), she subsequently suggested that forbidden foods, for example, represent not so much anomalies in classification, but rather point to a larger system of *justice* and *divine order*. In a study on clean and unclean animals in Leviticus, Douglas conveniently summarizes her provocative conclusions:

> Now we are in a position to make the connection between all three types of forbidden animal foods. First, out of honour to the blood and the life that is in the blood (Lev. 17.14), no flesh with blood in it is to be eaten. . . . Second, animal species that resemble in shape the sufferers from physical injury must not be eaten, that is, an equivalence is drawn between species and individuals lamed, or maimed or otherwise disfigured, and connects with the rule against offering blemished animals. Third, in the waters those creatures without fins or scales must not appear on the table as food. . . . Fishes hatch out naked, their fins and scales grow on them, so shoals of baby fishes, minnows, whitebait and larvae of insects, the orphans of the water world, would be forbidden by this rule.
>
> Holiness is incompatible with predatory behaviour. The command to be holy is fulfilled by respecting blood, the symbol of violent predation, and respecting the symbolic victims of predation. The forbidden animals in this perspective represent the endangered categories for whom Isaiah spoke, the oppressed, the

---

26. Ibid., 57.

fatherless, the widow (Isa. 1.17). Respect for them is a way of remembering the difference between the clean and unclean, the holy and the unholy.[27]

Douglas did not stop there. In her monograph that followed, *Leviticus as Literature*, she developed these ideas further and concluded that certain other Levitical impurities represent a larger divine order as well. In particular, she suggests that the laws of Leviticus show a reverence for all life in imitation of God himself. Furthermore, becoming impure through encounters with death or unclean objects or foods signifies a breaking of God's covenant with Israel. As she states, "The food purity rules and the touch purity rules are part of a unified doctrine in which corpse pollution, bloodshed, and unsanctified death are classed as breaches of covenant. . . . It has been a puzzlement to Christian readers that Leviticus puts unclean contact into the same bracket as breaches of the moral code. However, there is nothing puzzling about both kinds of disobedience to the Lord's command being treated together. To touch an unclean thing and then to approach the tabernacle puts the person in need of atonement."[28]

For Douglas, therefore, the impurities of Leviticus are in some way linked to a larger schema of a life lived under God. Though at times her readings border on being too symbolic, they certainly give us pause and force us to reflect on larger themes. God's high value placed on all life is signified in what is pure, while things that are impure or unclean in some way represent an encounter with death. As God's holy people, death must be avoided; when this is not possible, purgation is required. In some ways, all of this points back to the ideals of the early chapters of Genesis, especially texts such as Genesis 1:29–30, in which vegetarianism is mandated, undoubtedly out of respect for life. In these early chapters we also witness something of the divine hope that all life would be valued (and thus not taken). Following this comes the breakdown of that ideal, which resulted in the flood, followed by the life regulation of Genesis 9:1–7. Leviticus further regulates life and death through its laws even while it continues to uphold the original value placed on life in Genesis. In Leviticus every aspect of living with God points to life and death through a system of clean and unclean. Israel is to be a people of *life*, not death.

Although returning to Eden may strike the reader as a very Christian idea, it is an idea found in the Old Testament itself (see, e.g., Isa. 51:3; Ezek. 36:35); in some ways such thinking, as brought about by Douglas's work more generally, affirms various strands of traditional Jewish interpretation. Jewish

---

27. Mary Douglas, "The Forbidden Animals in Leviticus," *Journal for the Study of the Old Testament* 59 (1993): 3–23, here 22–23.

28. Mary Douglas, *Leviticus as Literature* (Oxford: Oxford University Press, 1999), 150–51. Compare the insightful reflection by Ronald S. Hendel, "Table and Altar: The Anthropology of Food in the Priestly Torah," in *To Break Every Yoke: Essays in Honor of Marvin L. Chaney*, ed. Robert B. Coote and Norman K. Gottwald (Sheffield: Sheffield Phoenix, 2007), 131–48. For a critique of Douglas's work, see Watts, *Ritual and Rhetoric*, 15–27.

interpretation has often viewed life and death as key to Leviticus and to the larger Hebrew Tanakh, or Jewish Scriptures.[29] This leads us to our next section.

Death and Life in Leviticus

Although the emphasis on life and death is important to traditional Jewish interpretation, it was Christian scholar Gordon Wenham who helped to explicate this idea more generally in Leviticus scholarship.[30] His work is important because he makes significant connections between states of impurity with death and states of purity with life. Wenham showed that in many of the laws found in Leviticus 12–15, for example (on childbirth, diseases, and discharges), there seems to be an attempt to rectify various symbolic encounters with death; in these passages certain types of sicknesses and other conditions diminish one's quality or sense of life and likely are viewed as a form of death. This explains why someone who experiences a severe skin disease becomes impure (Lev. 13–14), and it also helps to explain why a male or a female who has a genital discharge is unclean. Those with the deadening of skin or who suffer from discharges—expending life fluid: blood, semen, or otherwise—participate in a diminished form of life. This needs to be remedied through purification.

Such thinking may also help to explain why normal male-female intercourse, even if a new life results, still brings about impurity (Lev. 15:18). Again, perhaps the emission of semen that occurs during this act represented a diminishing of life in that life-fluid was expended. Such thinking may have been heightened within biblical culture due to the fact that the mechanics of semen production and pregnancy were not fully understood. Whatever the case, when certain laws in Leviticus are read in the light of life and death, they often (though not always) are illuminated and make more sense than if we simply view them as ancient superstitions or taboos. Furthermore, conceptions of life and death integrate well with other pentateuchal emphases, seen clearly in Deuteronomy, especially passages like Deuteronomy 30:15–20. In fact, the theme of life and death can be seen to animate much of the rest of the Old Testament and is an idea brought into particular focus in the New Testament.

Leviticus and the New Testament

This brings us to our final section before we move into our interpretation of Leviticus 16. It is with the New Testament that the interpretation of Leviticus

---

29. For an overview of Jewish ideas here, including those on "returning to Eden," see Jacob Neusner, *Handbook of Rabbinic Theology: Language, System, Structure* (Leiden: Brill, 2002), 243–75, esp. 260, 275.

30. See Gordon J. Wenham, *The Book of Leviticus*, New International Commentary on the Old Testament (Grand Rapids: Eerdmans, 1979).

becomes particularly difficult for the Christian interpreter: although Leviticus is quoted very little in the New Testament, it is of central importance in the debates between Paul and his fellow Jews regarding law keeping. Not only does Leviticus seem to contain the largest share of the Torah's laws concerning Israel's distinctives and religious identity among the nations (what scholars often call "boundary markers" or "identity markers"—circumcision, dietary laws, ritual observance), but it is also here that we most clearly come against questions about the nature of the law as it relates to *life*. To put the matter simply, Paul uses Leviticus to question whether the law brings life. His answer, in short, is that it does *not*. There is thus a great potential for conflict here since throughout this chapter I have maintained that keeping the way of the Torah, and laws of Leviticus in particular, brings life. Leviticus 26 makes this abundantly clear. Yet Paul uses Leviticus (specifically a statement in 18:5) to construct his argument that law keeping does *not* bring life; life comes only through *faith*. (Paul's use of Lev. 18:5 is found in Rom. 10:5 and Gal. 3:12.)

The issues here are complex. In fact, much of the current heated debate regarding "the New Perspective on Paul" is intimately tied up with these and related concerns. However, here is not the place to rehearse these arguments. For our purposes, I point to, and will engage briefly with, the recent work of Francis Watson in his *Paul and the Hermeneutics of Faith*.[31] Watson devotes a lengthy chapter to Leviticus and masterfully shows that there are two competing voices within the Torah itself regarding living by works and faith, voices that Paul discerns and exploits. Although Paul makes much of Habakkuk 2:4 in his Galatians and Romans discussions ("the just shall live by faith"; Rom. 1:17; Gal. 3:11), Watson shows how Paul also uses Deuteronomy 30:12–14 to bolster his agenda of faith righteousness by reading this text in opposition to Leviticus 18:5 ("The one who does these things will live by them"; Rom. 10:5). Watson states:

> Leviticus [18:5] represents one side of this inner-scriptural antithesis, which Paul here characterizes as "the righteousness which is by the law," which Moses "writes" (Rom. 10.5). The other side is here represented by a text that derives not from the prophets, as in Galatians, but from within the Torah itself (Deut. 30.12–14). This is here attributed not to Moses, as in the case of the Leviticus text, but to a personified "Righteousness of faith." . . . Paul aims here to show that, despite the impressive clarity of the Leviticus text, the soteriology of the Torah is not a singular, monolithic entity. Beneath the surface of Moses' text, a second, very different voice may be discerned.[32]

However, to be clear, Watson notes that Paul does more than simply regard the Leviticus and Deuteronomy texts as oppositional; Paul must *rewrite* the

31. Francis Watson, *Paul and the Hermeneutics of Faith* (London: T&T Clark, 2004).
32. Ibid., 330–31.

latter because in context, indeed directly therein, Deuteronomy 30:12–14 actually "offers eloquent support for the law's programme as summarized in Leviticus 18.5" (namely, the law leads to *life*).[33] Watson rightly points out that Paul can set the two texts against each other only by "drawing selectively on phraseology" from Deuteronomy 30, and Paul must rework this material for his purposes: "In Romans, the Deuteronomy passage is comprehensively rewritten . . . so that it testifies to the righteousness of faith, and against the righteousness of the law as articulated in the Leviticus citation."[34] This of course has the distinct advantage that Paul can promote *faith* as the means to life now that "the law's project has . . . been brought to an end by the divine saving action in Christ."[35] Watson conveniently summarizes: "The words of Deuteronomy become a witness against the Leviticus text in its literal sense. Those who zealously practice the law as the divinely appointed way to life, as instructed in Leviticus, are bluntly exhorted to desist by a strange new voice that avails itself of the words of Deuteronomy."[36]

It is tempting to explore this matter in more depth, especially given that the present volume is interested in theological interpretation of the Pentateuch as Christian Scripture. What better way to engage Leviticus than with Paul as our guide (in dialogue with Watson), working from the pages of the New Testament? However, my purpose in highlighting this discussion is not to come to definite conclusions on this matter but rather to illustrate some of the tensions inherent in interpreting the Pentateuch as a Christian reader. What are we as responsible readers of both canons to do? Does Leviticus bring *life* or *death*?

Clearly we must recognize that Paul's voice is extremely important, but so too is his context; further, other voices in the New Testament, as is the case in the Old Testament itself, create tension here, and Paul's voice is one amid others when it comes to matters of faith and works. To be sure, Paul's voice is vital, yet the decision of the early church to include New Testament authors like James in the canon, with his emphasis on justification through works and law-keeping—not faith alone (cf. Gal. 3:1–14 and James 2)—forces us to be especially careful. We also need to take note of those judgment passages in which one's actions make all the difference, such as Revelation 20:11–15 and Matthew 25:31–46. Perhaps there is a time to say that Leviticus brings life and perhaps there is another to say that it does not. One might argue that the Western Protestant church today is in more danger of resting in faith (or what one *believes*) rather than works, and for this reason we might choose to emphasize obedience to God over faith.[37] In this chapter I have chosen to focus

33. Ibid., 338.
34. Ibid., 336, 338.
35. Ibid., 334.
36. Ibid., 341.
37. To be sure, such dichotomies are not really satisfying or even all that helpful. Faith in the NT always implies more than intellectual assent and suggests the need for action, or a life

on life through obedience rather than on faith as found in Pauline debates, debates made in reference to Paul's Jewish law-keeping contemporaries. This does not rule out that another, new context will call for a different emphasis.[38]

We have by no means exhausted all the things that might be said to introduce Leviticus to readers interested in theological interpretation. We have simply highlighted five important themes that allow us some perspective in reading the book of Leviticus well. At this point I would like to move from this general discussion to a more specific, text-centered one through a theological exploration of Leviticus 16.

Leviticus 16: Purging the People

In this section we will look at a text that stands at the very heart of Jewish life, and in some sense of the Christian tradition too, even though it has in many ways disappeared from the Christian conscience. I propose to look at Leviticus's Yom Kippur (Day of Atonement, or Purgation) ritual. One might be tempted to look at culturally appealing texts like the ethical teachings found in the Holiness Code, in particular chapters such as Leviticus 19 with its "Love your neighbor as yourself" passage. Nevertheless, I choose Leviticus 16 because it seems sufficiently characteristic of the ethos of Leviticus as a whole—and yet foreign enough to modern readers—for it to be useful in bringing an ancient, seemingly primitive, and superstitious text into new light. My hope is that in doing so, we might come to see that interpretation of this sort is interesting, relevant, and actually necessary for Christian theology.

Structurally, Leviticus 16 comes in the first section of the book, one concerned primarily with rituals related to the priesthood. As I argue below, however, these verses do not address a private priestly affair but relate to the entire Israelite community. The event involves the purgation of all the sins of Israel, through an intriguing and elaborate ritual. As I also argue below, this chapter is indispensable for a New Testament understanding of Jesus and his work of bringing salvation to the whole world.

Leviticus 16:1 could suggest that at one time chapters 11–15 did not exist and were later inserted and now interrupt the otherwise flowing text. The narrator reminds the reader of the previous episode of Leviticus 10, the only real narrative episode in the book so far, concerning the deaths of Abihu and Nadab (and their offering "strange fire"; 10:1). This tragic event is largely unexplained and exceedingly terse; it has baffled interpreters and the rabbis

---

lived in relation to God. Such an idea is readily detected in reading Heb. 11–12. Consult the set of essays under "The Call to Faith in Hebrews," in *The Epistle to the Hebrews and Christian Theology*, ed. Richard Bauckham et al. (Grand Rapids: Eerdmans, 2009), 353–437.

38. This is also one way of saying that I do not necessarily think Luther got it wrong given *his* context. But it is also clear that we no longer live in sixteenth-century Europe.

for centuries because the precise nature of the offense is not clear. The text
itself, however, assumes otherwise. Immediately after the deaths of Aaron's
sons, Moses essentially tells Aaron that they should have known better; that
is, YHWH had instructed them in the business of treating God as holy. Aaron
remains silent (Lev. 10:3). Although Leviticus 16 will later make clear that the
Yom Kippur ritual is a once-a-year act that purges the sanctuary (vv. 29–34),
Milgrom suggests that the first verse's attempt to link the strange-fire episode
to the ritual may signal that severe or deliberate acts of pollution (in this case,
the sons' sin as well as the presence of their dead bodies in the sanctuary)
may bring about the need for emergency enactments of the ritual on other
occasions as well.[39] Whatever the case, the strange-fire incident is here linked
to the need to purge the sanctuary.

Verse 2 begins recounting the details of the procedure to take place on this
day. There is little left to the imagination; details are carefully given, from
precisely what, where, and when the high priest is to offer, to how the priest
should be dressed at different stages, to when he should bathe, to how he must
enter the sanctum and shield himself from the divine presence, and what takes
place in the holy room during the ritual itself. It is easy to overlook the fact
that these are *intimate* details of what is to take place between one representative person and God in a very sacred, rare, and exceedingly important ritual.
This text is not part of a secret priestly manual that is guarded and explained
only to the high priest upon his taking office, that is, guarded away from the
public. Rather, as Watts so rightly makes clear, such details are regularly to be
read publicly to the whole people of Israel. Nothing is kept from them. Every
person, from the high priest himself to the youngest of Israelite members—all
those with ears to hear—knows exactly what takes place in the holy of holies
when the priest disappears therein on this holy day. The priest works on the
people's behalf to cleanse the sanctuary and Israel, but the people are, in their
knowledge of the event and through their participation (e.g., through self-
affliction; see below), participants. Israel's religion, it seems, keeps no secrets.
These are communal matters.

Aaron, representing all future high priests who will lead work in the temple
and minister to Israel with the Levites (the priestly family), is instructed in a
number of ways. On this day he is to remove his usual highly ornate clothing
(described in Exod. 28) and put on simple dress. As Wenham observes, on this
day the colorful robes, the ornate jewelry, the gold, and the intricate embroidery
are all removed; instead of looking "like a king" on this day, the high priest
"looked more like a slave."[40] The priest will soon be in the presence of God,
and only modest linen clothing is appropriate. It is probably not coincidental,
as Wenham highlights, that such dress is regularly said to adorn the angels in

---

39. Milgrom, *Leviticus: A Book of Ritual and Ethics*, 167.
40. Wenham, *Leviticus*, 230.

heaven (e.g., in Ezekiel and Daniel) and the saints in Revelation 19.[41] Aaron is also to bathe. Perhaps it is not without some significance that in the Jewish tradition, death and burial rituals stipulate that simple linen clothing (or a shroud) is to be put on the deceased, who is also ritually washed before burial. Both are in preparation to meet God.

The verses that follow (5–10) describe the various activities to be performed by the high priest, particularly involving the killing of a sacrificial bull and one of the two he-goats. Verses 11–22 describe what is to happen in the holy of holies, as well as what is to happen to the second he-goat, which is released into the wilderness. The killing of the bull is to purify Aaron and his family, and the killing of the first goat, chosen by lot, is to purify the people. The priest is to take blood from both animals, in turn, and sprinkle it seven times upon and in front of the *kapporet*, an object not easy to identify, but probably the lid or covering of the ark—the very place where God is thought to dwell, or be enthroned (v. 14). The richness of this term is witnessed in the fact that in Greek translation the term is *hilastērion*, the same one used in Romans 3:25 to signify "propitiation," and is related to *hilasmos*, the term used in 1 John 2:2 and 4:10 to signify the same.[42] Aaron is carefully instructed in how to come near this most sacred place, only after a cloud of incense has covered it, making it safe to approach (v. 13).

When the blood of the goat is sprinkled on and in front of the *kapporet* (v. 15), it is important to note that the text indicates *what* is being purged or atoned. Verse 16 is key. It makes clear that the *sanctuary* is being cleansed "because of the uncleannesses of the people of Israel, and because of their transgressions, all their sins." The NRSV here does not quite capture the Hebrew sufficiently. The NIV is a little better with its rendering: "In this way he will make atonement for the Most Holy Place because of the uncleanness and rebellion of the Israelites, *whatever their sins have been*" (emphasis added). The words used here—*tum'ot* (impurities), *peshe'* (rebellions), and *khatto't* (sins)—work together to emphasize the fullness and comprehensiveness of the sins being addressed, especially through the author's addition of *kol* (all) to the final *khatto't*. It seems that every last sin that found its way into the sanctuary—unintentional and intentional—is in fact removed in this ritual.[43]

---

41. Ibid.

42. We will discuss 1 John 2:2 below. Unfortunately, we cannot explore the link in Romans more fully; see major commentaries on Romans, as well as the book by Daniel Stökl Ben Ezra, *The Impact of Yom Kippur on Early Christianity: The Day of Atonement from the Second Temple to the Fifth Century*, Wissenschaftliche Untersuchungen zum Neuen Testament 163 (Tübingen: Mohr Siebeck, 2003), 197–205.

43. That unintentional and intentional sins are in view is brought out nicely in the notes of Baruch J. Schwartz, "Leviticus," in *The Jewish Study Bible*, ed. Adele Berlin and Marc Zvi Brettler (New York: Oxford University Press, 2004), 203–80. Yet notice his idea (in line with the Mishnah) that intentional sins cannot actually be purified, hence the need for the goat of removal. In commenting on v. 22, he states, "The impurities (see v. 16) have disappeared, eradicated by

Such an idea will be mentioned again later in the text. No pollution or sin is left, and the sanctuary is left in a new, clean state.

It is from this verse (in conjunction with other passages) that Jewish tradition holds that the sins atoned for on this day are those brazen sins that were not atoned for previously. Throughout the year Israel has been making sacrifices for the sins it has committed, particularly inadvertent ones, yet on this day all other sins, those not addressed earlier—either because of a lack of acknowledgment or the death of the offender—are now removed. Again, if Milgrom and others are correct, this important rebalancing ensures that God will not leave a too-polluted sanctuary. Now that the sanctuary is clean, God's presence can remain in Israel. We will return below to the idea of whose sins are being atoned for when we discuss the communal nature of the sin purgation (or purification) here, especially in light of the fact that Israel is to repent collectively on this day. The idea that people might repent for the sins of others will undoubtedly strike modern individualistic readers as odd. In fact, some contemporary Christian faith communities may find any act of communal repentance foreign and unsettling.

If there is any aspect of Leviticus 16 that has gained widespread interest, it has to be that of the so-called scapegoat. It is with this idea that Leviticus 16 seems to become a superstitious text, even magical in orientation. The story comes to resemble others in the Old Testament where curses are written on paper and dissolved in water (along with temple dust) in order to determine whether adultery has occurred (Num. 5), or where a bronze snake is lifted on a pole to provide healing to the afflicted who look to it (Num. 21:4–9). It is no less strange that a goat could take upon its head the sins of the people and carry them into the wilderness. And yet, might there be more to this go-away-goat story, as there is to the other two stories just mentioned? Might the "scapegoat" have deeper implications as well?

It is not without significance that one goat dies and one goat lives. This may seem simple enough, yet it is key to the ritual. It is also significant that the fate of each goat is determined not by the priest or by the people, but through lots, something essentially understood in antiquity to be the work of God himself (cf. Prov. 16:33). In effect, the lives of both goats are in God's hands and the goat that is to live is said to "be left standing alive before the LORD" (Lev. 16:10 NJPS).[44] In Jewish tradition, the Day of Purgation is not only the day that cleanses the temple and takes away the sins of the people, it is also the day on which the fate—the life or death—of each member of Israel is decided for another year. In the Jewish calendar, Yom Kippur comes

---

the blood of the 'ḥaṭa't' offerings. Deliberate sins, however, are indestructible; they can only be sent away, in the hope that they may never return. The idea is that intentional acts of wrongdoing, once committed, can never really be undone" (246); cf. Milgrom, *Leviticus 1–16*, 1033–34.

44. Due to space constraints, we cannot enter into the rabbinic discussion and debates on whether the goat was to be killed in the wilderness, either by God or the person leading it.

as the last of the ten days of repentance, which began with Rosh Hashanah ("head of the year," New Year), and this period is regarded as an important decision time in each person's life. At the end of Yom Kippur, the fate of each person, like those of the goats, has been determined by God. Those who have been granted another year to live "shall be left standing alive before the Lord."

The rich symbolism of a goat being physically sent away and released, carrying away the sins of the people, should also not be overlooked. Although it may be difficult to appreciate in today's world, the act of stopping all activities to repent and fast, and then to see the sins of the entire community physically taken away into a place that is *gezerah*, "cut off" (16:22), would surely have left a deep impression. This supremely important event would likely have been a strong mnemonic device, something to aid the people in remembering the removal of their sins, whether in the minds of the very young or anyone else. That the goat would never be seen again, but was brought to the most desolate place known to the community, would surely have been an event to remember throughout the rest of the year.

Technically, there is a translational difficulty here. The text indicates that the priest is to cast lots to determine which goat is to be a sin offering to Yнwн, and which is to be kept alive "for *'aza'zel*" (Lev. 16:8). The Hebrew term used here, *'aza'zel*, is often translated "goat of removal," or "scapegoat," the latter having become a popular appellation in Western culture. However, the term is difficult to translate and may be a combination of the word for "rugged," "fierce," or "angry" (*'azaz*) and the word for "god" (*'el*). The resultant meaning is thus something like "fierce god." In this line of thinking, the sins of the people are sent to the wilderness (where demons were thought to dwell) to this "fierce god." To support this view, there is evidence that Azazel was an epithet for a demonic being in antiquity, something testified to in certain parabiblical texts from the Second Temple period such as *1 Enoch* and the *Apocalypse of Abraham*.[45]

However, there are also good reasons to be cautious here. Mary Douglas, building upon Levine's work in his commentary, expresses an understandable resistance to this idea and suggests that the traditional rendering of *la-'aza'zel* as "a scapegoat" (that is, it names the type of goat) is likely best. She puts it this way: "There is no need to invent a gift for a Goat-Lord of the wilderness, which would anyway be completely out of character for the book of Leviticus. For in the very next chapter, Leviticus 17:7 gives a strong injunction against what is assumed to be a popular custom of sacrificing to demons, satyrs, or spirits, in the fields. That Aaron be told in the middle of this very important rite for the consecration of the tabernacle to send a

---

45. The Azazel entry in the *Jewish Encyclopedia* (New York: Funk & Wagnalls, 1902), 2:365–67, remains a helpful resource on this topic. A more technical, up-to-date discussion appears in *DDD*, 128–31.

messenger or a gift to the demon Azazel is a very implausible translation."[46] Whatever translation we follow, the outcome is the same: the sins of the people are removed and sent to a place where they will not harm the community. Again, this ritual is clearly aimed at restoring society to a balanced and ordered state, something to which anthropologists like Douglas have rightly drawn our attention.

The ritual concludes with further instruction for the high priest regarding his clothing and washing, as well as for the disposal of the bull and the goat that were offered for purification. Their remains are to be burned outside the camp (Lev. 16:27–28); both the one who does this and the person who was appointed to take the goat into the wilderness are to wash and then return to society. The act of washing seems to have a dual purpose of cleansing, or removing the symbolic death associated with the ritual from the participant, as well as indicating when the ritual begins and ends.[47] To close the chapter, the narrator now gives an explanation regarding when the ritual is to take place, how often, and how the people of Israel are to participate. On this day no one is to work, and the people, along with resident aliens, are instructed to "deny themselves" (16:29), or more literally, afflict (*'anah*) their beings/souls (*nefashot*). It is not made explicit what exactly this entails, though it is not surprising that fasting and repentance came to be associated with this day, something seen in Acts 27:9, where it is simply called "the Fast." Also, the text makes it clear that, like the Passover, the observance of this ritual is perpetual, never to end: it is an "everlasting statute" (v. 34), and instruction is given for performing the ritual in subsequent years (vv. 32–33). Lastly, the narrator once again makes clear that this ritual "shall be made for you, to cleanse you; from all your sins you shall be clean before the LORD" (v. 30).

Significance of Yom Kippur to Christian Theology

> The historical past is never, for the believer, strictly or solely past; rather, the fulfillment of history governs and suffuses all history (because of the participation of time in the eternity of the providential Creator and Redeemer). This does not mean that the linear progression of history has no significance, but it does mean that earlier historical realities cannot be discarded once later historical realities have been unveiled. (Matthew Levering)[48]

46. Mary Douglas, "The Go-Away Goat," in *The Book of Leviticus: Composition and Reception*, ed. Rolf Rendtorff and Robert A. Kugler, Supplements to Vetus Testamentum 93 (Leiden: Brill, 2003), 127. She draws from Baruch A. Levine, *The JPS Torah Commentary: Leviticus* (Philadelphia: Jewish Publication Society, 1989).

47. So Douglas, "Go-Away Goat," 129.

48. Matthew Levering, *Jewish-Christian Dialogue and the Life of Wisdom: Engagements with the Theology of David Novak* (New York: Continuum, 2010), 21.

At this point I would like to reflect upon the significance of this passage as it relates to the larger book of Leviticus, the Pentateuch, as well as the whole Christian Bible. It may also be instructive to think through how our above discussion on understanding Leviticus corporately, and as a book that was heard, affects our reading.

If Leviticus sits at the center of the Torah, and Rendtorff and Warning are correct that Leviticus 16 in some sense sits at the middle of Leviticus theologically and literarily, what does this tell us about the significance of this passage?[49] Can anything be deduced regarding it, or is the fact that it sits at the center merely an interesting factoid, with little import for our theology? As mentioned above, the importance of this passage cannot be overestimated for Jews, past or present, as the day is, without question, the most important in the Jewish calendar.[50] But what about for Christians? Is it simply present in our Bibles for archival purposes, recounting an ancient practice of the past? Are not Good Friday and Easter the center of our religious life, days that commemorate the death and resurrection of Jesus?

The two events are not as far from each other as we might initially think, and it is not without significance that Jesus is introduced in John's Gospel as the one "who takes away the sin of the world" (John 1:29). In 1 John 2:2 the connection is even clearer: "And he is the atoning sacrifice [*hilasmos*] for our sins, and not for ours only but also for the sins of the whole world." The New Testament, it seems, especially in 1 John and its use of the term *hilasmos* (see above), would like to link Jesus to the events that take place on the day of purgation, only in later theology it is not only Israel's sins that are removed—and not only the particular location of Israel that is rebalanced—but all people and all places are set aright. Jesus' death on the cross clearly comes to be seen as a day of atonement much like that found in Leviticus 16.[51] We are also told in Matthew's Gospel that at the moment of Jesus' death, the temple curtain "was torn in two, from top to bottom" (Matt. 27:51). Based on the word used,[52] it seems likely that this refers to the innermost curtain, which concealed the holy of holies. The verb form here is passive, without subject specified (*eschisthē*, "was torn"), and the splitting of the curtain is clearly "from top to bottom"—all of which implies without question that the event is viewed as a divine action, something done by God himself. This act makes the holy of holies visible to all and thereby suggests that the yearly work of the high priest is now com-

---

49. Rolf Rendtorff, "Leviticus 16 als Mitte der Tora," *Biblical Interpretation* 11 (2003): 252–58. See above for discussion on Warning.

50. For a helpful summary of how Yom Kippur features in contemporary Judaism and the blessing it brings, see Joseph Telushkin, "Yom Kippur," in *Jewish Literacy* (New York: William Morrow, 2008), 638–41.

51. Much more could be said here; consult again the tour-de-force work of Stökl Ben Ezra, *Impact of Yom Kippur*.

52. *Katapetasma*, meaning curtain; cf. Exod. 26:31–35 LXX.

plete. In Jesus' death and resurrection, the world is cosmically rebalanced and cleansed by his blood. God's abode, once the holy of holies but now the earth, is cleansed of sin, and this purgation allows God to dwell there with his people, in his newly established kingdom. The book of Hebrews explains something of this. As it states, Christ's death on the cross brings about a hope of divine blessing for those who are in Christ, the very same hope that Abraham had in God, and this hope enters the holy of holies: "We have this hope, a sure and steadfast anchor of the soul, a hope that enters the inner shrine behind the curtain, where Jesus, a forerunner on our behalf, has entered, having become a high priest forever according to the order of Melchizedek" (Heb. 6:19–20).[53] These verses make little sense apart from an understanding of Leviticus 16.

In concluding his discussion on Leviticus 16, Wenham makes some important observations on how Christians might observe Good Friday more actively, a day that could be viewed in some ways as the Christian equivalent to Yom Kippur. Such an idea is not entirely novel: the churches of Rome and Byzantium have always refrained from work and fasted on this day. Yet in the Protestant tradition more generally there is no agreement on observing a fast in conjunction with Good Friday.[54] This may relate to the general reluctance concerning regulated ritual in Protestantism, which I noted earlier. I cannot help but think that recovering a fast and a day of repentance and self-affliction, in the light of God's taking away the sins of the world through Jesus' death, might be one way to ensure that Christians take seriously Leviticus 16:29 and 34 ("This shall be an everlasting statute for you") as well as Hebrews' emphasis on Christian repentance (again, see Heb. 6). But this also brings us back to earlier questions about communal life and corporate responsibility: it may be difficult for Protestants steeped in modern Western life to undertake communal repentance on behalf of themselves, let alone the entire world. It should hopefully be clear that Leviticus assumes communal repentance—even on behalf of others—and that the New Testament is not far from such an idea in its teachings on forgiveness being for the entire world (1 John 2:1–2). Such action surely is the church's duty.[55] However, we might also note that such activity also has the potential to nourish and transform the church each year, as the Day of Atonement does for the Jewish people who observe it. Recovering a connection to Yom Kippur as Christians can only help Christians who

53. Due to limitations of scope and space, here we cannot discuss the connection to Melchizedek. See the fine study by Douglas Farrow, "Melchizedek and Modernity," in *The Epistle to the Hebrews and Christian Theology*, ed. Richard Bauckham et al. (Grand Rapids: Eerdmans, 2009), 281–301.

54. As Stökl Ben Ezra makes clear, the history regarding when Christians ceased to observe Yom Kippur is complex; see esp. 212–25 and the conclusion of his *Impact of Yom Kippur*, 329–34.

55. I cannot explore this idea in full. Dietrich Bonhoeffer, *Life Together*, trans. John W. Doberstein (San Francisco: Harper & Row, 1954), provides a helpful starting point for these and related issues.

live in a fragmented and broken West to recover their communal identity and role in bringing forgiveness of sins to the whole world.

Yom Kippur in Creeds and Liturgy

Along these lines, it is not insignificant that the Apostles' Creed includes a statement testifying to the forgiveness of sins. In some ways Leviticus can be summarized as a book about purification, purgation, and forgiveness, a book that explains the rebalancing of the cosmos in order to permit God to dwell in his sanctuary. The shapers of the Pentateuch have placed Leviticus at the center of the Pentateuch, the center of God's instruction to his people after he delivered them from Egypt and provided for them in the wilderness. Leviticus makes sense only because the canon has already shaped this backstory, introduced God as creator and deliverer, and has testified to how he chose and delivered his people. In short, Watts is right that "list"—sections of instruction like those found in Leviticus 16—works in Leviticus because it has been carefully shaped in conjunction with the rest of the Torah's stories. Reading Leviticus as Christian Scripture takes seriously this literary position, takes seriously the content of Leviticus, and seeks to reread these ancient words as important for each new generation, for the people who live with and under God in the world. I have tried to read Leviticus and the Yom Kippur ritual in a way that stresses its communal aspects; I have suggested that there may be ways to recover the purgation ritual today as Christians, even though it cannot be observed as if the Christ event has not taken place. Christians can observe this day in the light of that event only if they are true to their identity in Christ. Whether in the Eucharist, Good Friday, or both, the church's recognition and observance of Yom Kippur in the light of Christ is one way of making real the words of the Creed: "I believe in . . . the forgiveness of sins."

In many traditions the liturgy of the church goes further than the creed's simple affirmation of the forgiveness of sins and makes a strong connection, similar to that found in the New Testament, between Jesus and the Yom Kippur event. Perhaps no words make this clearer than those of the Eucharistic Prayer found in the Book of Common Prayer, which is similar in content to other Western and Eastern liturgies: "All glory be to thee, Almighty God, our heavenly Father, for that thou, of thy tender mercy, didst give thine only Son Jesus Christ to suffer death upon the Cross for our redemption; who made there (by his one oblation of himself once offered) a full, perfect, and sufficient sacrifice, oblation, and satisfaction, for the sins of the whole world."[56] The words that follow this make clear that remembering this is no small matter but the essential and all-important duty of the church in perpetuity, as the Levitical

---

56. Church of England, *The Book of Common Prayer* (New York: Oxford University Press, 1928), 80.

text makes clear regarding the observance of Yom Kippur: "and [Jesus] did institute, and in his holy Gospel command us to continue, a perpetual memory of that his precious death and sacrifice, until his coming again."[57]

Although Jews and Christians cannot, by virtue of their differences, celebrate Yom Kippur together, it is remarkable that both groups are commanded, until the end of time, to observe God's forgiveness of all sins, in repentance, as a regular part of their religious life. In this we stand together, even while we stand apart. That YHWH abides with his people as a result of this purgation is also something worthy of further reflection. God can dwell only in a holy place, a place that has been made clean, and the Day of Atonement makes this possible. This idea is deeply rooted in Leviticus and is still maintained by both traditions. There may also be parallels, more than is often thought, in how the two groups view matters in Leviticus symbolically. Although by no means identical, Christians can appreciate that in contemporary Judaism, God is thought to dwell in the holy people Israel, rather than in a physical temple, and in some strands of Judaism, acts of loving-kindness (or at times prayer and suffering) function as symbolic substitutes for sacrifice as a means to forgiveness.[58] Such ideas are not so far from Christian ones whereby God dwells in his people through the Holy Spirit or, as Jesus taught, only those who act kindly and are willing to forgive others will receive forgiveness from God (Matt. 18:21–35).

Conclusion

Leviticus is a book of life and death, forgiveness, communal life, purgation, cleanliness, and also "list." It cannot be read apart from its larger pentateuchal context, yet we have also seen that the New Testament cannot really be understood apart from Leviticus either. The above references to the temple curtain being torn, the removal of all sins by way of one sacrifice, and a priest, Jesus himself, entering the holy of holies—these are all only understandable in the light of Leviticus, in particular the text we have examined, Leviticus 16. Although sometimes viewed as dry as dust and rarely read, Leviticus may well be the very backbone not only of the Pentateuch but also of the New Testament and its understanding of divine forgiveness. Here we have a book that could prove to be the primary source for deeper theological reflection on communal life, what it means to be the people of God, and the forgiveness of sins through the death and resurrection of Jesus. Leviticus may also prove to be a fruitful meeting ground for Jews and Christians who are open to exploring

57. Ibid.

58. On the former, see Michael Wyschogrod, *The Body of Faith: God in the People Israel* (Northvale, NJ: Jason Aronson, 1996); on the latter, consult the convenient summary of Telushkin, "Sacrifices," in *Jewish Literacy*, 46–48. See also Levine's chapter, "Leviticus in the Ongoing Jewish Tradition," in *JPS Torah Commentary: Leviticus*, 169–92.

their respective faiths in light of each other, even while there will always be a degree of separation between them, despite worshiping the same God.

Taking Leviticus seriously may be one avenue for the church to find its way as a communal people of God, called, in Christ, to live in and as the one "who takes away the sin of the world."

FURTHER READING

Leviticus

Cassik, Michael, trans. *The Commentators' Bible: The JPS Miqra'ot Gedolot; Leviticus*. Philadelphia: Jewish Publication Society, 2009.

Douglas, Mary. *Leviticus as Literature*. Oxford: Oxford University Press, 1999.

Levine, Baruch A. *The JPS Torah Commentary: Leviticus*. Philadelphia: Jewish Publication Society, 1989.

Milgrom, Jacob. *Leviticus: A Book of Ritual and Ethics*. Continental Commentary. Minneapolis: Fortress, 2004.

Radner, Ephraim. *Leviticus*. Brazos Theological Commentary on the Bible. Grand Rapids: Brazos, 2008.

Rendtorff, Rolf. "Is It Possible to Read Leviticus as a Separate Book?" In *Reading Leviticus: A Conversation with Mary Douglas*, edited by John F. A. Sawyer, 22–35. Journal for the Study of the Old Testament: Supplement Series 227. Sheffield: Sheffield Academic Press, 1996.

Schwartz, Baruch J. "Leviticus." In *The Jewish Study Bible*, edited by Adele Berlin and Marc Zvi Brettler, 203–80. New York: Oxford University Press, 2004.

Watts, James W. *Ritual and Rhetoric in Leviticus*. Cambridge: Cambridge University Press, 2007.

Wenham, Gordon J. *The Book of Leviticus*. New International Commentary on the Old Testament. Grand Rapids: Eerdmans, 1979.

Yom Kippur (Leviticus 16)

Douglas, Mary. "The Go-Away Goat." In *The Book of Leviticus: Composition and Reception*, edited by Rolf Rendtorff and Robert A. Kugler, 121–41. Supplements to Vetus Testamentum 93. Leiden: Brill, 2003.

Stökl Ben Ezra, Daniel. *The Impact of Yom Kippur on Early Christianity: The Day of Atonement from the Second Temple to the Fifth Century*. Wissenschaftliche Untersuchungen zum Neuen Testament 163. Tübingen: Mohr Siebeck, 2003.

Telushkin, Joseph. "Sacrifices." In *Jewish Literacy*, 46–48. New York: William Morrow, 2008.

———. "Yom Kippur." In *Jewish Literacy*, 638–41. New York: William Morrow, 2008.

4

⁓

The Book of Numbers

NATHAN MACDONALD

I n one of his sermons on the book of Numbers, the early church theologian
Origen compared Scripture to a feast of different foods. In the Bible there
is everything necessary to nourish the soul. Yet Origen had to admit that
some parts of the feast are more palatable than others. The book of Numbers
is an excellent example of a less desirable food. The reader is tempted to "reject
it and spit it out, as heavy and burdensome foods and as those that are not
suitable to a sick and weak soul."[1]

For Origen the book of Numbers was full of mysteries that required a high
level of spiritual maturity to decode. Young believers were best to keep to the
Gospels, the Letters of Paul, or the Psalms. Modern lectionaries and Bible reading notes follow Origen's counsel, though their composers likely do not realize
it. Wise though such practices may at first appear, the result is impoverishing.
The book of Numbers contains a rich catalog of stories and images. The cloud
and fiery pillar, the manna and quail in the wilderness, the sending of the spies,
water from the rock, the bronze serpent, and Balaam and his donkey—all are
to be found in the book of Numbers. In addition, the beautiful priestly blessing, "The LORD bless you and keep you; the LORD make his face shine upon
you, and be gracious to you; the LORD lift up his countenance upon you and
give you peace" (Num. 6:24–26), probably appears in more Christian services

It is a great pleasure to be able to offer this essay to my dear friend and teacher, Walter Moberly.
He is truly a teacher of Torah, instructed about the kingdom of heaven, and bringing forth
treasures old and new.

1. Origen, *Homily* 27.1.4; from Origen, *Homilies on Numbers*, Ancient Christian Texts,
trans. Thomas P. Scheck (Downers Grove, IL: InterVarsity, 2009), 168.

than almost any other part of Scripture with the exception of the Lord's Prayer. Finally, the book makes important contributions to our understanding of the people of God. Indeed, the whole book can be envisaged as an extended reflection on what it means to be a worshiping and serving community.

Undoubtedly though, the treasures of Numbers are hidden in jars of clay. The traditional Christian title, Numbers, draws attention to a different and unattractive side of the book. There are lengthy censuses, lists of sacrifices, and a series of way stations in the desert. Ancient legislation, both civil and cultic, is scattered throughout the book with no apparent logic. In addition, the book's story line seems to meander, with no obvious sense of direction, rather like the people of Israel themselves. This aspect of the book is neatly summarized in the Hebrew name for the book, taken from the first words in Numbers 1:1: *Bemidbar*, "in the desert." For Israel and for the reader, the book of Numbers is an unwelcome detour on the way to destinations more interesting. A brief rehearsal of the book's contents will highlight many of the difficulties that a reader confronts.

Outline of Numbers

The first third of the book is set in the Wilderness of Sinai (1:1–10:10). Various directions are given to Moses in order to organize the people in preparation for departure from Sinai. The tribes are counted and arranged around the tabernacle. The altar and the Levites are dedicated to divine service. Since it is a year after the exodus, Moses gives directions for the second celebration of Passover, with some clarification for those who cannot celebrate. In the middle of all this preparation of the camp are two chapters of ritual instructions (5:1–6:27). These include instructions for how to deal with a wife suspected of unfaithfulness, and the Nazirite, the individual who makes a temporary vow of heightened commitment to YHWH. It concludes with the priestly blessing.

Twenty days later the people depart for the promised land. The second third of the book tells of their travels. Their journey to the Wilderness of Paran, on the edge of the land, is fraught with rebellion. There are complaints at Taberah, dissatisfaction with the manna at Kibroth-hattaavah, and opposition to Moses from Aaron and Miriam (11:1–12:16). The reader is well prepared for ·the disaster that will ensue with the sending of the spies to inspect the land. The spies' report disheartens the people who refuse to march into Canaan. Moses' intercession saves them from complete destruction, but they are sent back into the wilderness to wander for a generation (13:1–14:45). The people's rebellion is only the beginning of a trend that will infect the Levites (16:1–17:9 [17:24 MT]) and even Moses and Aaron (20:1–13). Interspersed between these rebellions are various laws about offerings, tassels on garments, priestly and Levitical prerogatives, and purification from corpse impurity. In chapters 20–21 the people again begin to progress toward the promised land but are forced to make a long detour around Edom and approach the land from the east. They defeat Sihon and Og and take territory in the Transjordan.

The final third of the book is set on the plains of Moab (22:1), on the opposite side of the Jordan from Jericho (22:2–36:13). The Moabite king Balak summons a diviner named Balaam to curse the people, but under divine constraint Balaam can utter only prophecies about the glorious future of Israel. In sharp contrast, Israel becomes mired in idolatry through the actions of the Moabites. A census of the new generation is held in chapter 26. Various instructions are given about land inheritance, offerings and festivals, and vows. The reader is told of Israel's defeat of the Midianite tribes and the assignment of the Transjordanian territory to the tribe of Gad, tribe of Reuben, and half-tribe of Manasseh (Num. 31–32). A lengthy and detailed account of the stopping places in the wilderness is a counterpoint to the final chapters, which describe the division and ordering of the land and its various cities.

Numbers as a "Book" and as Part of the Pentateuch

The Structure of the Book of Numbers

Since the book of Numbers often has no clear sense of direction and contains such disparate materials as lists, narratives, and law, is it meaningful to talk about these thirty-six chapters as a book at all? For many critical scholars from the late nineteenth century onward, the book of Numbers was not a meaningful literary unit. Instead, they found coherence in the four sources that had been isolated through more than a century of careful scholarly investigation. The nineteenth-century documentary hypothesis that climaxed in the work of Julius Wellhausen discerned four documents that had been combined to form the present Pentateuch. The D document was restricted to the book of Deuteronomy and was rather unusual since it was predominantly a source of legal-cum-homiletical material. The three other putative documents, J, E, and P, were continuous narratives that ran from creation to the death of Moses. Scholars judged these four documents to be meaningful compositions and invested considerable labors into refining the analysis of them and assessing their shape and theological ideas.

From the perspective of proponents of the documentary hypothesis, the division of the Pentateuch into five books appeared to be a later imposition on the combined material. The division of the material was felt to be somewhat arbitrary, perhaps determined by the desire to have five fairly equal-sized books, or by the physical size of the scrolls. The division of Genesis from Exodus was natural enough, as was Deuteronomy from the books that preceded it. The divisions between Exodus, Leviticus, and Numbers appeared altogether less felicitous. The difficulties can be sensed by observing that the Israelites' encampment at Mount Sinai is found across all three books. The Israelites arrive in Exodus 19 and do not leave until Numbers 10. The division into three books separates material that clearly belongs together. With only Sinai material, Leviticus is the most coherent of the three books, while Exodus and especially Numbers appear to be rather fragmentary. As George Buchanan Gray put it at the turn of the twentieth century, "The book of Numbers is a section somewhat mechanically cut out of the whole of which it forms a part; the result is that it possesses no unity of subject."[2]

Not until the 1970s did scholars begin to reassess this judgment about the book of Numbers. Brevard Childs was by no means the only scholar to do so,[3] but his 1979 *Introduction to the Old Testament as Scripture* is a provocative and influential work, and his account of the book of Numbers is typically innovative. Childs was fully conversant with the critical understanding of the Pentateuch, including work that had most recently appeared, and he did not disagree with the argument that the fivefold division of the Pentateuch was a late development. Nevertheless, "it is quite clear that the five books were seen as separate entities by the final biblical editor in spite of the obvious continuity of the one story which extended from the creation of the world (Gen. 1:1) to the death of Moses (Deut. 34)."[4]

Childs identifies the crucial problem in Numbers to be the structure of the book.[5] This probably reflects Childs's interpretive instincts as someone trained in form criticism and whose canonical approach can be seen as form criticism applied to biblical books or the canon as a whole.[6] The decisive insight of form criticism is that the form or structure of the text is intimately linked to its function. Thus, as Childs sees it, a good sense of the structure of Numbers will help us to determine the canonical function of the book. Two features of the book suggest themselves as possible structuring devices. First are the chronological indicators found at various points in the book (1:1; 7:1; 10:11;

2. George Buchanan Gray, *Numbers*, International Critical Commentary (Edinburgh: T&T Clark, 1903), xxiv.

3. "The division into five books could have been motivated by technical reasons, as, for example, the length of the scroll needed for convenient reading. It should, however, be recognized that the division is not a purely external one but is inherent in Scripture" (Moshe Weinfeld, "Pentateuch," in *Encyclopaedia Judaica* 13 [1972]: 231–261, here 232).

4. Brevard S. Childs, *Introduction to the Old Testament as Scripture* (Philadelphia: Fortress, 1979), 129.

5. See also Dennis T. Olson's dissertation, completed under Childs's oversight: *The Death of the Old and the Birth of the New: The Framework of the Book of Numbers and the Pentateuch*, Brown Judaic Studies 71 (Chico, CA: Scholars Press, 1985). Olson writes, "The central problem in the interpretation of the book of Numbers . . . is the failure to detect a convincing and meaningful structure for the book" (31).

6. See now Daniel R. Driver, *Brevard Childs, Biblical Theologian: For the Church's One Bible*, Forschungen zum Alten Testament 2.46 (Tübingen: Mohr Siebeck, 2010).

20:1; 33:38). Second are the geographical indicators that place the people at
the Wilderness of Sinai (1:1), the Wilderness of Paran (13:3), and the plains
of Moab (22:1). Childs finds neither entirely satisfactory. The chronological
indicators are not complete or consistent, and the geographical indicators
do not always coincide with what appear to be major transitions in the text.
Nevertheless, the geographical indicators are significant; used critically, they
suggest a division of the book into three sections. Childs concludes that "in
spite of its diversity of subject matter and complex literary development the
book of Numbers maintains a unified sacerdotal interpretation of God's will
for his people which is set forth in a sharp contrast between the holy and the
profane."[7]

Childs's brief analysis adumbrates most of what is to be found in more
recent attempts to make sense of the book of Numbers as a discrete book. The
structure of the book continues to be a scholarly preoccupation, and there is
significant disagreement about how best to describe it. Gordon Wenham offers
a variation on Childs's proposal and seeks to account for the difficulties with
the geographical notices by recognizing transitional material in 10:11–12:16
and 20:1–22:1.[8] Dennis Olson divides the book into two halves, each introduced by a census (chs. 1–25; 26–36). The first half recounts the death of the
old generation, and the second half sees new life and hope in the following
generation. Unfortunately, Olson's proposal tends to minimize the positive
features in chapters 1–10 and 21–25.[9] Mary Douglas finds a "ring" (a literary
pattern often labeled "chiasm") centered on Numbers 16–17. In other words,
chapters 1–4 and 36 can be paired together, chapters 5–6 and 33–34 can be
paired together, and so forth. Many such "rings" or chiasms are in the eye
of the beholder, and this is no exception; it is sometimes difficult to discern
what one part of Douglas's ring has in common with its counterpart.[10] Won
Lee offers a "conceptual analysis" of the book of Numbers. He finds Numbers 13–14 to be the crucial chapters portraying Israel's failure to conquer
the land. Numbers 15–20 portray the punishment of the exodus generation,
and chapters 21–36 report the forgiveness of Israel and the call of the new
generation to fulfill the call to conquer the land. Lee tends to underplay the
negative features of chapters 21–25 and has little to say on Numbers 1–10.[11]

7. Childs, *Introduction*, 199.

8. Gordon J. Wenham, *Numbers*, Tyndale Old Testament Commentary (Leicester, UK:
Inter-Varsity, 1981); idem, *Numbers*, Old Testament Guides (Sheffield: Sheffield Academic
Press, 1997).

9. Olson, *Death of the Old*; Dennis T. Olson, *Numbers*, Interpretation (Louisville: John
Knox, 1996).

10. Mary Douglas, *In the Wilderness: The Doctrine of Defilement in the Book of Numbers*,
Journal for the Study of the Old Testament: Supplement Series 158 (Sheffield: JSOT Press, 1993).

11. Won W. Lee, *Punishment and Forgiveness in Israel's Migratory Campaign* (Grand Rapids:
Eerdmans, 2003). Lee's more recent treatment of the "conceptual coherence" of Num. 5–10
similarly says little about the relationship of these chapters to what follows: "The Conceptual

Unsurprisingly, different structures generate different senses of how the book functions. Childs's own proposal is rather short on details, and it is questionable whether the book can be adequately summarized with the word *sacerdotal* and the contrast between "holy and profane." Both Olson and Lee make much of the two generations that appear in Numbers. But as we have seen, the material in the book cannot be neatly divided between these two rubrics. For her part, Douglas sees the book as a manifesto for a unified people of God. God is willing to forgive both Israel and Judah and to begin again with both.

The most optimistic conclusion that can be drawn from this survey, I think, is that the quest to determine the structure of Numbers has been of limited value; more pessimistically, it has been a failure and a false trail. As critical scholars of an earlier generation sensed, the book has no clear structure. This necessarily implies that the structure of the book is not the way to approach the question of the book's function.

As we have seen, Childs's own approach is to begin with the critical consensus and to raise the question of canon. In the years since Childs's *Introduction*, literary-critical work, especially in Germany, has paid more attention to the fivefold canonical division of the Pentateuch. Childs's commitment to working within the literary-critical consensus of his day, while probing it critically, to a certain degree forced him to accept the sense that the Pentateuch and its fivefold form was an artificial imposition on the redactional unity of JEDP. This was the case even while his raising of the issue of canon pointed in a fresh and more radical direction. We will now turn to see how some recent literary-critical work has accepted the final canonical form as an important piece of evidence and how this has produced new ways to see the historical development of the Pentateuch. This will allow us to see the central role of Numbers and to understand its function within the Pentateuch.

Numbers in Recent Pentateuchal Criticism

As widely recognized, since the 1970s the classic documentary hypothesis has been increasingly questioned. There is no need to rehearse the whole of the history since then, but it is useful to highlight a number of important developments. These will help to show how a quite different understanding of the Pentateuch's formation has emerged.

First, Rolf Rendtorff's important work on the tradition history of the Pentateuch shows the lack of compatibility between form-critical and source-critical methods. Scholars such as Gerhard von Rad and Martin Noth assumed that at some level the work of form criticism, which worked with the smallest distinguishable unit of text, could be harmonized with source criticism, which

---

Coherence of Numbers 5, 1–10, 10," in *The Books of Leviticus and Numbers*, ed. Thomas Römer, Bibliotheca ephemeridum theologicarum lovaniensium 215 (Leuven: Peeters, 2008), 473–89.

worked with the comprehensive documents that arched from creation to conquest. This harmonization had never been shown, and Rendtorff questioned whether it could be done.[12]

Second, scholars had assumed that the pentateuchal writers were working according to a preexisting pattern and consequently produced similar documents. The pattern was something like patriarchs → exodus → wilderness → conquest. Gerhard von Rad famously argued that the pattern was found in Israel's earliest creedal statements, such as the so-called small historical credo of Deuteronomy 26:5–9. Recent scholarship has argued that von Rad had actually stood the history of the tradition on its head. The "small historical credo" is now widely regarded as a very late composition.[13]

Third, many scholars have now abandoned the hypothesis of a J or an E source. The existence of the E source has long been questioned. In the first half of the twentieth century, E's lack of distinctive characteristics and the difficulties in isolating it from J already suggested to some that it should be abandoned. In recent years a number of scholars have questioned whether the J document existed as a continuous source.[14] In addition, though earlier scholarship assumed that non-P material was written before P, this is no longer the case.

Fourth, in a seminal essay Lothar Perlitt argues that the priestly account of Moses' death in Deuteronomy 34 came not from P but from a later writer. This led to considerable efforts to determine the extent of the original Priestly document, which has increasingly been pushed back into Leviticus, or more often to the end of the book of Exodus.[15]

Fifth, the canonical divisions within the Pentateuch were perceived to be deep enough within the literature that they could not be explained merely as later artificial impositions on a unified Pentateuch. Instead, the division between the books was itself important evidence for the growth of the Pentateuch.

Sixth, earlier scholarship often proceeded by compiling lists of characteristic vocabulary or phrases and using these to associate more material with the relevant document. Recent scholarship is much more aware that one text may make deliberate allusions to another—the phenomenon of inner-biblical interpretation—which considerably complicates this mode of procedure. Similar vocabulary or style is not necessarily evidence of a single source: it could

12. Rolf Rendtorff, *The Problem of the Process of Transmission in the Pentateuch*, Journal for the Study of the Old Testament: Supplement Series 89 (Sheffield: JSOT Press, 1990).

13. Norbert Lohfink, "The 'Small Credo' of Deuteronomy 26:5–9," in *Theology of the Pentateuch: Themes of the Priestly Narrative and Deuteronomy* (Edinburgh: T&T Clark, 1994), 265–89.

14. Thomas B. Dozeman and Konrad Schmid, eds., *A Farewell to the Yahwist? The Composition of the Pentateuch in Recent European Interpretation*, SBL Symposium Series 34 (Atlanta: Society of Biblical Literature, 2006).

15. Lothar Perlitt, "Priesterschrift im Deuteronomium?" *Zeitschrift für die alttestamentliche Wissenschaft* 100 (1988): 65–88.

also be evidence of an interpretive process within the text by later writers or redactors.[16]

As a result of these developments, theories about continuous, parallel documents have become less convincing. Instead, scholars are coming to the view that the Pentateuch began as traditions which gathered around particular people or episodes. These collections were then brought together into more substantive literary texts. In particular, the Pentateuch's growth is best envisaged as having taken place around two poles: the priestly material and the Deuteronomic law code. We might liken this to two imbalanced star systems slowly gathering more and more material into each of their gravitational fields. At some point the two star systems converge upon one another, throwing out material between them as they merge. In our illustration the larger star system is the priestly material. The isolation of the priestly material remains the most durable hypothesis from the documentary hypothesis. Yet there is considerable disagreement about the extent of the original Priestly document, with various competing suggestions about whether its conclusion is to be found in Exodus 29, in Exodus 40, or in Leviticus 16. Whatever the original extent of the Priestly document, it appears to have gathered more and more material to itself over time. The smaller star system is the Deuteronomic law code. It too drew more and more material to itself over time. At some point the two documents were redacted together.

Recent investigations of the Pentateuch suggest that this was not the end of the compositional process. The existence of these two large complexes of material about Israel's constitution in the past demanded some sort of harmonization. A significant move in that direction was the composition of the so-called Holiness Code (Lev. 17–26). During the last few decades, scholarship has suggested that this legal code tried to mediate between the priestly instructions and the Deuteronomic law code.[17] Another attempt to do so incorporated both narrative and legal material: the book of Numbers.[18]

Numbers between Genesis–Leviticus and Deuteronomy

Examining recent scholarship on how the Pentateuch was composed provides, in my view, important clues to the canonical function of Numbers.[19]

16. For an excellent introduction to inner-biblical interpretation (sometimes, perhaps problematically, called "intertextuality"), see Bernard M. Levinson, *Legal Revision and Religious Renewal in Ancient Israel* (Cambridge: Cambridge University Press, 2008).

17. See Jeffery Stackert, *Rewriting the Torah: Literary Revision in Deuteronomy and the Holiness Legislation*, Forschungen zum Alten Testament 52 (Tübingen: Mohr Siebeck, 2007).

18. See Reinhard Achenbach, *Die Vollendung der Tora: Studien zur Redaktionsgeschichte des Numeribuchs im Kontext von Hexateuch und Pentateuch*, Beihefte zur Zeitschrift für Altorientalishe und Biblische Rechtsgeschichte 3 (Wiesbaden: Harrassowitz, 2003).

19. In passing we should note that it is quite mistaken to oppose the canonical approach to historical criticism. This misunderstanding has largely stemmed from John Barton's influential

The book of Numbers can be seen as the glue that joins the two major poles of the Pentateuch: the priestly literature and Deuteronomy. Thus the attempts to discern an independent structure for the book were misguided because the book was never intended to function independently of the other books in the Pentateuch. This is apparent in the geographical markers, which move the Pentateuch's narrative from the Wilderness of Sinai to the plains of Moab. In other words, the narrative of Numbers moves the reader of the Pentateuch from Leviticus to Deuteronomy, from one place of instruction to another. Furthermore, this mediatory function is also apparent in the ritual and legal material, which often draws from both priestly and deuteronomic sources.

In light of this reconstruction, it becomes apparent why, even though it lacks a strong structure, the book of Numbers has characteristics that are distinctive to it. It is not at all the case that Numbers lacks coherence or that it is not meaningful to give attention to the theology of the book of Numbers. Yet in doing so it is necessary to remember that Numbers is seeking to mediate between the existing theological complexes of the priestly material and Deuteronomy. In other words, the coherence of Numbers resides not in a self-contained literary structure, but in a distinctive theological vision that draws from the priestly material and Deuteronomy and mediates between them.

Some Central Themes in Numbers

If we consider some of the central themes in Numbers, we will appreciate how the book achieves this mediatorial role. We will examine three themes:

- The people of Israel
- The priests and the Levites
- The land

The People of Israel

The book of Numbers has a strong focus on the people of Israel. The instructions to Moses in the book of Exodus are concerned with the construction of the tabernacle. The first sixteen chapters of Leviticus regulate sacrificial practice and preventing uncleanness from polluting the sanctuary. The final chapters of Leviticus regulate social interactions and seek to ensure that the Israelites are a holy people, without moral impurity, in their intracommunal

---

Reading the Old Testament: Method in Biblical Study, 2nd ed. (London: Darton, Longman & Todd, 1996). For incisive criticism of Barton's misreading, see Driver, *Brevard Childs*.

relationships. In the book of Numbers, on the other hand, the organizational structures of Israelite communal life are the focus: the organization of the wilderness camp; the distinctions between laity, Levites, and priests; and the nature of proper leadership.

The importance of communal organization is apparent in the opening chapters. The Levites and priests are arranged around the tabernacle, with the rest of the Israelites camping farther out, according to their tribal affiliations (Num. 1–4). In these chapters the portrayal of the Israelites appears to blend two different ideas. On the one hand, Israel is a military camp, assembled and counted, prepared to conquer the promised land (e.g., Num. 1). On the other hand, Israel is a sacerdotal community, focused around the tabernacle. These two perspectives merge different visions of Israel that are found in the priestly material and Deuteronomy. In the priestly material the tabernacle is the central focus of the Israelites' life, and Israel is a community brought out of Egypt to offer worship to YHWH. In Deuteronomy the conquest of the promised land is firmly in view, and Israel is a war camp. The combination of these two perspectives on Israel transforms both. The book of Numbers combines the priestly vision of the tabernacle in Israel's midst and the deuteronomic war camp: thus we have an *ecclesia militans* (church militant) with the tabernacle at its heart and the land of Canaan as its goal.

The Priests and the Levites

The ordering of the Israelite camp in Numbers 1–4, with Levites and priests close to the center, reflects a hierarchical ordering of the Israelite community. The wilderness community is a theocracy, with clear divisions between laity and Levites, Levites and priests, priests and high priest. Korah's rebellion in Numbers 16–17 seeks to eliminate these distinctions. Korah and his cohort argue that the priests have no claim to special status: "All the congregation are holy, every one of them" (16:3). Divine intervention on behalf of Aaron validates the distinctions. The book also establishes clear instructions for the different responsibilities and privileges of the priests and Levites.

In Genesis–Leviticus there is hardly any mention of the Levites. The priests and high priests are given distinct roles in relation to the tabernacle. They offer sacrifices and ensure that the sanctuary's sanctity is preserved. In Deuteronomy, however, the Levites appear frequently as a marginalized group, deserving the charity of Israelite landowners. In addition, the priests are often described as "Levitical priests" in Deuteronomy. How is the reader to make sense of these different perspectives? The book of Numbers offers a solution by distinguishing priests from Levites. The priests belong to the tribe of Levi, but the Levites are a minor clerical order, with responsibility for aiding the priests and carrying the tabernacle.

The Land

From its beginning the book of Numbers is oriented toward the promised land. The military census that is undertaken in Numbers 1 has in view the conquest of Canaan. The central turning point in the book is the people's refusal to go into the land; as a result they are sent back into the wilderness. Elsewhere the limits of the land are described, and steps are taken to assign the land to the different tribes.

In Genesis–Leviticus the land promised to the patriarchs is "the land of Canaan." This designation appears to cover the area between the Jordan and the Mediterranean Sea (cf. Gen. 13:10–12), and there is no suggestion that territory across the river Jordan is to be included in the promised land. The book of Deuteronomy introduces a complication because in their journey to the promised land, the Israelites defeat the Transjordanian nations of Sihon and Og. Moses allocates the land to some of the Israelite tribes and describes it as God's gift to them (Deut. 3:12–20). The book of Numbers wrestles with the question of how these two different conceptions of the extent of the promised land are to be squared with each other. Its solution is to define Transjordan as outside the boundaries of Canaan proper (Num. 34:1–15). Nevertheless, Moses permits it to be settled by Israelites. This is not Moses' decision, as it is in Deuteronomy, but comes about as the result of a request by the tribes of Reuben and Gad and the half-tribe of Manasseh.

Our brief overview of some of the major themes of the book of Numbers has demonstrated how the book draws upon ideas in the priestly literature and Deuteronomy and combines them into new forms. The theology of Numbers is consequently distinctive and novel, while also assisting readers of the Pentateuch as they move from priestly texts to deuteronomic texts.

Numbers and Its Relation to History

It is readily apparent that since Numbers brings the priestly materials and Deuteronomy together, the book of Numbers must belong to some of the latest parts of the Pentateuch. The critical consensus that emerged at the end of the nineteenth century envisaged the composition of the Pentateuch as taking place during a period of about five hundred years, beginning at about the time of the united monarchy (ca. tenth century BCE) and being completed in the early Persian period (ca. fifth century BCE). A striking trend of critical work since the 1970s has been the tendency for most dates to be pushed later in Israel's history than was the case in previous scholarship. This is also true of the book of Numbers. If we can date the original Priestly code to the late Babylonian exile or early Persian period, as many scholars do, then this book is most likely to be dated sometime in the mid- to late Persian period (ca. 450–332 BCE).

The date of the book's composition in the Persian period does not preclude the possibility that earlier material is found within it. The writers of the book seem to have incorporated some traditional material, especially poetic fragments. How ancient these are is difficult to ascertain in most cases. To the writers of Numbers, they probably appeared ancient. Two good examples of texts with earlier histories are the story of Balaam (Num. 22–24) and the priestly blessing (6:22–27). The oracles of Balaam have archaic language, and the figure of Balaam is known from the Deir ʿAlla Inscription (ca. 800 BCE). A version of the priestly blessing, written on two silver plaques, was discovered in a tomb at Ketif Hinnom, just outside Jerusalem. The plaques have been dated by many scholars to the sixth century BCE and are the earliest physical evidence we have for any biblical text. The possibility of discerning earlier traditions has been a scholarly preoccupation for a long time. Exceptional discoveries such as those from Ketif Hinnom aside, the task is fraught with considerable difficulties. In many cases we can say no more than that the writers of Numbers may have utilized earlier material. Many texts in the book of Numbers are perhaps better understood, however, not as lightly edited deposits of traditional material, but as creative exegesis of texts from the Priestly corpus and Deuteronomy. In my view, studying them in light of recent work on inner-biblical interpretation elsewhere in the Old Testament holds out more potential for generating insight than using the tools of source, form, or tradition criticism alone.

Nevertheless, how is the book of Numbers to be related to the Persian period in which it was composed? We may identify two different approaches commonly taken. In the first view the book of Numbers is understood as a mirror of the Second Temple community of Jerusalem. The text is held to have a *transparency* to its compositional context. The encamped tribes around the tabernacle reflect the centrality of Jerusalem; the opposition of Korah to Aaronic leadership reflects internal political struggles between Aaronides and Levites. Eryl Davies is a representative of this view. In his commentary on the book of Numbers, he writes that for the book's priestly composers, "their concern was to legitimate the religious practices and institutions of their own day by projecting them back to the time of Moses."[20] In the second view, the book of Numbers is understood as a utopian document. The book does not reflect any historical reality, but is the ideal that the writers of Numbers believed should obtain in the Second Temple community. In her recent book Adriane Leveen sees the priestly material in Numbers as utopian, albeit modified by the more realistic nonpriestly material.[21]

In my view both approaches are mistaken since they envisage textual production almost entirely as a form of political will. Such approaches do not do sufficient justice to the distinctive intertextual nature of Numbers and the

---

20. Eryl W. Davies, *Numbers*, New Century Bible Commentary (Grand Rapids: Eerdmans, 1995), lxix.

21. Adriane B. Leveen, *Memory and Tradition in the Book of Numbers* (Cambridge: Cambridge University Press, 2008).

interpretive pressure of existing scriptural texts upon the writers of Numbers. This is not to deny the presence of political factors in the composition of Numbers; it is only to notice that such approaches reduce the complexity of textual production. We should also observe the effect of placing these stories and laws in the Mosaic past, particularly in the wilderness. The book of Numbers projects these materials into a period that has its own narrative logic. Thus while the book can reflect the political and socioeconomic circumstances of its time of production, it also reflects the narrative logic of the imagined Mosaic period. So, for example, the highly schematized camp, with the tabernacle in the center and the tribes arranged around it (Num. 1–4), makes sense only within the narrative of the Pentateuch. Such a scheme is neither a reflection of Persian period Yehud nor a realizable manifesto for the Second Temple community. Rather, it is a narrative portrayal that is fully realistic. The writer's imagination is, of course, unconsciously constrained by his own historical context, but also consciously by the existing texts of the priestly material and Deuteronomy and the felt need to bring them together coherently.[22]

We may distinguish this way of understanding the book from what we might call a "mythical" reading. The book of Numbers is not placed in a time or place completely detached from the Second Temple community. The book is not set before the flood, nor is it set in a mythical location such as Eden. In both those cases we have a "lost world" and a clear distinction made with the reader's world. In contrast, the book of Numbers is set in a place to the south of Yehud and in the earliest moments of Israel's history. It has a time and a place. This time and place gives the writers considerable imaginative freedom within the constraints imposed by the existing priestly and deuteronomic texts. Yet it is also not the time and place of the writers or earliest readers of Numbers. It belongs to the past. But it is also *Israel's* past, and as such that past has an authority over the Second Temple community.

Numbers and Its Early Interpretation

The pursuit of a coherent narrative about Israel's existence in the past has consequences for how the book is interpreted. The Mosaic legislation and

22. The narrative of Numbers began to present difficulties only when its narrative logic was examined according to a critical historiography. Thus the Israelites' time in the wilderness was taken as a serious historical account until the eighteenth century. With a belief in miraculous divine provision, the narrative did not appear inconceivable. Only with the posthumous publication of Reimarus's work (in 1774–78) did questions arise about whether it was at all conceivable that two million people could march through the wilderness. For the realistic narrative of the Bible and how the rise of critical historiography reframed the issues, see Hans W. Frei's seminal work, *The Eclipse of Biblical Narrative: A Study in Eighteenth and Nineteenth Century Hermeneutics* (New Haven: Yale University Press, 1974).

organization of the people has a unique authority, but it is also one that stands in need of interpretation. This feature is already embedded in the book of Numbers. Even for its writers and earliest readers, the book speaks of a past that really is past: the book does not directly address the Second Temple community; nor does it provide its readers with a future vision, such as Ezekiel does in the last nine chapters of his prophecy. The book of Numbers is, then, a text that creatively interprets the other parts of the Pentateuch yet also demands interpretation itself.

In his book on the rhetorical shape of the law, James Watts makes the astute observation that if we ask how the pentateuchal law was first used, the earliest evidence suggests that it was read publicly. Despite our presuppositions about the use of law, there is no evidence of the pentateuchal law being used for making judicial decisions, and the same thing is true of other ancient Near Eastern laws.[23] The difference is well summarized by the observation that the Hebrew word *torah* is perhaps better understood as "teaching, instruction" rather than "law." In the only account we have of the reading of the law in the Second Temple period, the law is read *and* interpreted. Ezra reads from the book of the law of Moses, and the Levites help the people to understand the law. "They read from the book, the law of God, section by section. They gave the sense, so that the people understood the reading" (Neh. 8:8).

An example of scriptural interpretation of the Pentateuch from that same period is found in Ezra 9–10, where Ezra confronts the difficulty of mixed marriages in the Jewish community. The deuteronomic legislation that the Canaanites be destroyed, neither marrying with them nor making treaties with them (Deut. 7:1–6), is interpreted by Ezra in relation to intermarriage with peoples from the surrounding nations. The list of Canaanite nations from Deuteronomy 7:1 is revised to include the Ammonites, Moabites, and Egyptians in Ezra 9:1. This interprets the text of Deuteronomy 7:1 together with 23:1–7 so as to go beyond the text of Deuteronomy 7, which concerns itself only with people who live within the boundaries of the promised land. It also interprets the deuteronomic commandment to destroy the Canaanites (*herem*) as forfeiture of property and expulsion from the community (Ezra 10:8). Thus, from the earliest point at which it is possible to see the Pentateuch being read as a scriptural text, it is being interpreted by means of analogy.

The narrative of Numbers is used to obvious effect in Ezra's prayer that follows the reading of the law. The wilderness stories from Exodus 15–18 and Numbers 11–21 provide examples of divine generosity and Israel's disobedience (Neh. 9:15–21). The history of Israel is a clear warning against disobedience for the people of Ezra's day. As a result they commit themselves to keep the law, including prescriptions found in the book of Numbers

---

23. James W. Watts, *Reading Law: The Rhetorical Shaping of the Pentateuch*, The Biblical Seminar 59 (Sheffield: Sheffield Academic Press, 1999).

(Neh. 10:36–40 [35–39]; cf. Num. 15:17–21; 18:8–32). The disobedience for which the Israelites are condemned in the wilderness is specific to their circumstances, but an analogy is easily drawn to the community that Ezra seeks to lead.

Thus, already in Ezra and Nehemiah we have evidence of a creative and supple hermeneutic when interpreting the Pentateuch. The application of texts can be extended through the combination of biblical texts (Ezra 9:1), texts can be applied in a literal and a nonliteral manner (Ezra 10:8; Neh. 10:36–40 [35–39]), and narratives can be appropriated through analogy (Neh. 9:15–21). If we turn to two later examples of early interpretation, Qumran and the apostle Paul, we find similar hermeneutics at work.

The difficulties in interpreting the book of Numbers are apparent in the disagreements between the Qumran sect and the Jewish leadership in Jerusalem over the meaning and application of the biblical idea of the "camp." In comparison to Leviticus the book of Numbers extends the locus of sanctity from the tabernacle to the wilderness camp (5:1–4). But how should the "camp" be interpreted in the Second Temple period? Both the *Halakhic Letter* (4Q394) and the *Temple Scroll* (11Q19) equate the wilderness camp with Jerusalem: "And we think that the temple [is the tent of meeting and Je]rusalem is the camp" (4Q394 2.16–17). It is probably at odds with nonsectarian interpretation of Numbers, as the letter writer's "we think" implies.[24] For both the Qumran sect and Jewish nonsectarians, the book of Numbers had authoritative force within their communities, and for both the text needed to be applied through analogy. The difference arises only in determining how the analogy should work. When Numbers describes the holiness of the camp, should this apply to the city or just to the temple courts?

In the New Testament, the wilderness stories in both Exodus and Numbers receive extended exposition from Paul in 1 Corinthians 10:1–12. Like Ezra, Paul uses the stories to highlight divine generosity and human disobedience. Typologizing the Red Sea, the manna, and the water from the rock, Paul argues that the Israelites had access to the same sacraments as the church (vv. 1–5; cf. vv. 14–22). Nevertheless, they were punished for the sins of idolatry, sexual immorality, testing Christ, and complaining (vv. 6–12). In the wilderness narratives Paul discovers exactly the same sinful practice that he has to confront at Corinth. It is perhaps no surprise that Paul should turn to Numbers in writing to the unruly Corinthian church, for no other Old Testament book is quite as concerned with the order of God's people as is this one. Nevertheless, the appropriation of the book is not straightforward. For Paul's understanding, an essential continuity exists between the Israelites in the wilderness and the

---

24. For discussion, see Hannah K. Harrington, *The Purity Texts*, Companion to the Qumran Scrolls (London: T&T Clark, 2004); Ian C. Werrett, *Ritual Purity and the Dead Sea Scrolls*, Studies in the Texts of the Desert of Judah 72 (Leiden: Brill, 2007).

nascent Christian community. Nevertheless, the new context means that Paul has to proceed through the use of typology and analogy.[25]

The interpretive strategies of analogy and typology that ancient readers employed are important pointers to how the book of Numbers was designed by its authors to be read. In certain cases the authors of Numbers may well have had particular views about how the narrative and laws of Numbers are to be implemented, and they could not have envisaged how the book would later be interpreted. Nevertheless, some form of analogizing was an essential feature for how the book was to function for its authors and first readers. Indeed, many concerns of modern historical-critical readings would have been more alien.

Numbers 20–21

The sheer diversity of material in the book of Numbers makes it difficult to find a text that can be described as representative of the book as a whole. For this reason I want to give attention to two chapters that play a pivotal role in the narrative and illustrate many characteristics of the book: Numbers 20–21. These chapters are a recognizable unit within the book. They trace Israel's journey from Kadesh, the point from which the Israelites sent out the spies, and end with the Israelites camped by the Jordan, just opposite Jericho, ready to enter the promised land (22:1). A block of legislative and ritual material (Num. 18–19) comes immediately before these chapters, and the three chapters about Balaam follow immediately after them. A number of features make Numbers 20–21 useful as an insight into the larger book.

First, throughout the chapters are scattered a number of different genres. The principal genre is narrative; as with the book of Numbers as a whole, that provides the framework within which the other genres are located. Thus these chapters have a narrative structure that drives the action forward, despite apparent twists and turns. Itineraries are embedded in the narrative in 21:4 and 21:10–20. These well illustrate a strong interest in details and lists that characterize the book of Numbers. It is not enough to say that Israel traveled from Kadesh to the banks of the Jordan; the exact route needs to be specified. There are also a few snippets of poetry in 21:14–15, 17–18, 27–30. In two cases these are presented as citations of existing songs; they are not freshly composed to be part of Numbers.

Second, most of what we find in Numbers 20–21 has a parallel elsewhere in the Old Testament, especially within the Pentateuch. The most important

25. Although Paul is selective, appealing only to the texts that address the needs of the Corinthian community, he does so within a coherent construal of the larger pentateuchal narrative. See Francis Watson, *Paul and the Hermeneutics of Faith* (London: T&T Clark, 2004), 354–411.

parallel is to be found in Deuteronomy 1–3, where the journey from Kadesh to the Jordan is rehearsed by Moses as part of his valedictory speech to the Israelites. Not only is the same ground covered, but also some of the events are told in a very similar manner. Israel requests passage through Edom (Num. 20:14–21//Deut. 2:1–8, 27–29) and does the same with Sihon and Og, though on these two occasions the Israelites meet their resistance with conflict and defeat them (Num. 21:21–35//Deut. 2:24–3:17). There are other parallels: the story of water from the rock (Num. 20:1–13) is quite similar to the provision story in Exodus 17:1–7; Aaron's death on Mount Hor (Num. 20:22–29) is recounted in Numbers 33:38–39, but also has some similarities to Moses' death on Mount Nebo (Deut. 34:1–12); the itinerary in Numbers 21:10–13 has parallels in Numbers 33:44–45 as well as Deuteronomy 2:14, 24; the poetic fragment in Numbers 21:27–30 has a parallel in Jeremiah 48:45–46; the settlement of Transjordan in Numbers 21:24–25, 31–32 has a parallel in Numbers 32. Other parallels could be mentioned; those listed above are just the most striking.

Third, these chapters introduce a number of apparent difficulties. There are, for example, a number of tensions when we compare the parallel passages that we have listed above. The Edomites refuse Israel passage through their territory, despite the fact that Deuteronomy 2:27–29 implies that Edom has allowed Israel through. As a result Israel makes a huge detour around Edom and Moab, though Deuteronomy 2:1–8 envisages Israel traveling the direct route through these nations along the King's Highway. More problematic still is the surprising appearance of a victory at Hormah in Numbers 21:1–3. After the failure of the spies, Israel had been sent back into the wilderness. At the beginning of chapter 21, then, it seems to make no sense to have Israel attacking a city to the south of the promised land—even more so when we realize that this is precisely the city that the people fought against in Numbers 14. On that occasion they did so contrary to Yʜwʜ's command (who had ordered them back into the wilderness) and as a result were defeated.

The challenge facing any reader of these chapters is to make sense of this complicated block of material. As Baruch Levine observes on Numbers 21, "It would be hard to conceive of a single chapter of the Hebrew Bible that poses more complex historical and literary problems."[26] In trying to make sense of these chapters, I will undertake a close reading of the text that pays attention to its narrative dynamic and its relationship with other parts of the Bible, especially other parts of the Pentateuch. A satisfactory reading of Numbers 20–21 needs to take full account of all the difficulties in the text. We will then see how these problems have been addressed, before considering what light is shed on the text by understanding Numbers as a book that mediates between the Priestly corpus and the book of Deuteronomy.

26. Baruch A. Levine, *Numbers 21–36*, Anchor Bible 4A (New York: Doubleday, 2000), 110.

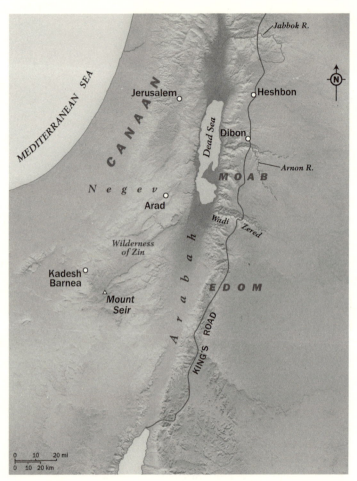

The Israelites' Detour around Edom

A Close Narrative Reading of Numbers 20–21

Chapter 20 opens ominously with Miriam's death. "In the first month the entire Israelite community came to the Wilderness of Zin, and the people settled at Kadesh. Miriam died and was buried there" (20:1). Death hovers over the central part of Numbers as a result of disobedience. This began in 11:2 at the edge of the camp, but penetrated the whole people with the spy episode (14:35), and even the Levites with the rebellion of Korah and his comrades (16:31–35). Now, finally, it even reaches Israel's leaders. This gloomy development is exacerbated for the reader by what immediately precedes the account of Miriam's death. The instructions for the red-cow ritual in Numbers 19 describe the virulence of impurity that stems from a corpse. For the book of Numbers, disobedience has resulted in death, and now further estrangement from God results, for death brings impurity and exclusion from the camp. There is, of course, a note of hope in Numbers 19 since impurity can be cleansed, but that is not the dominant note sounding forth at this point in the book.

In the narrative that follows, Moses and Aaron too find themselves joining their sister, condemned to die outside the land (20:2–13). The occasion is the bringing forth of water from the rock. The story has clear links to the earlier story in Exodus 17:1–7, including a number of identical phrases. This is perhaps clearest in the fact that both Exodus and Numbers locate the miracle at Meribah. The precise reason for Moses and Aaron's exclusion from the land has long puzzled interpreters. It is described in 20:12 as a failure of trust and in 27:14 as rebellion, highlighting the similarity of Moses and Aaron's conduct to that of the Israelites during the spy episode. The people's refusal to go into the land is likewise described as unbelief in Numbers 14:11 and as an act of rebellion in 14:9 (cf. Deut. 1:26, 43; 9:23). Moses is commanded to take the rod and speak to the rock. In the event he speaks to the people and strikes the rock twice. Is Moses' failure in the things he says, showing arrogance or unbelief? Or is it in striking the rock rather than speaking to it, a disobedience underlined by the second strike? It is difficult to choose between these two alternatives, and it is possible that this is a false choice. Thus we observe that the formula of obedient completion, "Moses did just as he commanded him," occurs not at the end of the narrative, but in verse 9. All that follows in verses 10–11 departs from Yhwh's commandment.

We might naturally expect the story of Aaron's death to follow immediately after the story of Moses and Aaron's sin. Instead, the natural flow of the narrative is disturbed by an account of Moses' sending messengers to the king of Edom to request passage through his territory (20:14–21). The appearance of this narrative at this point is surprising, for the people are still based at Kadesh, some distance from Edomite territory. Deuteronomy 2 suggests a different course of events: The Israelites are commanded to leave Kadesh. They wander for many days (2:1), presumably almost thirty-eight years (2:14), before they march through Edom. The encounter with Edom is also quite differently portrayed in Numbers and Deuteronomy, as we have already observed. There is no narrative comparable to Numbers 20:14–21 in Deuteronomy 2. The deuteronomic account assumes that Israel marched through Edomite territory, but in Numbers 20 Edom refuses Israel passage, forcing the Israelites to make a long detour east around Edom and Moab.

In Numbers the story of Israel's encounter with Edom is told mainly as a dialogue between Israel and Edom. The initial portrayal of an exchange of messengers between Moses and the king of Edom soon falls away, and the narrative becomes about the relationships of two "brother" nations, Israel and Edom. Israel's opening message recounts the previous experiences of the

Israelites (20:14–16). This has striking similarities to other creedal statements in the Old Testament, especially Deuteronomy 26:5–11. Yet the emphasis here is less on what YHWH has done and more on the troubles that Israel has endured. Rhetorically, the purpose is to rouse the sympathy of the Edomites for their "brother" Israel and to respond generously. This is a perspective strikingly similar to what we find in Deuteronomy, where rich Israelites are meant to show generosity to those without. The renouncement of any claim to Edom's crops or water supplies belongs to this same rhetorical move. It is meant to elicit from Edom the reply that the Israelites should by all means freely avail themselves of what Edom has. Yet Edom responds quite unexpectedly by refusing Israel passage. Israel changes tack and resends the messengers, offering to pay the Edomites for any inconvenience caused by its passage, but again Israel is rebuffed by the Edomites, who even assemble an army to defend their territory. In the story of Sihon, such actions lead to conflict. In the case of Edom, though, Israel turns away. Perhaps the reader is expected to know not only that Israel cannot attack a brother nation but also that Edom's territory is forbidden (cf. Deut. 2:5).

The Israelites travel on to Mount Hor, where death again makes an appearance. Aaron's death on Mount Hor and the appointment of Eleazer as his successor anticipate the death of Moses and the appointment of Joshua in Deuteronomy 34:1–12. The death of one of the leaders of the Israelite community is a significant moment of communal loss, marked by thirty days of mourning, but the appointment of Eleazer suggests the possibility of a new beginning. Here we have the juxtaposition of the death of the old and the birth of the new, a motif that characterizes the whole book of Numbers, as Dennis Olson argues.[27]

The development of the narrative unexpectedly shifts again with the attack of the king of Arad upon the Israelites (21:1–3). Arad is located in the south of Palestine, and it is difficult to understand why this king should now feel threatened since Israel has turned away from a southern entry into Canaan and has returned to the wilderness. The Israelites are said to be on the "road to Atharim" (21:1), but the location is otherwise unknown. Equally surprising, as we have already mentioned, is that the Israelites capture Hormah. This is the location mentioned in 14:45, when the Israelites are defeated after disobeying YHWH and yet trying to take the promised land without divine assistance. It is almost as if the narrative has been replayed so as to ensure a more favorable result the second time around. On this occasion the Israelites make a vow, a practice that frequently appears in the book of Numbers (e.g., Num. 30). They also put into effect the "ban" (Hebrew *herem*), according to which everyone is slaughtered (21:3). This is the first time this practice, more familiar from the book of Deuteronomy, occurs in the Bible.

---

27. Olson, *Death of the Old*.

In Numbers 21:4 the itinerary suddenly returns to Mount Hor, the place where Aaron has died, and the Israelites head back toward the Red Sea in order to begin their major detour around Edom and Moab. Faced with such a long journey, it is not surprising that the people grow weary. The Israelites' complaint is an amalgam of all their previous murmurings, even though contradictory. They have no bread; they have no water; the bread is detestable. The detestable bread is presumably a reference to the manna. As punishment God sends "fiery snakes," which are otherwise known only from Deuteronomy 8:15. These snakes bite the people and cause many to perish. The people appeal to Moses, who intercedes for them. At first glance the story appears to follow the pattern of the other murmuring stories in the book of Numbers: complaint → punishment → intercession → relief. But there are two novelties. First, the people confess their sin.[28] Second, God does not merely stop the plague of snakes, as the people request, but also provides a means of healing: the bronze serpent. As a result the standard murmuring narrative is quite transformed. For those who trust and look toward the bronze serpent, the overwhelming context of death is shattered. The narrative closes on a triumphant note, "and he *lives*" (21:9).

Before we leave the story of the bronze serpent, we should notice a couple of important intertextual links that are easily missed. First, the bronze serpent is placed upon a standard, better "the standard" (v. 9).[29] The only previous mention of a standard is in the story of the defeat of the Amalekites (Exod. 17:8–17). The identification of the standard is far from clear in that story, but it may be the rod that Moses holds high to ensure Joshua's victory.[30] Second, the story of the bronze serpent is one of the few narratives in the Old Testament where Yhwh is portrayed as a healer. Another such account in the Pentateuch is the story of the waters of Marah, where Yhwh reveals himself as "the one who heals you" (Exod. 15:26).[31]

The eleven verses that follow describe Israel's itinerary along the eastern borders of Edom and Moab, then to the banks of the Jordan (Num. 21:10–20). A careful reading reveals that we have two types of itineraries in these verses. The first type of itinerary in verses 10–12 uses a verbal sentence: "The Israelites traveled from X and camped at Y." As we have already observed, the Israelites' itinerary in these verses has parallels in Numbers 33:44–45 as well as in Deuteronomy 2:14, 24. These verses in Numbers 21 seem to have brought the two together, but they also make clear, as Numbers 33 does not, that the Israelites

28. The same words are uttered in Num. 14:40, but subsequent actions belie the Israelites' confession.

29. The MT has "*the* standard" only in v. 9; the Samaritan Pentateuch has it in both vv. 8 and 9.

30. This association was already noticed by the rabbis (Mishnah, *Rosh Ha-Shanah* 3.8).

31. For the rare attribution of healing to Yhwh, see Norbert Lohfink, "'I Am Yahweh, Your Physician' (Exodus 15:26)," in *Theology of the Pentateuch* (Edinburgh: T&T Clark, 1994), 35–95.

journey to the east of Moab. Thus we have an itinerary consistent with the rest of Numbers 20–21. The second type of itinerary is found in verses 19–20 and consists of a list of names with a preposition: "from X (to) Y." Between these two different types of itinerary are inserted two poetic fragments. The first fragment is said to be from "The Book of the Wars of YHWH." The Hebrew is rather difficult to read confidently, but it is interpreted to confirm that the Arnon River is Moab's border. The extent of Moab will again be a matter of concern in verses 25–30. The second fragment has no attribution, but its vocabulary is not typical of Numbers, and it seems likely to be a quotation. What we should not overlook, however, is the way the song is introduced. "Then Israel sang this song" appears to be an echo of the introduction to the Song of the Sea in Exodus 15:1, when Israel celebrated YHWH's victory over the Egyptian army at the Red Sea. In Numbers 21:17–18 the praise is not directed to YHWH. Instead, the song praises the leaders of Israel and their staffs. Although the fragment of poetry uses different vocabulary, we have a striking reversal of Numbers 16–17, where the staffs of the leaders reveal the failure of their leadership in rebelling against YHWH and Moses.

The story that follows concerns Israel's conflict with Sihon, king of the Amorites (21:21–31). It thus becomes clear why two types of itinerary appeared in 21:10–20. In the first type, the verbal sentence, Israel is said to have traveled and camped; in the second type, the locations are just listed. Thus the second list interrupts the narrative account of Israel's actions. It completes the itinerary all the way to the banks of the Jordan. For the narrative this still lies sometime in the future. When the story resumes in verse 21, the Israelites are still in the wilderness by the Arnon River, as they were in verse 13. In other words, the itinerary in verses 19–20 is clearly written in anticipation. It also creates the rather pleasing literary structure of two poetic fragments between two itineraries.

When Israel comes to Sihon's territory (21:21), north of Moab, messengers are sent to the king, requesting passage, as had been done with Edom. Sihon refuses and musters his army, but on this occasion Israel comes out to meet the Amorites in battle. The Amorites are defeated, and Israel takes over Sihon's territory (21:21–24). What follows is an account of Israel's occupation of Sihon's kingdom and a poem celebrating the same event. The poem is introduced as "That is why the poets say" (NIV) or "Therefore the ballad singers say" (NRSV). The varying translations highlight the difficulty of translating the Hebrew word *moshelim*. They are those who sing *mashal* compositions, where a *mashal* could be translated "proverb, wisdom saying" (cf. NASB). Here the *mashal* is perhaps best understood to be describing a reversal of fortunes, with similar examples in Isaiah 14:4 and Habakkuk 2:6. The fate that Sihon has inflicted upon Moab (21:28–29) has now been returned upon Sihon by the Israelites (v. 30). For this reason many commentators describe the poetry as a taunt song.

At this point the quotation of the poetry is to show that Sihon has occupied the former territory of Moab. As we have already seen in Numbers 21:13, there is an evident concern with the borders of Moab's kingdom. The poem is understood to show that the land on the east of the Jordan between the Jabbok and the Arnon was originally Moabite but had been taken by Sihon. It has long been appreciated that verses 28–29 are almost identical to Jeremiah 48:45–46, but in Numbers the poem has a different introduction and conclusion. A careful comparison suggests two important differences in the content. First, the poem in Jeremiah mentions Sihon once, and it is not entirely clear that this is a person. In contrast, the poem in Numbers mentions Sihon three times, and Heshbon is identified as his city. Second, there is a stronger emphasis on the geography of the territory. In Jeremiah 48:45–46 there are references to Heshbon and Moab, but in Numbers 21:27–30 there are additionally references to Ar, Arnon, Dibon, and possibly Nophah and Medeba. The differences in content between the poetic material in Jeremiah 48 and Numbers 21 underline the concern in Numbers 21 for the boundaries of the territory that Sihon is said to have captured from Moab. Again Numbers 21 appears to assume the perspective of Deuteronomy 2, that no part of Moabite territory has been assigned to Israel. Territory that Moab has previously held, but lost to Sihon, is clearly another matter.

The account of the defeat of Sihon replicates that found in Deuteronomy 2 with some overlap, but this is not the case for the brief account of the capture of Jazer (Num. 21:32). The story of the defeat of Og is told briefly, with a number of similarities to the defeat of Sihon (21:33–35). A comparison to the parallel in Deuteronomy 3:1–7 reveals a striking similarity between the two accounts. The defeat of Og is told in slightly shorter compass in Numbers 21, but almost every sentence in Numbers 21 has a verbatim parallel in Deuteronomy 3.

Making Sense of Numbers 20–21

How does one make sense of the bewildering mix of genres and narratives that we find in Numbers 20–21? As we have seen, the narrative progression of these chapters appears to make good sense at times. Yet there are also occasions where we think that we are finding our way, but then the ground appears to give way and we are left uncertain about our abilities to make sense of these chapters. There is, then, on the level of individual stories, some sense of order. But we cannot escape the presence of numerous problems, some of which we have identified in the previous section.

One way of making sense of these chapters and their difficulties is to try to discern different sources. Among the many strengths of the documentary hypothesis was its ability to do justice to both the sense of some narrative progression and the numerous problems that trouble the careful reader. Our sense of some order is justified; continuous sources are to be found in these chapters, and these make good sense. Nevertheless, numerous problems have resulted from trying to draw together sources that are, at some points, irreconcilable.

Here and elsewhere, the documentary hypothesis offered a solution to a text that did not make sense on any straightforward reading.

In his *Introduction to the Literature of the Old Testament*, S. R. Driver offers a classic analysis of these chapters with the insights of the documentary hypothesis. He avoids the difficult problem of distinguishing between the J and E sources, and divides the text between the Priestly source (P) and a combined JE source. The stories of Moses and Aaron's rebellion and Aaron's death on Mount Hor are attributed to P. The death of the high priest and succession of his son are clearly matters of concern to priestly writers. As we have seen, Aaron's death is closely linked to the story of Moses and Aaron's failure at the rock. Many of the itineraries are also attributed to P, including 20:1a; 21:4a, 10–11. The rest of the chapters are attributed to the combined JE source.[32] Driver's contemporary G. B. Gray attempted a more precise division of these chapters. He distinguished between J and E sources in the itineraries of 21:10–20 and the story of the conquest of Sihon. In the stories of Israel's encounter with Edom and the bronze serpent, it is not possible for Gray to detach the two sources from each other. The story of Og is attributed to the influence of Deuteronomy 3.[33]

Through careful and critical analysis, the documentary hypothesis sought to resolve the difficulties in Numbers 20–21. Here, as elsewhere in the Pentateuch, the cost of this exercise was the loss of a belief that the canonical text, esteemed by Jews and Christians, could make any sense on its own terms. The text made sense only if it could be separated into its individual sources. Though not a happy state of affairs, it did at least do justice to the real difficulties that confront the reader of these chapters in Numbers.

Another approach would be to argue that readers of the biblical text already have their own way of resolving the difficulties in Numbers 20–21. The reader of the canonical books finds the same events are repeated in Deuteronomy 2–3. The differences between the two passages are succinctly expressed by Perlitt in his comparison of the two passages: "The narrative materials of Deuteronomy 1–3 are also to be found in Numbers—with a significant difference. In Numbers they are scattered, disorderly, mixed up with legislative material, embedded in non-deuteronomistic layers, and arranged according to priestly concerns. In Deuteronomy 1–3, however, they are literarily condensed, geographically

---

32. Priestly source: Num. 20:1a, 2, 3b–4, 6–13, 22–29; 21:4a, 10–11. JE sources: 20:1b, 3a, 5, 14–21; 21:1–3, 4b–9, 12–35; see Samuel R. Driver, *An Introduction to the Literature of the Old Testament*, 8th ed. (Edinburgh: T&T Clark, 1909), 66. This lack of confidence about the ability to distinguish between J and E in these chapters has been characteristic of many recent discussions in Anglo-American scholarship; so, e.g., Baruch A. Levine, *Numbers*, 2 vols., Anchor Bible 4–4A (New York: Doubleday, 1993–2000).

33. J: Num. 20:1a*, 5; 21:1–3, 16, 18b–20, 24b, 25 (26), 32. E: 20:1b; 21:11b–13, 21–24a, 31. JE: 20:14–21; 21:4b–9. P: 20:1a*, 2–13*, 22–29; 21:4a. Redactor: 20:3–4, 8–11; Deuteronomist: 21:33–35. See Gray, *Numbers*, 256–307.

directed, rhetorically consistent and theologically unified."[34] Perceptive readers could understand the ordered account of Deuteronomy 1–3 as an authoritative commentary on Numbers 20–21, aiding them in making sense of those chapters and highlighting the key themes.

For Perlitt and many other interpreters, the only way to understand the confusion of Numbers and the orderliness of Deuteronomy is for the latter to be an interpretation of the former. As we have seen, however, the source and redaction criticism of the Pentateuch has changed significantly in recent years. In many ways the critical assessment of Numbers 20–21 changed in advance of the broader shifts in pentateuchal criticism. Already in 1940 Martin Noth had argued that significant parts of Numbers 21 were an editorial creation.[35] John Van Seters has argued extensively that the Deuteronomistic History was prior to, and a decisive influence upon, the Yahwist; he published his first explorations in this area on Numbers 20–21. This is no accident, for here we have some of the strongest evidence for the influence of Deuteronomy upon the earlier books of the Pentateuch.[36] Recent contributions to the question have suggested a complex interrelationship between Numbers 20–21 and Deuteronomy 1–3. The stories of an Israelite encounter with Edom (Num. 20:14–21) and with Sihon (21:21–24) are retold in Deuteronomy 2–3. The original stories were then incorporated into Numbers, with a great deal of additional material, some of which was influenced by the telling of these stories in Deuteronomy.[37]

If this account of the literature's history is correct, and a number of recent scholars seem to subscribe to this view, then it requires that we return to Perlitt's observation anew. Perlitt highlights the contrast between the orderliness of Deuteronomy and the disorderliness of Numbers. Another way of restating his observation would be to say that we have a much better idea of how Deuteronomy 1–3 works than we do of how Numbers 20–21 works. In Deuteronomy 1–3 we have a strong schematized contrast between the old generation that is defeated at Hormah and the new generation that is successful in defeating Sihon and Og.[38] The old generation is characterized by rebellion, and the new generation by obedience. The sharp divide between

---

34. Lothar Perlitt, "Deuteronomium 1–3 im Streit der exegetischen Methoden," in *Das Deuteronomium: Entstehung, Gestalt und Botschaft*, ed. N. Lohfink, Bibliotheca ephemeridum theologicarum lovaniensium 68 (Leuven: Peeters, 1985), 149–63, here 160–61 (author's translation).

35. Martin Noth, "Nu 21 als Glied der 'Hexateuch'-Erzählung," *Zeitschrift für die alttestamentliche Wissenschaft* 58 (1940/41): 161–89, referring esp. to vv. 10–20 and 32–35.

36. John Van Seters, "Conquest of Sihon's Kingdom: A Literary Examination," *Journal of Biblical Literature* 99 (1972): 182–97. See further idem, *The Life of Moses: The Yahwist as Historian in Exodus–Numbers* (Louisville: Westminster John Knox, 1994).

37. Achenbach, *Vollendung*; Eckart Otto, *Das Deuteronomium im Pentateuch und Hexateuch: Studien zur Literaturgeschichte von Pentateuch und Hexateuch im Lichte des Deuteronomiumrahmens*, Forschungen zum Alten Testament 30 (Tübingen: Mohr Siebeck, 2000).

38. See esp. Norbert Lohfink, "Darstellungskunst und Theologie in Dtn 1:6–3:29," *Biblica* 41 (1960): 105–34.

the two generations is highlighted in Deuteronomy 2:14. Only when the last member of the disobedient generation has died can the people cross over the Zered and begin the conquest of the promised land. In this way the chapters admirably introduce the book of Deuteronomy. They express the intrinsic connection between obedience and divine blessing that is central to Deuteronomy's presentation of the law.

If we are to make sense of Numbers 20–21 in a way that does justice to its literary, historical, and theological dimensions, I suggest that we build on these insights reflected in recent pentateuchal criticism. Thus I suggest understanding Numbers 20–21 as part of a larger attempt to mediate between the growing Priestly corpus (Genesis–Leviticus) and Deuteronomy. Viewing Numbers 20–21 in this way, we will be able to appreciate how these chapters function. First, these chapters reflect a careful reading of Deuteronomy 1–3 and seek to make sense of some confusing details in that text. Second, these chapters interweave the stories of Transjordan with allusions to the book of Exodus. In doing so, a more complicated account of the transition from the old generation to the new generation is achieved. Overall, this new account is not meant to replace what we find in Deuteronomy 1–3, but to complement and deepen it. We will explore this idea with reference to several specific details in the text.

The Problems with Edom and Moab in Deuteronomy

In the book of Deuteronomy, the journey of the Israelites is a model of simplicity. The Israelites march from Horeb to Kadesh-barnea, a journey that, we are told, takes eleven days. They send out spies from Kadesh but disobey God's command to take the land and are sent back into the desert. They wander there for thirty-eight years before being commanded to head north through Edom and Moab along their way to the territory of Sihon and the crossing of the Jordan.

As we have seen, one of the difficulties that confronts the attentive reader of Numbers 20–21 is the unexpected movements of the Israelites. They send messengers to Edom from Kadesh, though they are some distance from the historical heart of Edomite territory, and despite the fact that Deuteronomy locates Kadesh at the beginning of Israel's wilderness wanderings. They go around Edom and Moab, despite the clear implication of Deuteronomy 2 that they journey through those territories. As they undertake that long journey, they are attacked by the Canaanite king of Arad, even though they have moved away from his territory. After their victory the Israelites take the town of Hormah, though this is a town in the south of Palestine, and the expectation—after the incident of the spies—is that Israel needs to enter the promised land from the east.

Readers of the Bible have been burdened not only by the strange journey in Numbers but also by the apparent need to produce one coherent itinerary from the many different versions that are found in the Pentateuch. Many Bibles have maps of the wilderness itinerary that are eloquent testimony to the difficulties of this task. Lines loop all over the Sinai peninsula and the Arabah, trying to make sense of how the Israelites could be at Kadesh at the beginning of their wanderings and before approaching Edom, and how the Israelites came north past Edom in any one of three routes: up the Arabah, along the King's Highway, or entirely east of Edom. Unlike earlier generations of Bible readers, modern printing bequeaths to us the benefits of multiple colors so that the various "alternative routes" can be plotted.

Given the apparent failure to reconstruct a single, coherent itinerary, have we been taking the right approach to the biblical text? Is all this intense interest in the minutiae of southern Palestinian geography necessary? For the latter question, the answer for Numbers 20–21 is surely yes. After all, few books in the Bible are more geographically fixated than the book of Numbers. If we are interested in the book of Numbers, we should be concerned with the issues that animate it. And yet there is a paradox. Despite its strong interests in geography, the book of Numbers has produced an account of Israel's journey that is confused at best and maybe even just plain contradictory. Or perhaps we might better say that it is precisely because the writers of Numbers are so interested in geographical details that they have produced such perplexing results. They have read Deuteronomy 1–3 very carefully and encountered in it some difficult geographical problems.

There are two problems that the reader of Deuteronomy 1–3 encounters. First, according to 1:44 the Israelites were beaten "in Seir as far as Hormah." For readers likely to associate Seir with Edom (as occurs in Deut. 2 and elsewhere in the Old Testament), this reference to Seir is perplexing. What is Seir doing in a story about Israel's entry into the south of Palestine? Israel should be nowhere near Seir. The commentators have suggested various different solutions. Perhaps the reference to Seir was inadvertently introduced from Deuteronomy 2, or perhaps Seir is also a location in the south of Judah. For our purposes, what is important is not determining the correct solution to this problem, but merely identifying the existence of a problem that could have perplexed an ancient reader of Deuteronomy.

Second, there is an additional problem in the use of "Seir" in Deuteronomy. According to Deuteronomy 2:1 the Israelites are commanded to head back toward the Red Sea and go around "Mount Seir." After they have done this, they are commanded to head north and seek passage through "Seir," which is understood as Edomite territory (2:2–8). How does it make sense for Israel to go around Seir and then ask permission to go through it? If Israel can circumvent Edom, as it has been doing for the past thirty-eight years, why can it not do so now?

The problem arises from Deuteronomy 2:1, the instruction to go around "Mount Seir." The verb used here "to go around" (*sabab et*) means a partial circuit. It does not have the sense of a complete circuit unless further qualified. A good example of its use is found in Ezekiel 47:2, where Ezekiel goes around the temple from the north gate to the east gate. The location that Israel is to go around is identified as "Mount Seir." This does not refer to the historical heartlands of the Edomites, the mountains east of the Arabah. Rather, it is a location on the west of the Arabah, in the southern Negev. The biblical texts identify the original inhabitants of Seir as the Horites. It was probably only in the seventh century BCE onward that Edom expanded into this area. Not only did it displace the former inhabitants of the area, but in time Edom also came to be identified with Seir.[39] That Mount Seir is a location west of the Arabah is confirmed by Deuteronomy 1:2, which locates Mount Seir on the route between Horeb and Kadesh.

If this identification is correct then the itinerary described in Deuteronomy 2 is straightforward. Israel left Kadesh-barnea on the northwest side of the Negev plateau. They circled southward around it and entered the Arabah halfway along. This would then place the Israelites where they could climb up onto the Transjordan plateau and proceed on the King's Highway through traditional Edomite territory. To understand Israel's movement, it is crucial to distinguish between Mount Seir and Seir. Once this distinction is lost, the geographical logic of Deuteronomy 2 no longer makes sense.

I suggest that the writers of Numbers 20–21 paid very close attention to the text of Deuteronomy, but they struggled to make sense of these different references to Seir because they understood all of them as references to the same place, the kingdom of Edom. This explains many of the difficulties in these chapters. First, the writers of Numbers split the defeat at Hormah into two accounts. The first account in Numbers 14:40–45 plays a similar role to the account of the defeat in Deuteronomy 1:41–45. The second account in Numbers 21:1–3 is located close to Edom's borders, as the reference to Seir in Deuteronomy 1:44 requires, and on this occasion defeat is transformed into victory. The perplexing reference to Seir in Deuteronomy 1:44 allows the writers of Numbers 21:1–3 to replay the disobedience at Kadesh. Israel is now characterized by a faithful commitment to YHWH, seen in the completion of a holy vow to practice the *herem* of Deuteronomy.

Second, the writers of Numbers 20–21 read in Deuteronomy 2:1 that the children of Israel were forced to go around Mount Seir, and they understand this to mean not part of the southeastern Negev, but the entirety of Edom's territory. Thus in Numbers 21:4 we find Deuteronomy 2:1 cited, but with all ambiguity removed. "Then Israel left Mount Hor by the way of the Red Sea,

39. A rather revealing text is Ezek. 35. Ezekiel prophesies "against Mount Seir" (vv. 1–2, 7), which is clearly meant to be a cipher for the Edomites. Verse 15 removes any potential for misunderstanding by glossing "Mount Seir" with "you and all of Edom," but does so by assuming a distinction between you (= Mount Seir) and Edom. In Chronicles, the association of Mount Seir and Edom is complete (2 Chron. 20:10, 22–23).

in order to go around *the land of Edom*." This perspective is confirmed as the itinerary in Numbers continues in 21:10–13, which makes it very clear that Israel passes east of Edom and Moab. Thus, for Numbers 20–21 the Israelites are forced to make a huge detour around Edomite territory. But why is such an arduous journey necessary? The writers of Numbers attribute the reason to the Edomites themselves. The description of the messengers in 20:14–21 and their failure to secure passage for Israel through Edom provides an account that makes good sense of this need to go far out of the way on the journey to the promised land. But where should the sending of the messengers be located? The itinerary in Deuteronomy 1–2 allows for only one possibility. Since the circumambulation of Edom begins on departure from Kadesh (1:46–2:1), the messengers must have been sent from there.

The account of Edom's refusal does not just explain a geographical difficulty, but rather like the story of Hormah, it also becomes a vehicle for expressing deuteronomic theology. The Edomites refuse to show hospitality to Israel, even though Israel recounts some of the difficulties it has encountered to that point. Elsewhere in Deuteronomy the recounting of Israel's story results in generosity. This story begins with the people's landlessness and slavery and ends with their possession of the promised land. God's generous gift of a fruitful land is meant to stimulate matching acts of generosity. This message pervades Deuteronomy, with its focus on communal meals held at Yhwh's chosen sanctuary. In Numbers 20 Edom becomes a negative example. The unstated assumption is that *Israel* would not behave in such a way. In a subtle manner, then, the story engenders a set of moral values that the writers believe should characterize Israelite readers.

Thus while we can say that the writer of Numbers 20–21 misunderstood how the geographical references in Deuteronomy 1–3 were intended, he did seek to make sense of the ambiguous text that he had. More than that, we witness a close attention to the text, an attempt to read it as coherent and to understand one reference to Seir in light of another. Finally, the understanding of the itinerary leads to a richly developed narrative.

Numbers 20–21 between Exodus and Deuteronomy

Our examination of these chapters so far has primarily explored the way that deuteronomic stories and themes emerge. This is not the only influence upon these chapters, as our close reading has suggested. Instead, the book of Exodus has numerous echoes, in particular the stories found between the exodus from Egypt and the arrival at Sinai. The story of Moses and Aaron's failure is a striking retelling of Exodus 17; the bronze serpent alludes to the provision of water and manna in Exodus 15–17 as well as the "banner" of Exodus 17 and Yhwh as healer in Exodus 15. Finally, the discovery of the well in Numbers 21:16–17 leads to a song of praise like that sung after Yhwh's victory at the Red Sea. Unlike Exodus 15, the song of the well is not direct praise of YHWH. It does, however, celebrate the hierarchical structure of Israel functioning as YHWH intends it to do, and not indulging in the disobedience that has characterized it in recent chapters of the book. Two things are striking about these allusions. First, they are scattered throughout these chapters such that a careful interweaving between incidents inspired by Deuteronomy and incidents inspired by Exodus is achieved. Second, the allusions to Exodus come, by and large, from progressively earlier in that book: water from the rock (17:1–7), manna and Marah (15:22–16:36), the Song of the Sea (15:1–21). By careful narrative arrangement and subtle allusion, the writers present the failures of the wilderness as being undone and Israel as being led back from quarreling with God in the wilderness to the experience of praise. It is immediately after Israel has again learned to praise that the people begin to enter and conquer the land promised to them.

We might fruitfully compare the presentation of the wilderness wanderings in Numbers 20–21 to its literary precursor in Deuteronomy 1–3. In Deuteronomy we have a stark presentation of the demise of the old generation, with a clear boundary erected between the old, disobedient generation and the new, obedient generation. The boundary is marked by 2:14. "The period of time we wandered from Kadesh-barnea until the crossing of the Wadi Zered was thirty-eight years, until the entire generation of fighting men had perished from the camp, just as YHWH swore." God wipes the slate clean and begins anew with the next generation. The devastating annihilation of a generation is a common idea in biblical literature. The most famous example is the story of the flood, but it also finds striking expressions in the curses of Deuteronomy 28. In Israel's own experience, defeat of the nation and exile in Babylon was a catastrophe that affected a whole generation.

The book of Numbers does not abandon this perspective on divine punishment. The language and idea of Deuteronomy 2:14 are echoed in Numbers 32:13. But as Numbers 20–21 retells the narrative of Israel in the wilderness, the idea that the old generation has died out before they cross the Wadi Zered is conspicuously absent. This absence is highlighted when commentators, such as Levine, try to restore it: "To judge from the progress of the march, the end of the Exodus generation would have come in the text between verses 12 and 13 of Numbers 21."[40] But the final end of the old generation does not "come in the text." Nevertheless, Numbers 20–21 can be seen to provide a subtle commentary upon the idea of the punishment of a generation. It is not enough simply to wipe the slate and begin again. A more thorough, internal reorientation is needed. Numbers presents Israel confessing its sinfulness and receiving healing, as well as expressing gratitude and praise for divine provision. A similar perspective

40. Levine, *Numbers 21–36*, 79.

on the wilderness period is found in Deuteronomy 8, where the wilderness is seen as a time when Israel hungers in order to learn humility and dependence on God.

The nature of Numbers 20–21's commentary on the wilderness experience is not to displace the account in Deuteronomy 1–3. The possibilities opened through repentance and praise do not annul the punishment of the exodus generation. Their death in the wilderness is still a given. In a similar way, the emphasis on repentance and praise in Numbers does not replace Deuteronomy's insistence that disobedience leads to punishment. The book of Numbers will still be followed by Deuteronomy, with its insistence on the moral ordering of the world, seeing blessing coming to those who obey, but curse to the disobedient.

It might not be too difficult to imagine historical scenarios when such reflections might be generated, and that would also fit with the scholarly reconstruction of the literature's history. The original composition of Deuteronomy is usually placed around the end of the seventh century BCE, with various revisions and expansions taking place in the Babylonian exile and perhaps even afterward. The book of Numbers would be dated sometime in the Persian period. The idea of a whole generation being punished for its unfaithfulness and the hope of a subsequent new beginning for a following generation would fit well the Babylonian exile. Various biblical writers, such as the composer of Isaiah 40–55, imagine a fresh and glorious new start for the exiles in the land of Israel. Literature from the Persian period, such as Haggai or Ezra–Nehemiah, reveals that such hopes were quickly disappointed. The death of the old, sinful generation was not enough.

Such historical reconstructions have their value, but we should also observe that within the Pentateuch such reflections upon divine punishment, the collective failure of a whole generation, and the future possibility of grace and how that occurs are placed in Israel's distant past. These stories at the beginning of Israel's history are meant to be paradigmatic for the people's entire story with God; they are not exhausted in any one particular historical event. For every generation of God's people success in God's economy is not secured merely by having new leadership, new situations, or new people. Repentance, trust, and praise are also needed.

FURTHER READING

Davies, Eryl W. *Numbers*. New Century Bible Commentary. Grand Rapids: Eerdmans, 1995.

Douglas, Mary. *In the Wilderness: The Doctrine of Defilement in the Book of Numbers*. Journal for the Study of the Old Testament: Supplement Series 158. Sheffield: JSOT Press, 1993.

Leveen, Adriane B. *Memory and Tradition in the Book of Numbers*. Cambridge: Cambridge University Press, 2008.

Milgrom, Jacob. *Numbers: The Traditional Hebrew Text with the New JPS Translation*. The JPS Torah Commentary. Philadelphia: Jewish Publication Society, 1990.

Moberly, R. Walter L. *Can Balaam's Ass Speak Today? A Case Study in Reading the Old Testament as Scripture*. Grove Biblical Series 10. Cambridge: Grove Books, 1998.

Olson, Dennis T. *The Death of the Old and the Birth of the New: The Framework of the Book of Numbers and the Pentateuch*. Brown Judaic Studies 71. Chico, CA: Scholars Press, 1985.

———. *Numbers*. Interpretation. Louisville: John Knox, 1996.

Watson, Francis. *Paul and the Hermeneutics of Faith*, 354–411. London: T&T Clark, 2004.

Wenham, Gordon J. *Numbers*. Old Testament Guides. Sheffield: Sheffield Academic Press, 1997.

5

The Book of Deuteronomy

Rob Barrett

Deuteronomy prepares Israel for something new. As Moses' life—a thread of continuity from the beginning of Exodus—and Israel's desert wandering come to an end, the people look to their new life as a nation in the land that YHWH is giving them. At this new beginning, Deuteronomy again and again stresses the importance of laying a proper foundation. As YHWH's special people, Israel's every breath must be filled with loyalty to their God, the center of their life.

Beginnings do not, however, happen only once. Deuteronomy is no mere recounting of this moment in Israel's past. Rather, the people of YHWH regularly faced new challenges that required rethinking their foundations, and they usually did so with Deuteronomy's ideas in mind. Deuteronomic ideas grounded King Josiah's seventh-century reform. Jeremiah's failed struggle to save Judah from Babylonian exile reflects the book's priorities. After the exile, Deuteronomy provided Ezra a framework for understanding the devastation and building again. The New Testament frequently quotes and alludes to Deuteronomy as Jesus and the church reconceive life as God's people, both in continuity with and in distinction from existing tradition. Deuteronomy is an unboundedly reusable text, particularly in times of reform and reestablishment.

Communities today who identify with YHWH's people should continue to attend to the book's searching call to choose between life and death, between YHWH's blessing and curse. The book pulsates with the rhythmic repetition of

I am grateful to Walter Moberly for encouragement, probing questions, wise counsel, and a model for graciously bringing together faithfulness and inquiry.

the contemporizing "today" (occurring more than sixty times) as the day of decision, and commitment remains in the present tense. Moses goes so far as to marginalize prior generations as he draws his audience into Israel's story: "YHWH our God made with us a covenant at Horeb. Not with our ancestors did YHWH make this covenant, but rather with us, this *we* here today, all of us now living" (Deut. 5:2–3, emphasis added).

Each new day is a new "today" of living within YHWH's covenant and brings with it to each generation the hopes that accompany the bright promises given to the loyal and, at the same time, well-justified anxieties about the stark consequences of failure. Each new day offers new opportunities, either for obedience to the covenant or for missteps of disloyalty to YHWH. Disciplined vigilance is required. Deuteronomy reflects palpable concern about the future, cognizant of costly failure ahead, but with indefatigable confidence in YHWH's determination to bless Israel in a unique way that will lead to faithful loyalty, somehow, in the end.

Outline of Deuteronomy

Deuteronomy can be analyzed according to a variety of structures. The book contains division markers that separate three speeches by Moses (1:6–4:40; 5:1–28:68; 29:2 [29:1 MT]–30:20). These speeches are joined together by brief narrated passages (1:1–5; 4:41–49; 29:1 [28:69 MT]). Finally, there is a longer narrative section at the end, also containing brief speeches and a longer song and blessing by Moses (31:1–34:12). The book's narrator speaks from a position within the land, referring to Moses as being "across the Jordan in the wilderness" (1:1). The "action" of the book, however, is completely set on the plains of Moab, on the brink of Israel's entering the land. Moses' speeches are valedictory, the last words he will give to Israel before YHWH, from Mount Nebo, shows him the land he will not enter. The book closes with Moses' death and burial (34:1–8), and with Joshua succeeding—but in no way replacing—Moses (34:9–12).

Although the speech markers are significant, it is perhaps more helpful to observe the formal distinction between the detailed law in chapters 12–26 and the framework in chapters 1–11 and 27–34. The framework can also be divided into an outer portion (chs. 1–3; 31–34) and an inner portion (chs. 4–11, 27–30). Notice the seamless flow from the end of chapter 3 into the installation of Joshua in 31:1–8. The prologue in chapters 1–11 contains several identifiable pieces. After the narrator's introduction sets the scene in 1:1–5, Moses presents a selective retelling of Israel's movement from Horeb (= Sinai) to the plains of Moab, across the Jordan from the land (1:6–3:29). A sermon follows in chapter 4, which is largely distinct from the preceding historical summary but connected to it through reference to the rebellion and judgment at Beth/

Baal-peor (3:29; 4:3).[1] The sermon highlights the themes of Deuteronomy's framework: Israel's special relationship with Yhwh, the need to obey the law, provoking Yhwh to anger through disobedience, Yhwh's destructive judgment, and restoration in the end. After a brief narrative in 4:41–49, Moses' second speech begins with the Decalogue and Moses' role as mediator (ch. 5; cf. Exod. 20). A series of sermons follow, urging complete loyalty to Yhwh alone (6:4–25; chs. 7; 8; 9:1–10:11; and 10:12–11:32).

The detailed legal code follows in chapters 12–26. The organization of the laws is not easily discerned. There is a long tradition of seeing the laws as following the pattern of the Decalogue in general terms, though this is difficult to maintain in detail.[2] The first laws in chapter 12 place primary emphasis on the destruction of Canaanite worship sites and the centralization of Yhwh worship in one place. Chapter 13 maintains the focus on pure worship by prescribing harsh judgment upon those inciting Israel to worship other gods. Chapter 14 presents purity laws (vv. 1–21) and then begins a section of laws dealing with regularized events (tithing [14:22–29], canceling debt and freeing slaves [15:1–18], consecrating firstborn animals [15:19–23], and celebrating festivals [16:1–17]). Laws concerning leaders follow: judges (16:18–17:13), the king (17:14–20), priests and Levites (18:1–8), and prophets (18:9–22). Proposed thematic divisions of the laws in the next seven chapters have not been very successful. Gerhard von Rad's suggestion is as good as any: laws for criminal cases (19:1–21:9), regulations concerning families (21:10–22:30 [23:1 MT]), and then miscellaneous laws (23:1 [23:2 MT]–25:19).[3] Finally, 26:1–15 ordains ceremonies for presenting the firstfruits and the third-year tithe, with scripted testimonies about faithfulness between Yhwh and the giver. The lengthy legal section is concluded in 26:16–19.

The epilogue in chapters 27–34 does not read as smoothly as the prologue. Chapter 27 seems to interrupt the smooth flow from the law (chs. 12–26) to the blessings and curses (ch. 28) for obedience and disobedience. In this intervening chapter, Moses prescribes a series of ceremonies that Israel should perform as part of accepting the law in the land. Chapter 29 begins Moses' third speech. These words are marked as the covenant of Moab, established here with the wilderness generation, in distinction to the covenant of Horeb, which was

---

1. In "The Literary Criticism and Rhetorical Logic of Deuteronomy i–iv," *Vetus Testamentum* 56 (2006): 203–24, Nathan MacDonald argues for a subtle thematic connection in terms of divine presence, election, obedience, and land.

2. John Calvin classically arranged his *Harmony of the Law* according to the Decalogue. For more recent considerations of this approach, see Georg Braulik, "The Sequence of the Laws in Deuteronomy 12–26 and in the Decalogue," in *A Song of Power and the Power of Song: Essays on the Book of Deuteronomy*, ed. Duane L. Christensen, Sources for Biblical and Theological Study 3 (Winona Lake, IN: Eisenbrauns, 1993), 313–35; and Stephen A. Kaufman, "The Structure of the Deuteronomic Law," *Maarav* 1, no. 2 (1978): 105–58.

3. Gerhard von Rad, *Old Testament Theology*, vol. 1 (New York: Harper & Row, 1962), 226n86.

previously established with the exodus generation. This chapter contains a sermon reminiscent of those of the prologue, though with an unusual and temporary focus on an unfaithful individual (29:18–21 [17–20 MT]): the rest of the framework always understands Israel to be a unified collective. Chapter 30 seems to assume that the curses have already been experienced and focuses on restoring Israel to a place of obedience through circumcision of the heart (vv. 1–10). The chapter concludes with a closing appeal for obedience, for choosing life over death (vv. 11–20). The focus then moves to preparations for Moses' death (31:1–8) and the writing and regular reading of the law (31:9–13, 24–29). There follows a prediction of Israel's disobedience and YHWH's provision of a song to testify about his judgment in that day (31:14–32:47). Moses then ascends Mount Nebo to see the land that he may not enter (32:48–52). Chapter 33 inserts Moses' blessing of Israel, and then chapter 34 recounts his death and presents Joshua as his successor.

Deuteronomy in the Canon

Deuteronomy plays a central role in the canon of the Old Testament. Lines flow both inward and outward. Von Rad describes Deuteronomy as "gather[ing] together practically the whole of the assets of the faith of Israel, re-sifting them and purifying them theologically" and thus forming "as complete and perfect unity as can well be conceived."[4] In particular, Deuteronomy draws upon several major pentateuchal themes: YHWH's commitment to the patriarchs and their descendants, the exodus, the giving of the law, and the wilderness wanderings. It completes the rich tradition of Moses and marks this prophet and the events of his time as unique, for "never since has there arisen a prophet in Israel like Moses, whom YHWH knew face to face" (34:10; cf. vv. 11–12). It also draws proleptically from the conquest and settling in the land. Some of the prophets also flow into Deuteronomy. Hoseanic themes are particularly prominent, such as becoming satisfied and arrogant in the land and forgetting YHWH, YHWH's love for Israel, YHWH as Israel's educator, and the family unity of Israel.[5]

The lines flowing out of Deuteronomy into the rest of the Old Testament are so many and varied that scholars now call for more care in determining the criteria for accounting a text to be "deuteronomistic."[6] It is easy to fall into the

4. Gerhard von Rad, *Studies in Deuteronomy*, Studies in Biblical Theology 9 (London: SCM, 1953), 37.

5. Hans Walter Wolff, *Hosea*, 3rd ed., Biblischer Kommentar 14 (Neukirchen-Vluyn: Neukirchener Verlag, 1976), xxvi. See also n. 47 below.

6. Richard Coggins, "What Does 'Deuteronomistic' Mean?" in *Those Elusive Deuteronomists: The Phenomenon of Pan-Deuteronomism*, ed. Linda S. Schearing and Steven L. McKenzie, Journal for the Study of the Old Testament: Supplement Series 268 (Sheffield: Sheffield Academic

trap of "pan-Deuteronomism," reading Deuteronomy's particular emphases into texts throughout the Old Testament. Although traditional four-document (JEDP) analysis finds little D material in the other four books of the Pentateuch, recent critical studies claim significant quantities of deuteronomistic material to be there.[7] Looking in the other direction, Martin Noth famously argued for strong connections between Deuteronomy and Joshua, Judges, Samuel, and Kings, with Deuteronomy acting as an introduction to this collection, which he named the "Deuteronomistic History" and which carries the story of Israel up to the exile.[8] So Deuteronomy forms an important hinge that connects the four books of the Tetrateuch (Genesis–Numbers) to the four Former Prophets. It presents a theology that draws upon essential elements of the Tetrateuch and then drives the story of national Israel forward. In Kings, for example, the narrator explains the downfall of the northern kingdom of Israel in a strongly deuteronomistic style, particularly in the way Israel's destruction is explained by pointing to Israel's failure to follow Yhwh's commandments—with following other gods being the primary offense (2 Kings 17:7–18). Further, each monarch in Kings is evaluated largely by deuteronomistic criteria. Hezekiah and Josiah, who destroy the high places to centralize worship in Jerusalem, receive the narrator's rare, unreservedly positive evaluations (2 Kings 18:3–6; 22:2). Josiah even implements his reforms with a book likely resembling Deuteronomy in his hand (2 Kings 22–23).[9]

Deuteronomy also seems to have influenced many of the Latter Prophets. Only Joel, Obadiah, Jonah, Nahum, and Habakkuk appear to be free of any deuteronomistic influence.[10] There is a significant presence of Deuteronomy's

---

Press, 1999), 22–35. As Coggins observes (23), it is helpful to distinguish "deuteronomic"—what pertains to the book of Deuteronomy—from "deuteronomistic," which identifies ideas related to Deuteronomy that seem to be evidenced in other portions of the OT, such as the Joshua–Kings history and Jeremiah. The essays in this volume are instructive both for grasping the magnitude of interrelatedness between Deuteronomy and the rest of the OT and the problem of overplaying that point.

7. For a survey of approaches and literature, see Marc Vervenne, "The Question of 'Deuteronomic' Elements in Genesis to Numbers," in *Studies in Deuteronomy: In Honour of C. J. Labuschagne on the Occasion of His 65th Birthday*, ed. F. García Martínez et al., Supplements to Vetus Testamentum 53 (Leiden: Brill, 1994), 243–68, esp. 246–51. Nathan MacDonald's contribution in this present volume argues that the authors of Numbers sought to present their material in a way that remained faithful to both P and D.

8. Martin Noth, *The Deuteronomistic History*, Journal for the Study of the Old Testament: Supplement Series 15 (Sheffield: JSOT Press, 1981).

9. Wilhelm M. L. de Wette ("Dissertatio critica-exegetica, qua Deuteronomium a prioribus Pentateuchi libris diversum, alius cuiusdam recentioris auctoris opus esse monstratur" [DPhil diss., University of Jena, 1805]) first connected Josiah's law book with Deuteronomy. For a summary of the correspondence between Deuteronomy and Josiah's reforms, see Samuel R. Driver, *A Critical and Exegetical Commentary on Deuteronomy*, International Critical Commentary (Edinburgh: T&T Clark, 1902), xlv.

10. Robert A. Kugler, "The Deuteronomists and the Latter Prophets," in Schearing and McKenzie, *Those Elusive Deuteronomists*, 127–44, here 130–31.

ideas in all the rest of the prophets. Jeremiah and Ezekiel are most commonly mentioned, with Jeremiah presenting Deuteronomy's ideas in strongly related language while Ezekiel wraps the ideas in more priestly verbal forms.[11]

Finally, although the Wisdom literature seems to express little interest in deuteronomic emphases—such as the uniqueness of the relationship between Yhwh and Israel, the promises to the patriarchs, the establishment of the nation, and the law of Moses—Weinfeld has argued that "wisdom substrata" undergird the deuteronomic tradition.[12]

Theological Interests

Exploring Deuteronomy's theological edifice is a daunting task. For present purposes, I highlight three foundational themes. First, Deuteronomy is ultimately concerned that Israel remain loyal to Yhwh. Second, it frames its understanding of Israel's dynamic life with Yhwh around the ideas of blessing and curse. Third, Deuteronomy's long, central "law" section fills out what loyalty to Yhwh implies. All three themes illuminate the character of the relationship between Yhwh and Israel and relate to the idea of covenant. Furthermore, in Deuteronomy the relationship between Yhwh and Israel is patterned after the political relationship between an ancient Near Eastern high king and his vassal, possibly signaling a conscious transposition of this practice into Israel's religious key.[13] These same themes of loyalty, blessing and curse, and stipulations feature in these treaties.

Loyalty to Yhwh

Deuteronomy's central concern is Israel's loyalty to Yhwh alone. Without this, Israel ceases to be Israel. No other gods and no other ideas can take priority over Yhwh, his ways, and his intentions for Israel. Yhwh is the chief actor in Israel's life, bringing the nation out of Egypt, founding it in the land, and blessing it there. Yhwh is also the lawgiver and judge who sets Israel's rules and evaluates their adherence.

The centrality of the Yhwh-alone idea for Deuteronomy's Israel gains initial expression in the first two commandments of the Decalogue (5:6–10).

11. Driver (*Deuteronomy*, xcii–xciv) summarizes the connections between Jeremiah and Deuteronomy.

12. Moshe Weinfeld, *Deuteronomy and the Deuteronomic School* (Oxford: Clarendon, 1972), 244–81.

13. The original articulation of the connection is George E. Mendenhall, "Covenant Forms in Israelite Tradition," *Biblical Archaeologist* 17, no. 3 (1954): 50–76. For a critique of Deuteronomy's dependence on these treaty forms, see Ernest W. Nicholson, *God and His People: Covenant and Theology in the Old Testament* (Oxford: Clarendon, 1986), 56–82.

Yнwн's opening statement here bases his claim to Israel's allegiance on the exodus (5:6). Verses 7–9a then stipulate three negative commands, which form a single unified prohibition: "no other gods."[14] Although making images may seem to be a separate matter, the grammar of the passage envelops the second commandment's prohibition of images in verse 8 amid the first commandment's prohibiting "other gods." Notice the way the plural pronoun "them" in verse 9 ("You shall not bow down to them or worship them") refers not to the singular idol of verse 8 ("You shall not make for yourself an idol") but to the gods of verse 7 ("You shall have no other gods"). Thus the first and second commandments are composed as a unit. Jeffrey Tigay rightly argues that images were not only symbols of gods, but were also identified as gods themselves, and since Yнwн must not be imaged, they must represent forbidden gods.[15] In verses 9b–10, Yнwн explains his demand in terms of his jealousy and promises multigenerational punishment or reward for those who reject or embrace this demand.[16]

The Shema (6:4–9) provides a positive form of these negative commandments. Israel accepts Yнwн's commands with these words: "Hear, O Israel: Yнwн is our God, Yнwн alone" (6:4). Although alternate translations could suggest that this is an expression of monotheism and perhaps denies the existence of other gods, this difficult verse is best understood as an affirmation of Israel's singular devotion to Yнwн and no other.[17] This single-mindedness is commanded in the next verse: Israel must love Yнwн with the entire heart, soul, and might (6:5). While "love" in English primarily refers to feelings, within the context of Deuteronomy—as with ancient Near Eastern vassal treaties—the focus is loyalty.[18] The following verses of the Shema emphasize the importance of Israel's filling their days and their world with this idea, surrounding themselves with Israel's inviolable commitment: loyalty to Yнwн alone (6:6–9). Not only does Jesus identify the Shema as the greatest commandment (Matt. 22:36–38; Mark 12:28–30), in addition, his interlocutors

14. On the variety of interpretations of the preposition "before" in the first commandment, see Moshe Weinfeld, *Deuteronomy 1–11: A New Translation with Introduction and Commentary*, Anchor Bible 5 (New York: Doubleday, 1991), 276–77.

15. Jeffrey H. Tigay, *Deuteronomy: The Traditional Hebrew Text with the New JPS Translation*, Jewish Publication Society Torah Commentary 5 (Philadelphia: Jewish Publication Society, 1996), 65.

16. On this interrelatedness of the first commandments, see S. Dean McBride, "The Essence of Orthodoxy: Deuteronomy 5:6–10 and Exodus 20:2–6," *Interpretation* 60 (2006): 133–50, esp. 140–48.

17. R. W. L. Moberly, "'Yнwн Is One': The Translation of the Shema," in *Studies in the Pentateuch*, ed. John A. Emerton, Supplements to Vetus Testamentum 41 (Leiden: Brill, 1990), 209–15; idem, "Toward an Interpretation of the Shema," in *Theological Exegesis: Essays in Honor of Brevard S. Childs*, ed. Christopher Seitz and Kathryn Greene-McCreight (Grand Rapids: Eerdmans, 1999), 124–44.

18. William L. Moran, "The Ancient Near Eastern Background of the Love of God in Deuteronomy," *Catholic Biblical Quarterly* 25 (1963): 77–87.

agree (Mark 12:32; Luke 10:25–28) and parallel first-century Jewish literature suggests that this is not a new idea. Indeed, Jewish tradition has consistently held the Shema in extremely high regard, reciting it twice daily, teaching it to children as soon as they can speak, and reciting it on one's deathbed.[19]

Beyond these brief but critical words in Deuteronomy, the framework of the book focuses on loyalty to YHWH alone, advocating it in sermons (Deut. 4; 6:10–15; 7; 8; 9:1–10:11; 10:12–11:32) and even in a song (Deut. 32). In many places the problem of following "other gods" (an important deuteronomic phrase) is cited as the reason for YHWH's destructive force being levied against Israel (6:13–15 is a good example). Indeed, turning to other gods is equated with Israel's breaking its covenant with YHWH (31:16).

Concern for Israel's fidelity to YHWH is also prominent in the law code of Deuteronomy 12–26, where the first laws command the destruction of places where the land's previous occupants worshiped their gods (12:2–3; cf. 12:29–31). In the strongest terms the next chapter outlaws incitement to follow other gods (Deut. 13), and in later chapters the death penalty is prescribed both for individuals following other gods (17:2–7) and prophets speaking in their names (18:20).

Although Deuteronomy displays little interest in nations other than Israel, it does emphasize the incomparability of the YHWH–Israel relationship, thus highlighting from a different angle that Israel should be loyal to YHWH.[20] Deuteronomy is not "monotheistic" in the sense of denying the existence of other gods or advocating that all peoples should follow YHWH instead of other gods. The other gods may exist in some fashion, but they bear no comparison with YHWH, who allocates them to other peoples and stands completely unchallenged by them (cf. 4:19; 32:8, 17, 37–39).[21] The Israelites' God is closer than any other (4:7), their law is more righteous (4:8), their birth out of another nation is unprecedented (4:34), and other gods do not compare to theirs (32:31, 37–38). When living in harmony with YHWH, Israel will sit "high above all the nations of the earth" (28:1; cf. 26:19; 28:13), unconquerable by military or economic power (28:7, 10, 12). Despite these superlatives, Deuteronomy

19. Tigay, *Deuteronomy*, 440–41.

20. On deuteronomic interest in YHWH's dealings with other nations, see Patrick D. Miller, "God's Other Stories: On the Margins of Deuteronomic Theology," in *Israelite Religion and Biblical Theology: Collected Essays*, Journal for the Study of the Old Testament: Supplement Series 267 (Sheffield: Sheffield Academic Press, 2000), 593–602. Christopher Wright's commentary (*Deuteronomy*, New International Biblical Commentary 4 [Peabody, MA: Hendrickson, 1996]) tries to find a missiological theme in Deuteronomy (xi, 8–17), but see the critique of Wright's approach in Joel N. Lohr, *Chosen and Unchosen: Conceptions of Election in the Pentateuch and Jewish-Christian Interpretation*, Siphrut: Literature and Theology of the Hebrew Scriptures 2 (Winona Lake, IN: Eisenbrauns, 2009), 176–80.

21. On the question of monotheism in these passages, see Nathan MacDonald, *Deuteronomy and the Meaning of "Monotheism,"* Forschungen zum Alten Testament 2.1 (Tübingen: Mohr Siebeck, 2003), 78–95.

fears the irrational allure of the other gods and implicitly acknowledges the attractiveness of the ways of other nations. Therefore the current occupants of the land must be utterly destroyed (7:1–2) and their worship sites likewise obliterated (7:5; 12:2–3). Anxiety about assimilation leads to a xenophobic "cleansing" that is deeply problematic for modern readers.

Deuteronomy's commitment to Israel's uniqueness has led some scholars to search for unusual or even unique features of Israel's life and religion against its ancient Near Eastern background. Prominent examples within Deuteronomy include worship of a single god, prohibition of divine images, prohibition of divination (18:10), and the limitation of the king's power (17:14–17).[22] Cult centralization in "the place that YHWH your God will choose" is also a striking feature of Deuteronomy (12:5, 11, 14, 21; 14:23–24; 16:2, 6, 11; 18:6; 26:2). Centralization is striking not only because it is unusual across the ancient Near Eastern world but also because it is unusual within Israel's own Scripture. The patriarchs were unconcerned with later legal protocol and built altars in a variety of places (Gen. 12:7–8; 35:1–7). Exodus seems to envision multiple cultic sites (Exod. 20:25–26). Though regularly critiqued by those adopting Deuteronomy's priorities, popular religion in Judah and Israel had many cultic sites, most notably the "high places" that are condemned throughout Kings and many of the prophets. This centralization is doubtless another expression of Deuteronomy's concern about maintaining loyalty to YHWH alone.[23]

Blessing and Curse

YHWH's "blessing" and "curse" not only provide a carrot and stick for achieving Israel's loyalty but also animate his relationship with Israel. Blessing is no mere incentive to obedience but enables Israel's distinctive life with YHWH. YHWH's curse is a tool for devastating disloyal Israel and, through destruction, restoring them to loyalty.

Unfortunately, these ideas are commonly distorted by scholars. Quite often they are reduced to a tit-for-tat proportional response by YHWH to good and bad actions by individuals, sometimes labeled "retribution theology." YHWH does nothing so trivial; after all, this would reduce Israel's existence to a series

22. On kingship, see Henri Frankfort, *Kingship and the Gods: A Study of Ancient Near Eastern Religion as the Integration of Society and Nature*, Oriental Institute Essay (Chicago: University of Chicago Press, 1948). The so-called Biblical Theology Movement focused on the uniqueness of ancient Israel, though many of its claims have subsequently suffered significant critique. A classic example from the movement is G. Ernest Wright, *The Old Testament against Its Environment*, Studies in Biblical Theology 2 (London: SCM, 1950). A summary of the critiques can be found in Brevard S. Childs, *Biblical Theology in Crisis* (Philadelphia: Westminster, 1970), 13–87.

23. As a starting point on the significance of centralization in Deuteronomy, see Bernard M. Levinson, *Deuteronomy and the Hermeneutics of Legal Innovation* (Oxford: Oxford University Press, 1997), 23–52 and throughout.

of mechanical exchanges. Deuteronomy's vision is quite different. Blessing is bestowed at a national level, contingent upon the nation's obedience. This is obviously difficult to measure, and the history in Kings, which is strongly influenced by Deuteronomy, tends to evaluate the national responsiveness to YHWH by the king's actions. Curses are likewise threatened against the nation when it turns away from YHWH, but not in some proportional way that would typically result in a middling blessedness/cursedness that leaned one way or the other from year to year. Rather, if the nation is judged to be disloyal to YHWH—the exact criteria are nowhere spelled out—YHWH threatens near-complete destruction, to the brink of oblivion. The price for disobedience is not decreased blessing but an utterly destructive curse. With considerable similarity to neo-Assyrian treaty curse lists, Deuteronomy authorizes horrifying reprisals for treachery against YHWH, the Great King. One small example will suffice. Apparently reflecting a macabre ceremony, one Assyrian treaty warns a potential traitor: "Just as this ewe is cut open and the flesh of its young placed in its mouth, so may he (Shamash?) make you eat in your hunger the flesh of your brothers, your sons, and your daughters."[24] Moses similarly warns disloyal Israel of a siege where "you will eat the fruit of your womb, the flesh of your own sons and daughters whom YHWH your God has given you" (28:53). Such terrible curses are deeply problematic but seem to be an inevitable result of Israel's refusal to yield and YHWH's willingness to impose his will through force.[25] In the larger canon, the destruction of the northern kingdom is connected to these curses (2 Kings 17:7–23), and the fall of Jerusalem follows a similar though more complex path. Blessing and curse in Deuteronomy are national and absolute, not individual and proportional.

A second misunderstanding is that blessings and curses flow naturally out of the actions that precipitate them. Klaus Koch has famously argued for an "act-consequence nexus" in the Old Testament, where YHWH acts only as a midwife, guiding the delivery of consequences that naturally follow actions.[26] Thomas W. Mann suggests a modern analogy, where the sinful act of enslaving Africans in America led to the curse of modern racism.[27] While undoubtedly

24. From *VTE*, lines 547–50 (in *ANET*, 539d). On ANE treaty curses more generally and their relationship with Deut. 28, see Delbert R. Hillers, *Treaty-Curses and the Old Testament Prophets*, Biblica et orientalia 16 (Rome: Pontifical Biblical Institute, 1964), chs. 2–3.

25. For an exploration of the difficult deuteronomic themes of disloyalty to YHWH and the resulting destruction, with an analogy to the ways modern states impose their will upon the disloyal, see Rob Barrett, *Disloyalty and Destruction: Religion and Politics in Deuteronomy and the Modern World*, Library of Hebrew Bible/Old Testament Studies 511 (New York: T&T Clark International, 2009), 160–201 and throughout.

26. Klaus Koch, "Is There a Doctrine of Retribution in the Old Testament?" in *Theodicy in the Old Testament*, ed. James L. Crenshaw, Issues in Religion and Theology 4 (Philadelphia: Fortress, 1983), 57–87.

27. Thomas W. Mann, *Deuteronomy*, Westminster Bible Companion (Louisville: Westminster John Knox, 1995), 151–54.

actions have their consequences, this is not what Deuteronomy teaches. Idolatry does not lead naturally to drought or defeat in warfare, but idolatry provokes YHWH, who then chooses these punishments (cf. 28:15–68). Though YHWH may sometimes choose forms of blessing and curse that do "poetic justice" by bearing some analogy to the action, YHWH chooses and causes. The blessing and curse of Deuteronomy are not built into the fabric of creation.

This leads to a third misunderstanding that conflates YHWH's universal blessing of creation with Israel's blessing. Although loyal Israel does experience more and better forms of these common blessings (28:1–14), such is not the point.[28] YHWH's blessing for Israel provides an assured and secure plenty that affords Israel the "luxury" of living according to a pattern set by YHWH, which does not necessarily make practical sense in and of itself. For example, Deuteronomy does not envision a powerful king; the exercising of military, economic, or political strength over its neighbors; or an international policy based on alliances with other nations. Indeed, such power plays are largely forbidden (e.g., 17:14–17; note that multiplying wives likely refers to royal marriage alliances) or ignored in Deuteronomy. In a competitive world where empires fight for dominance over their neighbors, Israel's choosing not to focus on becoming strong and fighting off would-be conquerors would seem to be a recipe for disaster. Assimilation into the ancient Near Eastern world and national disappearance would seem to be the inevitable result.[29] But YHWH's "unrealistic" promise is that he can be trusted to take care of Israel, to bless them, despite their walking out of step with everyone else. It is not discordant for Jews today to make the claim that their continued existence, despite oppression and historic lack of a homeland, testifies to God's commitment to them. Deuteronomy's framework of blessing for Israel enables Israel's loyalty to YHWH and his special ways.

Claus Westermann helpfully clarifies the complementary roles of YHWH's blessing and saving activities.[30] "Saving" involves YHWH's sweeping into a dangerous situation and miraculously rescuing from peril. "Blessing" is the quieter, continuing activity where YHWH dwells with and provides for regular needs in an almost unnoticeable way. Deuteronomy transitions Israel from focus on the saving mode to recognizing the blessing mode. In Deuteronomy 26:5–10, an Israelite recounts the work of YHWH, highlighting saving—his rescue of the suffering Israelite slaves in Egypt—but ending with blessing in the settled land: "And he brought us into this place, and gave us this land, a

---

28. Pace Terence E. Fretheim, *The Pentateuch*, Interpreting Biblical Texts (Nashville: Abingdon, 1996), 48–49.

29. Norman K. Gottwald, *The Tribes of Yahweh: A Sociology of the Religion of Liberated Israel, 1250–1050 B.C.E.* (Maryknoll, NY: Orbis Books, 1979), 617–18.

30. Claus Westermann, *Elements of Old Testament Theology*, trans. Douglas W. Stott (Atlanta: John Knox, 1982), 52; see more generally parts 2 and 3 of this volume, as well as his *Blessing in the Bible and the Life of the Church*, trans. Keith Crim, Overtures to Biblical Theology (Philadelphia: Fortress, 1978).

land flowing with milk and honey" (v. 9). The "rescuing Yhwh" brought Israel there; the "blessing Yhwh" gives milk and honey. The quiet blessing can easily be misunderstood; the ground does not acknowledge Yhwh, so Israel must: "I bring the first of the fruit of the ground that you, O Yhwh, have given me" (v. 10). Blessed Israel risks forgetting Yhwh the provider.

Clear throughout Deuteronomy is that Yhwh's blessing is conditioned on obedience. But perhaps surprising is that, in line with this, Israel (almost) never needs to appeal to Yhwh for blessing. If Israel is obedient, the land will be productive, and Israel will live in prosperity. There is no pleading, no seasonal ritual to refresh the blessing, and no forms of prayer for rain during drought. Given Canaan's particular weather sequence of wet and dry seasons, which must not deviate far from the expected pattern in order for farmers to grow crops successfully, this absence is surprising, for surely anxiety about agricultural provision would find expression in prayer. But Deuteronomy paints a picture of anxiety-free surplus, with Yhwh being attentive to the necessary details. The one exception is the prayer at the end of Deuteronomy 26, where the tithe is presented with an affirmation of obedience to the law and a simple request that Yhwh will continue to bless (vv. 13–15). This stands in stark contrast to anthropologists' reports of primitive religions and their rain rituals, the prescriptions for responding to drought in the rabbinic Mishnah, and historic practice in the church during times of drought.[31] But far beyond rain and crops, anxiety about other areas of life normally requiring "blessing" is also absent in Deuteronomy (and in much of the OT, as well): concerns over sickness and death, finding good marriage partners, success in business ventures, protection from accidents, and so on. The concerns that often fill church prayer lists are absent here as Yhwh quietly takes care of Israel's needs. The one thing needful is careful obedience to Yhwh's will.

Yet an important question remains: what exactly is entailed by obedience and disobedience, loyalty and disloyalty? To explore that question, we turn to the detailed law, which constitutes the large central portion of Deuteronomy.

The Nature of Deuteronomy's Law

Despite the substantial and significant framework material, Deuteronomy is also fundamentally a book of laws. The conundrum is the ambivalent place of law—this or any other—in Israel's story. On the one hand, it is central: life and death hang in the balance as Israel is measured according to the question of obedience to the law (e.g., 28:14–15). On the other hand, here the nature of

31. On seeking rain in primitive religion, the Bible, and rabbinic literature, see Raphael Patai, "The 'Control of Rain' in Ancient Palestine: A Study in Comparative Religion," *Hebrew Union College Annual* 14 (1939): 251–86, esp. 278–81. In modern times, the 1868 edition of the Anglican Book of Common Prayer lists prayers for rain and fair weather first in its list of occasional prayers.

"law" is not transparent; this "law" does not indicate the specialized text of legislators and lawyers, as in the modern world. The Hebrew term "torah" is difficult, including more than explicitly legal texts and encompassing YHWH's larger will and instruction for Israel. So what is this law code that makes up the central part of Deuteronomy (chs. 12–26)? I consider three aspects that are particularly relevant for the present introduction to the book, all of which are interrelated: the context of the laws, their genre, and their relationship to the book's framework.

First, laws as behavioral requirements and prohibitions require a context for adherence. Already on the surface of Deuteronomy are two drastically different contexts for obedience: the wilderness and the land. Obedience in the wilderness is required to enter the land, and obedience in the land is required in order to stay there (11:8–9). The large societal differences between wilderness nomadism and settled life seem to require considerably different legal stipulations. Josiah's seventh-century reign and Ezra's postexilic setting provide additional, strongly varied contexts. Furthermore, later readers of Deuteronomy's laws live in their own contexts and must work to appropriate the ancient laws for themselves. Within the Pentateuch itself, which reflects multiple contexts, "the law" is neither monolithic nor static, but seems amenable to adaptation as demonstrated by the differences between Deuteronomy's law code and the two other major law collections, the Covenant Code in Exodus 20:23–23:33 and the Holiness Code in Leviticus 17–26.[32] What is meant by "the law" that must be obeyed is far from straightforward.

The second issue concerns genre. What sort of text is this? The casuistic laws (in "if . . . then" form) might seem to be straightforward: if one's son is stubborn and rebellious, then the men of the town should stone him to death, subject to all of the details of that particular law (21:18–21). The modern reader naturally imagines a lawcourt context, with the parents and their son standing before a judge, describing the difficult situation, with lawyers arguing two different sides of the story, and the judge consulting the law code to determine the proper course of action. Standing in stark contrast with this scenario is the fact that there is not a single Old Testament example of such an occurrence. Simply put, the law code does not seem to be used as a law code. Rather, Israel's law is described as being used in a very different way: public readings. James Watts lists accounts of public readings of the law by Moses (Exod. 24:3, 7), who also prescribes new public reading every seven years (Deut. 31:11), and by Joshua (Josh. 8:34–35), Josiah (2 Kings 23:2; 2 Chron. 34:30), and Ezra (Neh. 8:1–5).[33] Beyond public reading, the law is also taught to the people (Lev. 10:11; Deut. 33:10; 2 Chron. 17:7–9).[34] Only twice is the

---

32. On relationships between the law codes, see Driver, *Deuteronomy*, iii–xix, xxxvii–xli.

33. James W. Watts, *Reading Law: The Rhetorical Shaping of the Pentateuch*, The Biblical Seminar 59 (Sheffield: Sheffield Academic Press, 1999), 15–20.

34. Ibid., 21.

law commended for continual study by leaders who might act as judges (Deut. 17:19; Josh. 1:8), but the explicit reason given for Joshua and the deuteronomic king to study the law is to ensure their own loyalty to Yhwh.[35] They appear to act as models of such studious, obedient loyalty for the people. It is striking that the Old Testament's presentations of legal complaints before Moses, elders, and priests never describe appeals to written laws.[36] It seems that these "law codes" are best understood as persuasive, rhetorical texts that aim to inculcate core components of Israel's behavioral identity as Yhwh's people. They erect a building, a lifespace, that is built upon the foundation of loyalty to Yhwh, putting flesh on that skeleton.[37] Tensions between the various law codes suggest—although one could perhaps harmonize them—that the canonical text is comfortable with some degree of imprecision in what it means to "obey the law." This is also reflected in the developments of Christian and Jewish traditions, each of which in different ways makes drastic changes to the content of obedience to Yhwh's laws while maintaining an essential continuity with the law in the canonical texts. There is no one straightforward way for taking seriously the demands of the text that Yhwh's law is to be obeyed, but the demand that the law be taken seriously is unavoidable.

The third issue concerns the relationship between Deuteronomy's framework material (chs. 1–11, 27–34) and the legal center (chs. 12–26). Again, the relationship might seem clear because the introduction closes with Moses' demand that Israel "must diligently observe all the statutes and ordinances that I am setting before you today" (11:32), and the legal corpus picks this up: "These are the statutes and ordinances that you must diligently observe" (12:1). The law closes with a similar demand (26:16–19) and connects the law to the blessings and curses that are triggered by obedience or disobedience to the law (27:1, 10; 28:1). But what is meant by observing the entire law? Perhaps significant is the way both the final sermon of the prologue and the hinge between blessings and curses in chapter 28 smoothly connect obeying the entirety of the law to the core issue of following Yhwh alone (11:28; 28:14). Alternatively, the curse list of Deuteronomy 27 narrows the core of the law to twelve matters (27:15–26). Even grammatically, the large variety of legal details are sometimes reduced to the singular "the commandment" or "the entire commandment" ([kol] hammitsvah; 5:31; 6:1, 25; 7:11; 8:1; 11:8, 22; 15:5; 17:20; 19:9; 27:1; 30:11; 31:5). Sometimes the singular commandment is joined to the detailed "statutes and ordinances," but far from always (5:31; 7:11). In one place an absent conjunction implies that "the commandment" and "the statutes and the ordinances" are to be equated (6:1). One clearly incorrect way of handling these complexities in the law would be to discard

---

35. Of course, meditating on Yhwh's law is highlighted in other places, such as Ps. 1:2.

36. Watts, *Reading Law*, 21–22; however, he notes in 135n11 that Ezra (9:11–12) cites an otherwise unattested commandment of Yhwh against intermarriage with the people of the land.

37. Compare ibid., 135–37.

the law, for the clearest point of all, dripping from nearly every part of Deuteronomy—as well as much of the rest of the Bible—is that YHWH is very focused on directing the behavior of his people.

But what in the end does adherence to YHWH's law mean? Can it really be the case that a single Israelite failing in one detail will lead to the devastating curses (28:15; cf. vv. 16–68)? If so, one might reasonably expect the code itself to establish effective mechanisms for ensuring such obedience. Further, one would expect a legal system based on careful scrutiny of the law books to be described within the written tradition. But such does not appear. Perhaps Niels Peter Lemche's analysis is correct that recourse to written laws within the ancient social systems in view within Deuteronomy would obstruct more than promote justice, for social obligations and prohibitions, structures, and punishments were built on basic cultural ideas, understood by the people, and well maintained by those leaders judged to be just.[38] Despite the strong language about obeying the entire law, modern readers must be careful to avoid anachronistic readings that impose modern ideas of law and justice. It seems best to read Deuteronomy's legal material as a reflection on basic social priorities, a filling out of YHWH's vision for Israel's life.[39] Von Rad rightly concludes, "All the commandments are simply a grand explanation of the command to love [YHWH] and to cling to him alone," a command that Deuteronomy insists be held at the center of both individual and communal life (6:4–9).[40]

Summary of Themes

These three elements of the YHWH–Israel covenant are critical for Deuteronomy's theology. Israel is required to be single-mindedly loyal to YHWH, to do so in accordance with YHWH's law, while supported by YHWH's blessing yet under the threat of YHWH's curse of destruction. Although Deuteronomy is sure that Israel will fail along the way, it expresses confidence that Israel will indeed be loyal to YHWH in the end. Deuteronomy itself is an important component in assuring this end. The book functions to pull Israel together and center the nation on YHWH. Sociologists observe that all societies are bound together by common commitments that are required of all members of the society.[41] Most of the time, a society's unity is tacitly assumed, with most people living according to the society's structures without question, seeing the way things

38. Niels Peter Lemche, "Justice in Western Asia in Antiquity, or: Why No Laws Were Needed!" *Chicago-Kent Law Review* 70 (1995): 1695–1716.

39. Bruce Wells ("What Is Biblical Law? A Look at Pentateuchal Rules and Near Eastern Practice," *Catholic Biblical Quarterly* 70 [2008]: 223–43) helpfully outlines five ways to understand pentateuchal law, evaluating them based on records of ANE legal practice.

40. Von Rad, *Old Testament Theology*, 1:230.

41. See Peter L. Berger's classic study *The Sacred Canopy: Elements of a Sociological Theory of Religion* (New York: Doubleday Anchor, 1967).

work as simply the way things must be, or at least ought to be. But powerful rhetoric is needed when the societal priorities become unsettled. Those who challenge the society's "sacred" foundation stones must be reprimanded and punished in order to maintain the commitments as inviolable. Public explanation is made for why it is good and right that the society does what it does and why alternatives are harmful and wrong. Deuteronomy reflects such a conflict over the shape of Israel's society. Sweeping aside all alternatives as invalid and dangerous, the deuteronomic view of Israel's identity and future is presented as the only right option. Deuteronomy urges a recentering of Israel around YHWH and his ways.

Theological Exegesis

I now turn to two passages of Deuteronomy to illustrate these ideas in a concrete way: the sermon of Deuteronomy 8 and the law of release in Deuteronomy 15:1–11. Since one comes from the framework and one from the law, the question of the relationship between these two major structural units arises. Theologically, the passages illustrate the handling of the covenantal issues of loyalty to YHWH, the dynamics of blessing and curse, and the nature of the law. Canonically, the passages demonstrate the way other biblical traditions flow into Deuteronomy and then how the deuteronomic principles are adopted by other parts of the Bible. Thematically, both passages concern the economics of Israel's life with YHWH. Since economics is so central to modern life, I also briefly reflect on continuing implications of these texts for communities who take them as Scripture.

Deuteronomy 8

Deuteronomy's basic theological pattern is almost fully exhibited in chapter 8. YHWH has rescued Israel from Egyptian slavery, makes nonnegotiable demands for obedience, and promises overflowing blessing in the land. But Israel runs the very real risk of failing to meet YHWH's expectations, resulting in YHWH's destroying them. The sermon labors to avoid this fate by pressing Moses' interpretation of Israel's past onto the reader. Reading communities of every age are to reexperience eating from YHWH's miraculous provision in the wilderness and then to live responsively.

The structure of the sermon is difficult, leading to suggestions of a complex compositional history and to chiastic analyses of the material.[42] Despite the

---

42. Though often modified in various ways, the classic chiastic analysis is that of Norbert Lohfink, *Das Hauptgebot: Eine Untersuchung literarischer Einleitungsfragen zu Dtn 5–11*, Analecta biblica 20 (Rome: Pontifical Biblical Institute, 1963), 194–95. Timo Veijola (*Das fünfte Buch Mose:*

complexity, as it stands the sermon displays a clear logic, without significant tensions. Yet this does not mean that the message is simple. There are important and even troubling gaps in its demanding message. The sermon voices a dire warning, with life-and-death consequences, but critical details about both the danger and the remedy are lacking. But this difficult "incompleteness" allows the sermon to be recontextualized. By giving only the general shape of the threat that Israel faces, a wide variety of particular threats are encompassed, all of which bear a family resemblance, but with none specified explicitly. Its message rises above any single setting and raises the specter of unfaithfulness to Yhwh over a wide variety of circumstances, demanding continual interpretation and vigilance.

·   The sermon begins with Moses' demand of Israel: obey "the entire commandment that I am commanding you today" (8:1). But what does this mean? As discussed above, the term "entire commandment" is strikingly singular when Deuteronomy is filled with so many different commands. The difficulty of the term is revealed by translators' efforts to interpret it for modern English readers. The NRSV renders it literally ("this entire commandment"); the NIV and NASB choose plurals ("every command," "all the commandments"); and the NJPS uses opaque English by means of capitalization ("all the Instruction"). The Hebrew text of the sermon reflects ambivalence about the distinction, choosing an expanded plural in verse 11 ("his commandments and his judgments and his statutes"), retaining two different traditions in verse 2 (written: "his commandment"; oral: "his commandments"), and a plural in verse 6 that could be rendered singular with adjusted vowel pointing ("commandment(s) of Yhwh your God").[43] Yhwh's requirement upon Israel is also expressed metaphorically as "to walk in his ways" (v. 6) and in high imagery as "liv[ing] by . . . everything proceeding out of the mouth of Yhwh" (v. 3). In verse 19 the key offense of disloyalty appears: to "follow after other gods and serve them and bow down to them." Once again, there rises into the foreground the obligation to remain loyal to Yhwh alone, and the necessity of living according to the wide array of instructions that flow out of Yhwh's mouth lies not far behind. Loyalty is determinative, but it finds expression in every aspect of the lives of individuals and communities.

Deuteronomium. Kapitel 1,1–16,17, Das Alte Testament Deutsch 8 [Göttingen: Vandenhoeck & Ruprecht, 2004], 208–21) proposes a redaction history that also helpfully distinguishes the sermon's concerns for obedience, the richness of the land, and the wilderness memory.

43. The two traditions preserved in Deut. 8:2 follow the Masoretic convention of recording, where the two differ, both an oral tradition (Qere, the way the text is to be read out loud) and a written tradition (Kethib, the way the text is to be written). In v. 6, the issue surrounds the greater reliability of the consonantal text over the much later record of vowel points around the consonants. In the MT tradition, the vowels indicate that Israel must keep "the commandments of Yhwh," but a single vowel change, with no consonantal changes, would lead to the reading "the commandment of Yhwh."

Verses 7–10 detail a properly functioning relationship between Yhwh and Israel. Yhwh is bringing Israel into a wondrously special land. There will be no scarcity of life's necessities there. Verses 12–13 expand on Israel's prosperity with the luxuries of fine houses, large flocks, and precious metals. Israel will eat, be satisfied, and—most important—bless Yhwh, their provider (v. 10). Acknowledging Yhwh signals the danger point. Here is where everything can fall apart. Paradoxically, Yhwh's blessing tempts Israel to forget Yhwh amid the blessings (vv. 11–14), thus suffering Yhwh's curse (v. 20). The Talmud warns, "Filled stomachs are a type of evil,"[44] and indeed, Moses connects filled stomachs to utter destruction. But why is prosperity a problem? The very grammar of the multiplying material goods in verse 13 suggests an answer: Israel's things multiply with no explicit agent. "All that you have will multiply." Prosperity does not bear the identifying stamp of its source. There is no "gift from Yhwh" label; Israel just prospers. Of course, the land is no magical place. Crops and herds do not care for themselves. Ore must be mined and processed. Gold and silver multiply through entrepreneurial trading. Israel does the same things as any other nation, but alongside this ordinary life, Israel experiences the peculiar blessing of Yhwh's care for their well-being. Israel's unique relationship with Yhwh leads to the requirement that they explicitly connect this positive life to Yhwh.

Moses' strategy for maintaining this connection is to press upon them the memory of life in the wilderness. The wilderness was the polar opposite of the land (vv. 15–16): fearful, thirsty, and filled with snakes, serpents, and scorpions instead of flocks and herds. But critically, Yhwh was with Israel there. In these verses, Yhwh's presence is woven into the description of desert dangers; he was there at every turn. Life in the wilderness would seem to be impossible, but Yhwh's miraculous provision was sufficient. It is exactly the unexpected survival for forty years that should impress future generations: this was indisputably Yhwh's doing. There is no other explanation. The ambiguous experience of prosperity in the land—whence come these good things?—must be interpreted through the lens of Yhwh's unambiguous provision in the desert.

Unfortunately, within the "blessed ordinariness" of life in the land this reality is easily forgotten. In order to counter forgetfulness, Moses exhorts Israel: "Remember!" (v. 2). Moses expresses his recollection of the past in a succession of purpose clauses: "in order to humble you, to test you, to know what was in your heart" (v. 2). Israel's humbling, being forced into a submissive, bent posture, came not only from being unable to feed themselves, but also perhaps more from being fed (v. 3). Certainly the hungry welcome food. Receiving a handout, however, requires acknowledgment of the superiority of the giver. The gift shames the recipient, who can give nothing in return but thanks and

---

44. Babylonian Talmud, *Berakhot* 32a. On this theme, see also Weinfeld, *Deuteronomic School*, 280–81.

an admission of inadequacy. Humiliation is not an end unto itself, though, but a "test." This test produces two outcomes. For Israel, the testing is "in the end to do you good" (v. 16). For YHWH, it is designed "to know what was in your heart, whether or not you would keep his commandments" (v. 2). Testing is a difficult concept, and Moberly carefully examines this passage to argue that YHWH is no dispassionate investigator, but uses testing "for a deepening of the encounter between God and people."[45] Although a flat reading might see YHWH as having a bad case of nonomniscience and resorting to a desert experiment to fill a gap in his knowledge, the wilderness test actually illuminates YHWH's relationship with Israel and thereby strengthens that relationship. In particular, the humiliation of hungering and being fed causes Israel to know that a human lives not through food alone, but through everything that comes out of the mouth of YHWH (v. 3). Though some commentators identify the outflow of YHWH's mouth as his continuing providence, it is better within the context of Deuteronomy to interpret it as YHWH's commands.[46]

YHWH wants to know, "Will you follow my commands?" But how did this test work in the wilderness? What commands were to be obeyed? Moses does not explain what YHWH was looking for, nor does YHWH ever announce the end of the wilderness test as he did when testing Abraham (Gen. 22:12). For Deuteronomy, the test of concern is not the one in Israel's past but in the ever-present today. As wilderness Israel learned "the way that YHWH your God has led you" (v. 2), today's Israel must respond to YHWH in the rich land. This is no right/wrong examination, or a simple demonstration of willingness to follow some rules, but the construction of a relationship of nonreductive dependence upon YHWH. In other words, Israel must live in conscious response to YHWH's blessing.

In its final movement, the sermon changes to a future perspective (relative to the setting on the plains of Moab) as it demands that Israel steel itself for the challenge of prosperity, for their hearts may become proud—literally, "rising up" (v. 14)—in contrast to the stooped-over humiliation of the wilderness. Such pride leads to forgetting YHWH and saying, "My strength and the might of my hand made this wealth for me" (v. 17). YHWH vanishes from Israel's thought as the self becomes the only point of reference. But Moses admonishes them to remember that YHWH is behind their ability to make wealth (v. 18). The ambiguities of prosperous life are deceptive. Humans can see only their own efforts and the results; the one who is providing the productive context is

45. R. W. L. Moberly, *The Bible, Theology, and Faith: A Study of Abraham and Jesus*, Cambridge Studies in Christian Doctrine 5 (Cambridge: Cambridge University Press, 2000), 106; also see 97–107 for the larger context.

46. Lothar Perlitt, "Wovon der Mensch lebt (Dtn. 8,3b)," in *Die Botschaft und die Boten: Festschrift für Hans Walter Wolff zum 70. Geburtstag*, ed. Jörg Jeremias and Lothar Perlitt (Neukirchen-Vluyn: Neukirchener Verlag, 1981), 403–26. Note the Hebrew wordplay between the "thing coming out" (*motsa'*) and the word for "commandment" (*mitzvah*).

invisible. The purpose of the prosperity is also invisible. Gold does not reveal its goal, but Yhwh has a goal: the establishment of a prosperous people in a prosperous land, a people in a unique relationship with him. Israel faces the temptation of replacing Deuteronomy's story with an opposing one: productivity comes from the self; productivity is for the self. Will Israel forget that the blessed life must remain tied to Yhwh's interests?

Replacing focus on Yhwh with focus on the self is unusual in Deuteronomy (though cf. 9:4), which is usually concerned with the problem of other gods. The sermon suddenly shifts to this primary anxiety in its closing summary (v. 19). The commonality between pride and apostasy is forgetting Yhwh. Yhwh and Yhwh alone provides the context for prosperity and directs its purpose. The implied connection to other gods is that Israel might credit them with providing the nation's prosperity and therefore reckon that it is the other gods' favor that must be sought to continue that prosperity. Yhwh will have none of this. Confusion about this will cause Yhwh to destroy Israel. As the earlier civilizations of Canaan disappeared, so will Israel (v. 20). Although the sermon ends on this point, when read together with the rest of the framework material, restoration after destruction is surely also in view (see, e.g., 4:27–31; 30:1–10). But as throughout Deuteronomy, Israel has no freedom to choose their gods. Yhwh insists.

With respect to the larger canon, the sermon of Deuteronomy 8 demonstrates that lines flow both into Deuteronomy and outward. In terms of flow into this chapter, the command to remember requires reference to Israel's presettlement traditions: the covenant with the fathers, slavery in and exodus from Egypt, and forty years in the wilderness, with miraculous provisions, including the novel manna and water from the rock. Interestingly, no reference is made to the Sabbath aspect of the manna tradition as developed in Exodus 16:5, 22–30. Such an idea would have illustrated an important aspect of Israel's peculiar life with Yhwh, but perhaps in too narrow a fashion to fit Deuteronomy's interest in the broader law. Two other aspects of the manna tradition are also omitted: the "neither excess nor lack" (Exod. 16:16–18) and daily provision (16:19–21), both running counter to the chapter's concern with faithfulness amid great prosperity. The sermon also anticipates the traditions of Israel's movement from its deuteronomic setting in the plains of Moab and into the promised land: destruction of the Canaanite nations, settling in the good land, luxurious living in fine houses, religious conflict with self-sufficiency and idolatry, and eventual destruction. For a postdestruction (exilic and postexilic) audience, memory and the larger tradition sharpen the sermon as the specter of offending Yhwh again arises (e.g., Ezra 9:1–15).

The sermon also has an afterlife in the canon, providing an intertext for ongoing struggles with properly living under Yhwh's blessing. I consider three passages. Hosea 2 bears a tight relationship with Deuteronomy 8 and likely predates it.[47] I then examine postexilic Haggai's first oracle, which concerns response to national poverty, thus inverting the problem of Deuteronomy 8. Finally, Jesus' first temptation in Matthew 4 makes explicit reference to Deuteronomy 8.

Hosea 2 engages the problem of Israel's confusion over the source of its prosperity, using the powerful, extended metaphor of an unfaithful wife and her outraged husband. Although the sexualization of the wife's unfaithfulness in chasing after lovers and acting as a prostitute exercises most interpreters, bearing Deuteronomy 8 in mind guides one's focus to the wife's motivation for her promiscuity. The husband explains her offensive thinking: "She said, 'I will go after my lovers; they give me my bread and my water, my wool and my flax, my oil and my drink'" (Hosea 2:5 [7 MT]). He then explains the reality: "She did not know that it was I who gave her the grain, the wine, and the oil, and who lavished upon her silver and gold" (2:8 [10 MT]). As in Deuteronomy 8, there is confusion over the source of prosperity, with Israel wrongly crediting themselves or other gods, just as the wife in Hosea 2 credits her lovers. Although these lovers are never clearly identified, the most natural interpretation is that they are other gods, with the name Baal appearing in several places (2:8, 13, 17, and in a different sense, 16 [10, 15, 19, 18 MT]). Some interpreters intriguingly suggest that even within its primary context, the wife's lovers actually point to societal "gods," such as political alliances or oppressive economic structures that generate wealth but oppose the way of Yhwh.[48] The wife pursues lovers for profit (in vv. 5, 7a [7, 9a MT]) and decides to return to her first husband only when she can no longer find her lovers (v. 7b [9b MT]). The strange irony in the oracle is that the husband has been providing for her all along, but the wife does not perceive it. This is a masterful presentation of the same ambiguity observed in Deuteronomy 8. Yhwh's ordinary provision is invisible, his purposes unclear. Fields of grain do not self-identify as Yhwh's blessing.

In both Hosea 2 and Deuteronomy 8, the nature of life with Yhwh is clear only in the wilderness. But Hosea 2 reverses the place of the wilderness experience. In Deuteronomy 8, the wilderness is a training ground for future

---

47. Driver (*Deuteronomy*, xxvii–xxviii) highlights this debt to Hosea by referring to Deuteronomy as the prophet's "spiritual heir."

48. In *Hosea 2: Metaphor and Rhetoric in Historical Perspective*, Academia biblica 20 (Atlanta: Society of Biblical Literature, 2005), Brad E. Kelle argues that Hosea is condemning Israel's rulers for making alliances during the Syro-Ephraimite War, using the term "baal" to refer to Israel's Aramean ally, not to a Canaanite god. On the economic side, see the proposals by Gale A. Yee ("'She Is Not My Wife and I Am Not Her Husband': A Materialist Analysis of Hosea 1–2," *Biblical Interpretation* 9 [2001]: 345–83) and Marvin L. Chaney ("Accusing Whom of What? Hosea's Rhetoric of Promiscuity," in *Distant Voices Drawing Near: Essays in Honor of Antoinette Clark Wire*, ed. Holly E. Hearon [Collegeville, MN: Liturgical Press, 2004], 97–115). For a summary of these and other views, see Brad E. Kelle, "Hosea 1–3 in Twentieth-Century Scholarship," *Currents in Biblical Research* 7 (2009): 179–216, esp. 202–8.

dependence upon Yhwh. In Hosea's oracle, Yhwh drives failed Israel into the wilderness again (2:3, 9, 12, 14 [5, 11, 14, 16 MT]) to relearn the forgotten lesson of dependence. This is the wilderness of destruction and exile. In this new wilderness, Yhwh will restore his marriage to Israel to its proper form. He will seduce her and speak to her heart, re-creating the former days after the exodus when the Yhwh–Israel relationship was originally forged (vv. 14–17 [16–19 MT]), culminating in Yhwh saying, "You are my people" and Israel rightly responding, "You are my God" (v. 23 [25 MT]). Israel's blessed life in the land is beautiful and enviable, but it is also a life filled with danger and ambiguity. It is the wilderness and the memory of Yhwh's care that forms, protects, and preserves Israel's relationship with Yhwh.

The second outworking of Deuteronomy 8 that I consider is Haggai's first oracle (1:1–11), spoken to the Jews of the early postexilic period. Haggai inverts Deuteronomy's sermon in a different way, though focusing again on the problem of Israel's being confused over Yhwh's provision. As befits reappropriation of Deuteronomy, Haggai faces a critical transition in Israel's life: the reconstruction period following the destruction of Jerusalem and the temple. For Haggai, Israel's problem is misunderstanding not prosperity but futility: the people's practical efforts strangely produce disappointing results.[49] Haggai pinpoints the problem: "Is it a time for you yourselves to live in your paneled houses, while this house [Yhwh's temple] lies in ruins?" (1:4). Yhwh testifies, "You have looked for much, and, lo, it came to little; and when you brought it home, I blew it away. Why? . . . Because my house lies in ruins, while all of you hurry off to your own houses" (1:9). Like Deuteronomy 8, the people are focused on themselves rather than on Yhwh, but in a situation of lack rather than prosperity. As in Deuteronomy 8 (and Hosea 2), scarcity produces the teachable moment. The people are focused on generating wealth, but Yhwh works against them because they have decentered him. Haggai works to reverse their priorities, promising Yhwh's blessing to be the result (2:19). Their postexilic "wilderness" provides an opportunity to learn that life with Yhwh is not always economically logical; an "impractical" focus on Yhwh's temple will produce economic benefits because Yhwh is the hidden source of Israel's prosperity.

In a third example, Jesus directly refers to Deuteronomy 8 near the end of his own humbling hunger in the wilderness (Matt. 4:1–4//Luke 4:1–4). The devil raises the question of what sort of Son of God Jesus might be and suggests that he make bread for himself from the stones (v. 3).[50] Jesus refuses and quotes Deuteronomy 8:3b. Commentators commonly assert that the devil is tempting Jesus to misuse his divine powers to satisfy his own needs rather than serving

---

49. Haggai's second and third oracles engage the problem of futility in different ways and, though relevant here, are not considered.

50. The devil is not seeking proof that Jesus is God's Son but questions the kind of son he is (see Moberly, *Bible*, 199).

others. But I suggest that, as with Israel in Deuteronomy 8, the wilderness is for confirming and even deepening the relationship between Father and Son, thus the issue is about short-circuiting this lesson of dependence.[51] The issue here is Jesus' choice—at the Spirit's direction—to be hungry and in need, and to wait for the heavenly provision that appears in verse 11. Although the idea of Jesus' being disciplined and trained for obedient service challenges some theologies, this idea also appears in Hebrews 5:8. Moberly's careful development of the idea of "testing," as discussed above, applies here as God the Son and God the Father both come to "know" something that was in some way unknown because it had not been "tested" before. Jesus accepts the—logically unnecessary—humiliation of hunger here as he will accept the greater—and likewise logically confounding—humiliation of crucifixion later. While Jesus is on the cross, mocking voices will challenge him to distrust God and save himself, echoing the devil's challenge: "If you are the Son of God . . ." (Matt. 27:39–44; cf. 4:3). Jesus asserts his unbounded loyalty to God in the clearer case of wilderness hunger as he prepares for the dark, pained, and ambiguous challenge of loyalty he will face on the cross.

Finally, modern communities seeking to live within Deuteronomy's traditions can ask if there still exist related temptations to confuse self or other gods with the God who is the true source of prosperity. Can the sermon of Deuteronomy 8 probe faithful and affluent people in the modern West who dwell in a good, rich land? Indeed, it is perhaps even less obvious today what might be meant by God's providing blessings. In economic terms, the modern West understands prosperity to come from "the market," a subtle human construct that yields potent blessing for those abiding by its demands. In the context of recent world financial turmoil, Rowan Williams, archbishop of Canterbury, has criticized trust in the market as our provider:

> We find ourselves talking about capital or the market almost as if they were individuals, with purposes and strategies, making choices, deliberating reasonably about how to achieve aims. We lose sight of the fact that they are things that we make. They are sets of practices, habits, agreements which have arisen through a mixture of choice and chance. Once we get used to speaking about any of them as if they had a life independent of actual human practices and relations, we fall into any number of destructive errors. We expect an abstraction called "the market" to produce the common good or to regulate its potential excesses by a sort of natural innate prudence, like a physical organism or ecosystem. We appeal to "business" to acquire public responsibility and moral vision. And so we lose sight of the fact that the market is not like a huge individual consciousness, that business is a practice carried on by persons who have to make decisions

51. Others see contrast rather than analogy here, claiming that Jesus succeeds in the wilderness where Israel failed: e.g., see George H. P. Thompson, "Called—Proven—Obedient: A Study in the Baptism and Temptation Narratives of Matthew and Luke," *Journal of Theological Studies* 11 (1960): 1–12, here 3. Yet Deut. 8 does not portray Israel as failing in the wilderness.

about priorities—not a machine governed by inexorable laws. . . . And ascribing independent reality to what you have in fact made yourself is a perfect definition of what the Jewish and Christian Scriptures call idolatry.[52]

Indeed, an expectation that the market will provide the blessing of prosperity leads to a concern for fulfilling the market's demands and directing human energy toward accomplishing the market's goals. This must be idolatry. The idolatrous people of God run the risk of reenacting the macabre comedy of the unfaithful wife of Hosea 2 as she chases after her lovers to gain the blessing her husband already provides, only to be intentionally impoverished in order to learn afresh what God demands of his relationship with his people. But what might it mean then to "remember YHWH your God, . . . who gives you power to get wealth" (Deut. 8:18)? Primarily, it means focusing on God's ways rather than the market's, being willing to make choices against market "laws" in order to prioritize God's sometimes impractical concerns and interests. The community—this text does not address isolated individuals—that lives with the sermon of Deuteronomy 8 must be willing to step outside its economic environment and live according to alternative rules, as Israel was called to live apart from its wider Near Eastern environment. Deconstructing the idolatrous self-aggrandizement of a market-centric view within the community that is honoring the text of Deuteronomy requires the difficult liberation of choice from the demands of the market and the surrender of those choices to the demands of God.

To begin exploring what some of those demands of God might be, I turn to the economic laws of Deuteronomy 15:1–11. As suggested earlier, the detailed law of Deuteronomy's central portion puts flesh on the skeleton of the framework's generalized demand that Israel be completely loyal to YHWH alone.

Deuteronomy 15:1–11

YHWH's promise to bless the nation of Israel with prosperity in the land stands together with an intent to structure Israel's society in a way that befits the national blessing. The law thus contains commands that shape the society in peculiar ways around the idea of blessing. The law for canceling debts every seven years (Deut. 15:1–11) provides a useful example.[53] This law stands in opposition to both modern practice and, as will become clear, to ancient common sense as well. It is a "dangerous" law in the sense that it is vulnerable both

---

52. Rowan Williams, "Archbishop's Article on the Financial Crisis," *The Spectator*, September 27, 2008, http://www.archbishopofcanterbury.org/articles.php/629/archbishops-article-on-the-financial-crisis.

53. Although Deut. 15:1–18 belongs together as a unit that covers both canceling debts and releasing debt slaves, in the interest of space I focus here only on the former, in vv. 1–11. Both mitigate the extreme problems of the poor.

to serious abuse by those who request loans and to serious resistance from those who are commanded to surrender their claims. But Yhwh asserts that his people do not have ultimate control over the goods he provides in his blessing. Yhwh blesses in order to enable Israel to live in a surprisingly different way.

This passage well illustrates Deuteronomy's hortatory legal style: only a few verses contain legal stipulations; the rest urge and justify compliance. These "laws" lack means of enforcement and penalties for violators. As discussed above, the implied audience is neither judge nor lawyer but Israelite society. The community of lenders and borrowers attends to the way their economic world should function. As with most of Deuteronomy's laws, the addressees are the wealthy and powerful. The poor are to hear their rights in the proclamation of the law, but the message is aimed at those who control the shape of the society.

Verses 1–3 present the legal requirements. The passage opens with an over-arching prescription: "Every seventh year you shall do release [*shemittah*]." The term *shemittah* refers to dropping something and is related to the word for leaving a field fallow in the Covenant Code law of Exodus 23:10–11. The Deuteronomic Code extends this concept to refer to freeing debtors from working off loans. Characteristic of the Deuteronomic Code, a verbal link with the Covenant Code provides a starting point for moving in a new direction. Canceling debts was a familiar concept in the ancient world, being particularly connected with the rise of a new king.[54] Such royal decrees could be mere propaganda or, if real, head off economic and political disaster, popularize the new king with the indebted masses, contrast the new king with his predecessor's ways, and take steps toward a more just society. In contrast to this occasional custom, Deuteronomy 15 theologically grounds the practice and regularizes it, which changes the dynamics considerably. For one thing, a regular release depoliticizes the practice by disconnecting it from the monarch's decree.[55] Regular debt release also discourages creditors who can foresee an upcoming debt cancellation, as will become clear later in the text.

Verse 2 goes on to explain the way the release works: "Every creditor holding a loan that is loaned to his neighbor is to release it, not pressing his neighbor or his brother, because a release belonging to Yhwh is proclaimed." The final clause makes the general point that this release is Yhwh's idea and hints at the grounding concept that everything Israel and individual Israelites own ultimately belongs to Yhwh, who can stipulate the transfer of these resources. There has been considerable argument about the meaning of "releasing" a loan,

54. For an introduction to the practice and an analysis of the most important Mesopotamian example, see Johannes P. J. Olivier, "Restitution as Economic Redress: The Fine Print of the Old Babylonian *mēšarum*-Edict of Ammiṣaduqa," *Zeitschrift für altorientalische und biblische Rechtsgeschichte* 3 (1997): 12–25.

55. Joshua A. Berman, *Created Equal: How the Bible Broke with Ancient Political Thought* (Oxford: Oxford University Press, 2008), 102.

whether it means complete cancellation or (less radically) delaying repayment for a year. While an analogy with leaving a field fallow for a year might support the idea of delayed repayment, the "release" here aims not at softening the burden of poverty but eliminating it, suggesting the radical cancellation of the debt. Driver discounts cancellation because such a law "would seem calculated to defeat itself; for upon such conditions it is difficult to understand how any would have been found ready to lend."[56] Indeed, this problem drives the exhortation to lend that follows. It is precisely the impracticality of the law that grows increasingly shocking as the exhortation continues.

The law is missing some critical details, such as the date of the release and the types of loans that are covered by it.[57] It is implied that the law does not concern business investments, such as providing goods for a trader to sell, with an obligation to repay based on the proceeds. Rather, it concerns loans to those in physical need. Perhaps surprisingly, there is no distinction based on the reasons for becoming poor, such as different provisions for the lazy, the unwise, and the unfortunate.

Verse 3 exempts debts to foreigners from this law. This distinction between "brother" and foreigner is startling at first, because of the regular deuteronomic concern for the resident alien (ger). The retained loans are not those to the ger, however, but rather those to the "stranger" (nekar), which most likely means those passing through Israel, perhaps traders, rather than non-Israelites who live in the land.[58] The exclusion places the focus on Israelite society (of which the ger is a member) but need not imply abuse of outsiders. The term "brother" appears no less than six times in these eleven verses, highlighting the importance of the "family" of Israel. While this "family" is primarily determined by blood, it is more generally a boundary marking those living under YHWH's blessing, who are required to live according to YHWH's ways. Deuteronomy makes other provisions for the widow, orphan, and resident alien—the triad who do not have access to the standard economic system of agricultural production. These receive long-term provision through the third-year tithe and gleaning (Deut. 14:28–29; 16:11, 14; 24:19–20). The law of Deuteronomy 15:1–11 for alleviating debt poverty is separate, being aimed at those who do have ways of supporting themselves as farmers or laborers, but for one reason or another have fallen into an economic mire and need help to regain their footing and become productive again.

Instituting a predictable pattern for debt release produces predictable problems. Verses 4–6 address the societal problem of poverty, while verses 7–11 address the individual issue of losing money because of this law. At the societal level, regular debt release raises the possibility of large segments of the

---

56. Driver, *Deuteronomy*, 179.
57. Within a later Jewish context, the rabbis supplied these details in order to complete the law (Tigay, *Deuteronomy*, 145n8).
58. Ibid., 146.

population regularly falling into debt. After all, as supply-demand analysis would suggest, if debt does not have a high cost to the debtor, there will be lots of it. Can the nation afford this inefficient economy that allows debtors to get away without paying? Modern economic theory warns of cushioning failure because of its effect on overall economic efficiency. Might Israel become a land of demanding poor, who chase after the few with surplus resources? Moses proclaims the opposite: there will be no poor in Israel because YHWH will bless obedient Israel (vv. 4–5). YHWH, the blessing one, insists on this peculiar economic pattern; conventional economics is not Israel's provider. Verse 6 promises—against naysayers who would claim this law unworkable— that Israel's collective wealth will be overflowing, rising above that of other nations. Israel will be a creditor nation, not a debtor (cf. this same contrast in 28:12, 44).[59] Israel has nothing to fear but disobedience.

Next, 15:7–11 moves to the problem of lenders' losing their money. Only a very wooden reading would complain of a contradiction to the assertion that "there will be no poor among you" in verse 4 and the casuistic possibility raised in verse 7: "If there is among you a poor person from one of your brothers in one of your towns. . . ." The repeated "one of" emphasizes the exceptional nature of this poverty. But how should this aberration be handled? The law preaches, heaping disgrace upon any who would deny the needy one: "Do not harden your heart; do not shut your hand"—after all, he is "your brother" (v. 7). Despite giving a loan having no practical advantage to the creditor—interest is forbidden to other Israelites (23:19–20 [20–21 MT])—the one with enough is urged not just to soften the needy one's troubles but also to lend him whatever he needs (15:8).

The critical test of obedience comes as the debt cancellation time approaches. The characteristic deuteronomic warning, "Guard yourself, lest . . . ," signals a critical temptation (15:9; cf. 4:9, 23; 6:12; 8:11; 11:16; 12:13, 19, 30). In YHWH's economy, it is not prudent to deny a loan because the proclamation of release is near and the lender is sure to lose the principal. Instead, such thinking is worthless and reflects an evil attitude toward the needy brother (v. 9). The preaching law warns that the helpless poor will cry out not to a court, but to YHWH, who is an interested party in the financial transaction.[60] After all, YHWH is the one promising to provide sufficient blessing to enable adherence to the law (v. 10). Although the blessing here might be read individualistically, where

59. "Ruling" in v. 6 likely points to financial and material superiority since an Israelite empire is not in view in Deuteronomy.

60. See also YHWH's interest in the abuse of a day laborer (Deut. 24:15) and the fuller, harsher description of YHWH's response to abuse of the vulnerable in the Covenant Code (Exod. 22:21–24 [20–23 MT]). Eckard Otto ("Programme der sozialen Gerechtigkeit: Die neuassyrische (*an*-) *durāru*-Institution sozialen Ausgleichs und das deuteronomische Erlaßjahr in Dtn 15," *Zeitschrift für altorientalische und biblische Rechtsgeschichte* 3 [1997]: 26–63, here 54) observes that the appeal to YHWH accords with human institutions being unable to enforce the law.

the creditor will personally be granted overflowing supply, Deuteronomy's generally collective viewpoint suggests that the blessing is societal.

The passage closes with an assurance that there will always be such poor in Israel, providing another opportunity to complain of a contradiction with verse 4. As Deuteronomy paints the picture of Israel's life under YHWH, however, both are true, for while the poor are always surfacing, this transient trouble is easily rectified through obedience to the law, fueled by YHWH's promised blessing. Generosity and blessing circulate uninterrupted, an economic engine driven by YHWH's particular interest in Israel, the wonder of economists everywhere.[61] The cycle is broken only by disobedience, which results in destruction.

As with the sermon of Deuteronomy 8, the law of release has a continuing life in the canon. Jeremiah 34:8–22 focuses on the related issue of slave release (cf. Deut. 15:12–18) and is a prime portrayal of Israel's failure to comply with YHWH's economic challenge. It seems that Nebuchadnezzar's siege of Jerusalem led King Zedekiah to proclaim the release of Judean slaves, a onetime royal action under duress (Jer. 34:8–10, 13–14). The narrative does not ascribe a motivation to Zedekiah, though commentators regularly suggest a panicked attempt to gain YHWH's favor under military pressure ("foxhole religion"), possibly a shrewd choice under the pressing siege to release slaveholders from the problem of feeding their slaves, or a strategy to make normally exempt slaves available for military service.[62] Despite previous neglect and questions of motive, YHWH praises the decision (34:15). But YHWH's moment of praise is as brief as the slaveholders' charity; apparently when the siege was temporarily lifted, the slaves were forced back into servitude, leading to YHWH's condemnation of the city and promise to grant them a different sort of release: "a release to the sword, to pestilence, and to famine" (34:17). Zedekiah's abuse of release economics is a parody of YHWH's intention, with the deuteronomic curse being YHWH's response to such profaning of his name (34:16). What might have seemed to be economically and politically prudent actually leads YHWH to bring economic and political destruction.

A broad concept of "release" is also prominent in Jesus' ministry. He announces a release in programmatic terms by reading Isaiah 61:1: He has been sent—among other things—"to bring good news to the poor" and "to proclaim release to the captives" (Luke 4:18). This is now the year of release (Isa. 61:2; Luke 4:19). Jesus seamlessly proclaims release of disparate varieties of unbearable burdens that crush people. The Matthean account of the Lord's Prayer sets "forgive . . . as we forgive" in terms of debts, while the Lukan form rekeys the tune in terms of sins (Matt. 6:12; Luke 11:4). In economic terms

---

61. The idea of cyclic generosity and blessing comes from Richard D. Nelson, *Deuteronomy: A Commentary*, Old Testament Library (Louisville: Westminster John Knox, 2002), 191.

62. John Bright, *Jeremiah: A New Translation with Introduction and Commentary*, Anchor Bible 21 (New York: Doubleday, 1965), 223–24; Jack R. Lundbom, *Jeremiah 21–36: A New Translation with Introduction and Commentary*, Anchor Bible 21B (New York: Doubleday, 2004), 559.

and in harmony with Deuteronomy 15, Jesus insists that his followers live by an economic policy of generosity, replacing judicious calculation with god-like generosity. "If you lend to those from whom you hope to receive, what credit is that to you? Even sinners lend to sinners to receive as much again. But . . . lend, expecting nothing in return" (Luke 6:34–35). Economic realism is for "sinners," not for followers of Jesus.[63] This liberality is justified by a noneconomic return: "Your reward will be great, and you will be children of the Most High; for he is kind to the ungrateful and the wicked. Be merciful, just as your Father is merciful" (Luke 6:35–36). Lending money to the wicked and ungrateful, even the day before debt release is announced (figuratively speaking), will result in financial loss, but gains godlikeness for the giver, who reflects the God who is profligate in his distribution of blessing.[64] For Jesus' followers, unlike blessed Israel, there is no promise of overflowing material blessing for obedience. Rather, there is a specter of poverty, hunger, and weeping; of being hated, excluded, reviled, and defamed; of losing both coat and shirt; of being struck on both cheeks (Luke 6:20–29). This is the context of the Golden Rule: "Give to everyone who begs from you. . . . Do to others as you would have them do to you" (Luke 6:30–31). Jesus endorses the economics of Deuteronomy 15, but while Deuteronomy looks to build Israel's version of the Great Society in such a way, Jesus envisions a Great Society that appears only by journeying through the cross.

Modern communities reflecting on economic life under God must first struggle to recognize and critique reigning economic assumptions, which elevate particular notions of fairness, the necessity of economic incentives for productivity and disincentives for low productivity, and the absolute right to private property. Deuteronomy 15:1–11, alternatively, privileges the relief of economic need. Nevertheless, debt relief is not itself a societal foundation stone, but an outworking of community values governed by the logic of God's blessing. Debt relief can make economic sense in other contexts as, for example, when Solon in sixth-century BCE Athens canceled debts in order to save the people from an economic catastrophe.[65] This is not what Deuteronomy's law is about. Rather, it represents courageous community moves that embody core values possibly in conflict with the ways of other societies.

---

63. Joachim Jeremias (*The Sermon on the Mount*, trans. Norman Perrin [London: Athlone, 1961]) helpfully outlines three approaches that have been used to blunt Jesus' ethical claims (that they are an unbearable yoke, that Jesus' demands are unrealistic and meant only to highlight human insufficiency to meet God's standard, and that this idea of the Christian life was meant only for a brief time before the imminent apocalypse) but then persuasively argues, much as I do here for Deuteronomy, that such ethical teachings are intended to explain how to make God's gifts a basis for a new life.

64. Notice Jesus' teaching in Matt. 18:23–34 that Christians must release others as God has released them.

65. George Grote, *A History of Greece* (London: John Murray, 1862), pt. 2, ch. 11. For an analysis of a Babylonian debt release program, see Olivier, "Restitution."

The example of the Jerusalem church in Acts 4:32–35 (see also 2:44–45) is instructive. The church shared its property in order to eliminate poverty within the community. Luke probably consciously refers to the realization of Deuteronomy 15:4 in Acts 4:34 ("There was not a needy person among them") as deuteronomic thinking yet again inspires the faithful. The practice is reported as successful, at least for a time, although the balancing narrative in Acts 5:1–11 makes clear that life was not idyllic.

What could it mean to reform church life today with these ideas? When reflecting upon the modern West, it quickly becomes clear that there is substantial truth in labeling ourselves *Homo economicus*. A huge proportion of modern behavior is driven by individuals rationally maximizing their personal utility through economic transactions.[66] A significant counterexample is the household of the nuclear family, where, as Ched Myers describes it, "Labor is cooperative, assets and possessions are shared equitably, and consumption is done without payment." He goes on to observe, "Before the rise of the great civilizations and empires—which is to say, for 99% of the history of *homo sapiens*—all human communities operated this way, practicing what anthropologists call 'generalized reciprocity.'"[67] The surprising decision by the Jerusalem church was to expand the idea of "household" to include the family of believers, bound together not by their own blood but by the blood of Christ. Although Adam Smith famously observed, "It is not from the benevolence of the butcher, the brewer, or the baker, that we expect our dinner, but from their regard to their own interest," this is not the spirit of Deuteronomy.[68] But it would be dangerously naive for modern churches to implement such economic policies without a foundation of strong and not easily severed community ties. Underlying such economic behavior should be mutual commitment that resembles something like marriage, where the community's fortunes all rise and fall together, and where there are significant barriers that impede the breaking of communal relationships. In transient modern societies, people's loyalties to social networks, jobs, geographies, and faith communities are similarly transient and nonbinding; hence the building of long-term mutual responsibility within the church—both locally and globally conceived—might need to precede or at least accompany the kind of economic moves that grow out of Deuteronomy 15:1–11. On the other hand, perhaps Jesus teaches apparently naive obedience that depends

66. On the concept of *Homo economicus*, see Joseph Persky, "The Ethology of *Homo Economicus*," *Journal of Economic Perspectives* 9 (1995): 221–31.

67. Ched Myers, interviewed by Kayla McClurg, as reported in Michael Schut's *Money and Faith: The Search for Enough* (Denver: Church Publishing, 2008), 160. Martin Luther's *On Trading and Usury* and *A Treatise on Usury* provide insightful Christian critiques of early capitalism as it began to take hold as a social order.

68. Adam Smith, *An Inquiry into the Nature and Causes of the Wealth of Nations* (Dublin: N. Kelly, 1801), vol. 1, bk. 1, ch. 2.

on God's superintending blessing and does not seek to avoid the costs of the cross. Regardless of the serious impediments of practicability and the pressure to conform to the status quo of the larger society (thus serving the world's economic idols), Deuteronomy continues to implore God's people to center themselves on loyalty to God and a life of obedience, fueled by blessing, which has the potential to be the wonder of other nations, who will say, "Surely this great nation is a wise and discerning people!" (Deut. 4:6).

Conclusion

Deuteronomy envisions a life for Israel driven by loyalty to the incomparable Yhwh, framed by obedience to his law, fueled by his blessing, and demanded by threats of his curse. This vision is portrayed as framing Israel's original settlement of the land and inspiring later reform movements. Deuteronomy's vision has also grounded critical reflection on life under God up until today. Though the book's challenge may seem to be overwhelming and its vision utopian, that is not its own view. God calls his people to walk in his ways, and he promises to fulfill his oath to make their efforts into the reality he envisions.

> This commandment that I command you today is not hard for you, nor is it too far away. It is not in heaven, that you should say, "Who will go up to heaven for us, and get it for us so that we may hear it and observe it?" Neither is it beyond the sea, that you should say, "Who will cross to the other side of the sea for us, and get it for us so that we may hear it and observe it?" No, the word is very near you; it is in your mouth and in your heart so you may obey it (Deuteronomy 30:11–14).

Further Reading

General

Barrett, Rob. *Disloyalty and Destruction: Religion and Politics in Deuteronomy and the Modern World*. Library of Hebrew Bible/Old Testament Studies 511. New York: T&T Clark International, 2009.

Jeremias, Joachim. *The Sermon on the Mount*. Translated by Norman Perrin. London: Athlone, 1961.

Miller, Patrick D. *The God You Have: Politics and the First Commandment*. Minneapolis: Augsburg Fortress, 2004.

Wells, Bruce. "What Is Biblical Law? A Look at Pentateuchal Rules and Near Eastern Practice." *Catholic Biblical Quarterly* 70 (2008): 223–43.

Deuteronomy 8

MacDonald, Nathan. *Deuteronomy and the Meaning of "Monotheism."* Forschungen zum Alten Testament 2, no. 1. Tübingen: Paul Mohr, 2003.

Moberly, R. W. L. *The Bible, Theology, and Faith: A Study of Abraham and Jesus.* Cambridge Studies in Christian Doctrine 5. Cambridge: Cambridge University Press, 2000.

Deuteronomy 15:1–11

Hamilton, Jeffries M. *Social Justice and Deuteronomy: The Case of Deuteronomy 15.* Society of Biblical Literature Dissertation Series 136. Atlanta: Society of Biblical Literature, 1992.

Houston, Walter J. *Contending for Justice: Ideologies and Theologies of Social Justice in the Old Testament.* Library of Hebrew Bible/Old Testament Studies 428. London: T&T Clark, 2006.

———. "'You Shall Open Your Hand to Your Needy Brother': Ideology and Moral Formation in Deut 15:1–18." In *The Bible in Ethics: The Second Sheffield Colloquium,* edited by John W. Rogerson, Margaret Davies, and M. Daniel Carroll R., 296–314. Journal for the Study of the Old Testament: Supplement Series 207. Sheffield: Sheffield Academic Press, 1995.

Oosthuizen, Martin J. "Deuteronomy 15:1–18 in Socio-Rhetorical Perspective." *Zeitschrift für altorientalische und biblische Rechtsgeschichte* 3 (1997): 64–91.

Sider, Ronald J. "An Evangelical Vision for Public Policy." *Transformation: An International Journal of Holistic Mission Studies* 2, no. 1 (1985): 1–9.

Appendix

Walter Moberly's Contributions to the Theological Interpretation of the Pentateuch

NATHAN MACDONALD WITH RICHARD S. BRIGGS

I t is difficult to describe succinctly the influence and importance of a teacher under whom you studied for a number of years and have known as a friend and colleague since then. As Philip said to Nathanael, "Come and see." There is no substitute for personal encounter. For most, however, the way in which they will encounter Walter Moberly is through his writings. Hence there is a place for trying to introduce his books and essays, though the primary purpose must be to encourage readers to turn to these themselves.

There is no doubt that Walter ranks among the foremost theological interpreters of the Pentateuch in the present. Several characteristics of his work should be recognized, some of which have already been explored in the introduction to the present volume:

- First, there is a deeply held conviction that the text must be carefully examined. As a biblical scholar Walter is first and foremost an interpreter of biblical texts, with all the necessary competencies that this entails. Arguments must always be well grounded exegetically.
- Second, there is a strong interest in the narrative and literary dimensions of the text. Walter's work belongs in the turn to narrative that began in the 1970s. He is attentive to the problems that have struck earlier critical interpreters, but has often found his own way to approach these issues, particularly through attention to the dynamics of narrative.

177

- Third, there is a belief that sustained engagement with key texts—the Akedah (ʿAqedah, Binding of Isaac, Gen. 22), the Shema (Shemaʿ, "Hear," Deut. 6)—is the best place to work out larger hermeneutical issues and theological conclusions.

- Fourth, the principal character of the biblical narratives is God. This God is none other than the One whom Christians worship as the Father of our Lord Jesus Christ. Consequently, to speak about the biblical texts is to speak about God and requires from the interpreter humility, faith, and theological discipline, combined with a deep respect for the text as sacred Scripture.

- Fifth, the biblical texts reveal this God to be, above all, trustworthy and gracious, generously dealing with creatures who too often are willful and blind to their own limitations.

The centrality of these convictions runs through his contributions to the interpretation of the Pentateuch, as well as his other writings. What follows is not a complete bibliography, but rather a guide to his writings that relate to the broader concerns of the present volume.[1]

The Pentateuch and the Concerns of Theological Interpretation

We should begin with Walter's extended *New Interpreter's Dictionary of the Bible* article, "Pentateuch."[2] This essay neatly encapsulates Walter's awareness of the critical problems in the Pentateuch, his belief that they must be taken seriously, and his own attempt to reframe an introduction to the Pentateuch in a way that prioritizes theological interests over historical concerns.

His more general hermeneutical writings, which give careful thought to the proper framing of the interpretive task in theological and other terms, are too wide-ranging to all be listed here, but among them the following bear particularly on the nature of theological interpretation. He tackles the matter directly in his article "What Is Theological Interpretation of Scripture?"[3] to which reference has been made in the introduction to this book. During the past ten years, he has also offered discussions of several associated areas in a series of articles that explore the following interrelated questions: What constitutes

---

1. In addition, see the listing of all his published books in the "Further Reading" recommendations in the introduction, above. Unless specifically noted, all further works cited in the footnotes of this appendix are by R. W. L. Moberly.

2. "Pentateuch," *NIDB* 4:430–38.

3. "What Is Theological Interpretation of Scripture?" *Journal of Theological Interpretation* 3 (2009): 161–78.

"biblical theology"?[4] What does it mean to "read the Old Testament as Christian Scripture"?[5] In what sense should religious belief be seen as a help or a hindrance to the practices of biblical criticism?[6] Is it really true that the Bible should be "interpreted like any other book"?[7] Taken together, all these writings represent a sustained attempt to rethink the appropriate conceptual categories within which the reading and study of scriptural texts may best be pursued. Overall they walk a fine line: Christian biblical interpretation is properly critical while also making judicious use of the resources of Christian theology. On most matters of substance, the Bible is not to be interpreted like any other book.

Genesis

The majority of Walter's exegetical work has focused on the book of Genesis. The book's attractiveness lies in its theological richness and narrative depth. Such a text requires attentiveness and time, and Walter has sought to give the text its due in a series of studies from the 1980s to the present. Three distinct phases may be discerned in Walter's engagement with Genesis, bearing fruit in three significant books.

The first book, *The Old Testament of the Old Testament*,[8] sought to use the relationship between Genesis 12–50 and the rest of the Old Testament as a way of thinking about how Old and New Testaments relate to each other. This consciously theological approach was not achieved by jettisoning the typical questions of critical scholarship, such as the use of different divine names in Genesis or the nature of patriarchal religion, but by careful reflection upon them. Yet in many respects this is a book swimming against the tide in its willingness to address questions of religious language, Jewish-Christian relationships, typology, and promise and fulfillment. In the preparation of *The Old Testament of the Old Testament*, Walter also wrote a brief book designed as an introduction to Genesis 12–50 for students.[9] More important

4. "How May We Speak of God? A Reconsideration of the Nature of Biblical Theology," *Tyndale Bulletin* 53 (2002): 177–202.

5. "Christ in All the Scriptures? The Challenge of Reading the Old Testament as Christian Scripture," *Journal of Theological Interpretation* 1 (2007): 79–100.

6. "Biblical Criticism and Religious Belief," *Journal of Theological Interpretation* 2 (2008): 71–100.

7. "'Interpret the Bible Like Any Other Book'? Requiem for an Axiom," *Journal of Theological Interpretation* 4 (2010): 91–110.

8. *The Old Testament of the Old Testament: Patriarchal Narratives and Mosaic Yahwism*, Overtures to Biblical Theology (Minneapolis: Fortress, 1992; repr., Eugene, OR: Wipf & Stock, 2002).

9. *Genesis 12–50*, Old Testament Guides (Sheffield: JSOT Press, 1992); reissued and updated in John W. Rogerson, R. W. L. Moberly, and William Johnstone, *Genesis and Exodus*, with an introduction by John Goldingay (Sheffield: Sheffield Academic Press, 2001), 99–179.

for the subsequent development of his thinking, he produced two significant studies on Abraham as exemplar of faith and righteousness: "Abraham's Righteousness (Gen. 15:6)"[10] and "The Earliest Commentary on the Akedah,"[11] which seeks to draw attention to Genesis 22:15–18, at the end of the chapter, as the earliest and canonical interpretation of the story itself.

This essay on the Akedah (Binding of Isaac) or, as known in the Christian tradition, the Sacrifice of Isaac, sees the beginning of Walter's sustained focus on the famous story found in Genesis 22. In what sense could or should this strange story be a paradigm for Christian living? In a subsequent essay, "Christ as the Key to Scripture,"[12] he takes issue with the familiar Christian interpretation of Isaac as a type of Christ. Such an interpretation too easily becomes rather superficial and skates over the issues that Genesis 22 raises. However, von Rad's celebrated and imaginative reading of the story, where Abraham is on the road of godforsakenness, might easily degenerate into the subjective and psychological. As we follow Walter in addressing Genesis 22, it becomes clear that the chapter is important to him not only for the many exegetical and theological puzzles it poses but also as a crucial text for thinking about the hermeneutical challenges of theological interpretation. This becomes apparent in a second major book, *The Bible, Theology, and Faith*,[13] written under the working title *God's Friend and God's Son*. In some ways this volume can be viewed as a hermeneutically oriented prolegomena for Christian theological interpretation. For Walter, careful hermeneutical thinking cannot be done apart from engagements with specific texts. Genesis 22 is a paradigmatic case because of its complexity, theological richness, and importance within the history of interpretation. A succinct summary statement of his understanding of the chapter may also be found in an essay from 2003: "Living Dangerously: Genesis 22 and the Quest for Good Biblical Interpretation."[14]

The third significant book on Genesis by Walter is *The Theology of the Book of Genesis*.[15] In this volume he brings together the insights of more than

10. "Abraham's Righteousness (Gen. 15:6)," in *Studies in the Pentateuch*, ed. John A. Emerton, Supplements to Vetus Testamentum 41 (Leiden: Brill, 1990), 103–30; repr. in *From Eden to Golgotha: Essays in Biblical Theology*, University of South Florida Studies in the History of Judaism (Atlanta: Scholars Press, 1992), 29–54.

11. "The Earliest Commentary on the Akedah," *Vetus Testamentum* 38 (1988): 302–23; repr. in *From Eden to Golgotha*, 55–73.

12. "Christ as the Key to Scripture: Genesis 22 Reconsidered," in *He Swore an Oath: Biblical Themes from Genesis 12–50*, ed. R. S. Hess, P. E. Satterthwaite, and G. J. Wenham (Cambridge: Tyndale House, 1993), 143–73.

13. *The Bible, Theology, and Faith: A Study of Abraham and Jesus*, Cambridge Studies in Christian Doctrine 5 (Cambridge: Cambridge University Press, 2000).

14. "Living Dangerously: Genesis 22 and the Quest for Good Biblical Interpretation," in *The Art of Reading Scripture*, ed. Ellen F. Davis and Richard B. Hays (Grand Rapids: Eerdmans, 2003), 181–97.

15. *The Theology of the Book of Genesis*, Old Testament Theology (Cambridge: Cambridge University Press, 2009).

twenty years of careful reflection on Genesis. One of the notable concerns of
the book is to engage with issues above and beyond the more familiar range
of "technical" matters that often occupy biblical scholarship, allowing questions brought from various more-popular quarters to impinge upon the work
of the careful biblical interpreter.

Several chapters in *The Theology of the Book of Genesis* reformulate material from some of the earlier studies already described, but the preparation of
this volume also saw Walter apply his nuanced theological analysis to various
texts from Genesis 1–11.[16]

His discussion of these chapters in "How Should One Read the Early
Chapters of Genesis?"[17] is not especially characteristic of his work. The difference is to be attributed to the special attention Genesis 1–3 has received,
especially in conservative forms of English-speaking Christianity, and in
the modern world more generally. Writing for a broader audience, Walter
offers several examples of the importance of genre recognition in handling
the early chapters of Genesis, an essential competence assumed in his other
essays. Much more typical of his own style and interests is "Did the Serpent
Get It Right?"[18] In this essay Walter tackles the apparent nonfulfillment of
God's threat of death if Adam eats from the forbidden tree. Despite some
commentators' view that this is not a matter of particular concern, Walter
insists that the apparent mendacity on God's part demands reflection in
light of the rest of the canon, where God's trustworthiness is affirmed.
His solution is to interpret death metaphorically and to reflect upon what
biblical texts mean when they speak about God's "repenting" of an action,
a topic to which he returns later (see below). The essay received a belated
and perhaps unexpected response from James Barr, partly in connection
with a book review that Walter had written on Barr's work on the Eden
narrative.[19] Barr argues that reading Genesis 2–3 with concerns about truth
and lying brings unhelpful modern categories to the text, although Barr
does not particularly engage with the actual reading of the text that Walter
offers. Walter's response, "Did the Interpreters Get It Right? Genesis 2–3

16. Yet engagement with the ancestral narratives was not absent, including two wide-
ranging studies of Gen. 12:1–3. An indication of Walter's approach to Gen. 12–50 may be
found in his briefer article "Patriarchal Narratives," in *Dictionary for Theological Interpretation of the Bible*, ed. Kevin J. Vanhoozer et al. (Grand Rapids: Baker Academic; London:
SPCK, 2005), 564–66.

17. "How Should One Read the Early Chapters of Genesis?" in *Reading Genesis after Darwin*, ed. Stephen C. Barton and David Wilkinson (New York: Oxford University Press, 2009), 5–21.

18. "Did the Serpent Get It Right?" *Journal of Theological Studies* 39 (1988): 1–27; repr.
in *From Eden to Golgotha*, 1–27.

19. James Barr, "Is God a Liar? (Gen. 2–3)—and Related Matters," *Journal of Theological
Studies* 59 (2006): 1–22. See also R. W. L. Moberly, review of *The Garden of Eden and the
Hope of Immortality*, by James Barr (London: SCM, 1992), in *Journal of Theological Studies*
45 (1994): 172–77.

Reconsidered,"[20] accepts the need to utilize language about truth and lies more carefully, but insists that other biblical texts do show a strong concern with the question of whether God's words are trustworthy and reliable.

The Cain-and-Abel story receives attention in two very different essays: "Exemplars of Faith in Hebrews 11: Abel"[21] and "The Mark of Cain—Revealed at Last?"[22] In the first Walter presents the writer of Hebrews as an attentive reader of the Greek translation of Genesis 4. In the second he argues that the sign to Cain is nothing other than the words that God speaks to him in 4:15. Finally, two essays tackle the flood story: "Why Did Noah Send Out a Raven?"[23] and "On Interpreting the Mind of God: The Theological Significance of the Flood Narrative (Gen. 6–9)."[24] In the first essay Walter reflects on why Noah sends out a raven *and* a dove. He seeks to avoid the symbolic moralizing of early interpreters and the modern tendency to see it as merely a traditional fragment. In the second essay Walter puzzles over why the same assessment about human beings' propensity to evil can result in judgment following Genesis 6:5 and in mercy at 8:21. This leads Walter to reflections on the relationship between divine mutability and divine benevolence.

Exodus

Walter's academic work began with the book of Exodus and a Cambridge doctorate under Graham Davies on the story of the golden calf and its aftermath, later published as *At the Mountain of God*.[25] His attempt at a fresh reading of Exodus 32–34 adumbrates the concerns that would animate his subsequent work. There is an awareness of the critical problems in these chapters, an attention to narrative analysis as an alternative lens with which to view these problems, and a deep sensitivity to theological paradox.

Walter's following book, *The Old Testament of the Old Testament*, can be seen as an attempt to tackle the critical problems that revolve around the revelation of the divine name in Exodus 3 and 6. As we have seen in the previous section, this took him back toward Genesis, where he has produced some of his

20. "Did the Interpreters Get It Right? Genesis 2–3 Reconsidered," *Journal of Theological Studies* 59 (2008): 22–40.

21. "Exemplars of Faith in Hebrews 11: Abel," in *The Epistle to the Hebrews and Christian Theology*, ed. Richard Bauckham et al. (Grand Rapids: Eerdmans, 2009), 353–63.

22. "The Mark of Cain—Revealed at Last?" *Harvard Theological Review* 100 (2007): 11–28.

23. "Why Did Noah Send Out a Raven?" *Vetus Testamentum* 50 (2000): 345–56.

24. "On Interpreting the Mind of God: The Theological Significance of the Flood Narrative (Gen. 6–9)," in *The Word Leaps the Gap: Essays on Scripture and Theology in Honor of Richard B. Hays*, ed. J. Ross Wagner, C. Kavin Rowe, and A. Katherine Grieb (Grand Rapids: Eerdmans, 2008), 44–66.

25. *At the Mountain of God: Story and Theology in Exodus 32–34*, Journal for the Study of the Old Testament: Supplement Series 22 (Sheffield: JSOT Press, 1983).

most important academic work. This focus upon Genesis means that Walter has written little on Exodus until quite recently. How he might approach the book theologically is apparent in the dictionary article "Exodus."[26] In brief compass, Walter discusses every part of the book, along with its major theological issues. A striking feature of the discussion of Exodus is the appreciation of the book's theology in both Jewish and Christian contexts. More recently he has offered a detailed study of the manna narrative in Exodus 16, "On Learning Spiritual Disciplines: A Reading of Exodus 16,"[27] where he identifies the main issues to be those of divine grace and the pedagogical intent of God's testing of Israel.

Numbers

Walter's instincts have seen him consistently drawn to narratives that enlighten the relationship between God and humans. Consequently, the books of Leviticus and, to a lesser degree, Numbers have not enjoyed as much of his attention. The story of Balaam is a striking exception, for here we have two issues with which Walter has wrestled for a long time. First, how should we understand biblical language about divine repentance? Second, how might we recognize the voice of God as speaking to us, even if it comes from unexpected corners? The first question, already canvassed in his discussion of Genesis 3 (see above), receives sustained attention in "God Is Not a Human That He Should Repent."[28] Here Walter considers in what way God can and cannot change his mind, showing his sense of divine paradox and the Bible's affirmation of both God's faithfulness *and* his responsiveness. The second question is addressed in two essays on Balaam's donkey, one written for an academic audience ("On Learning to Be a True Prophet: The Story of Balaam and His Ass"[29]), and the other at a more popular level, with an eye on the implications for the church's reading of the Old Testament today (*Can Balaam's Ass Speak Today?*).[30] Both essays reflect on the moral responsiveness necessary to hear

26. "Exodus," in Vanhoozer et al., eds., *Dictionary for Theological Interpretation of the Bible*, 211–16; repr. in *Theological Interpretation of the Old Testament: A Book-by-Book Survey*, ed. Kevin J. Vanhoozer et al. (Grand Rapids: Baker Academic, 2008), 42–51.

27. "On Learning Spiritual Disciplines: A Reading of Exodus 16," in *Reading the Law: Studies in Honour of Gordon J. Wenham*, Library of Hebrew Bible/Old Testament Studies 461, ed. J. G. McConville and Karl Möller (New York: T&T Clark International, 2007), 213–27.

28. "'God Is Not a Human That He Should Repent' (Num. 23:19 and 1 Sam. 15:29)," in *God in the Fray: A Tribute to Walter Brueggemann*, ed. Tod Linafelt and Timothy K. Beal (Philadelphia: Fortress: 1998), 112–23.

29. "On Learning to Be a True Prophet: The Story of Balaam and His Ass," in *New Heaven and New Earth: Prophecy and the Millennium: Essays in Honour of Anthony Gelston*, ed. Peter J. Harland and Robert Hayward (Leiden: Brill, 1999), 1–17.

30. *Can Balaam's Ass Speak Today? A Case Study in Reading the Old Testament as Scripture*, Grove Biblical Series 10 (Cambridge: Grove Books, 1998).

God's word in human words, a subject that finds more extended exposition in his more recent book-length treatment, *Prophecy and Discernment*.[31]

Deuteronomy

Walter's published work on Deuteronomy has also been rather focused. The possibility of a broader engagement is found in his response to Gordon Mc-Conville's Deuteronomy commentary. This response was delivered in a colloquium to launch both the commentary and the Apollos Commentary Series, of which it is a part.[32] Though it may not be immediately apparent, this is perhaps as good a place as any for the reader to understand Walter's hermeneutical and theological concerns. McConville's historically and theologically conservative commentary is one with which Walter has various sympathies, yet one that he also finds unsatisfactory. In particular, Walter emphasizes the challenges of the hermeneutical and theological task, thereby registering a disagreement with both conservative and liberal ideas that the biblical scholar's task is merely exegetical.

It is appropriate to end our review of Walter's writings on the Pentateuch with his work on Deuteronomy 6:4–9, on the Shema. Generations of undergraduate students at Durham know the importance of these verses to Walter and have written their first essays in Old Testament on its interpretation. For Walter, the passage has significance not only because of the highly esteemed place it holds within both the Jewish and Christian traditions but also because it has considerable heuristic value in highlighting key interpretive issues. First, there are basic issues of lexicography and understanding a text written in Hebrew. How should "one" or "heart" or "soul" be understood? Theological interpretation is no substitute for careful grammatical exegesis. Second, what is the appropriate context or contexts for understanding these verses: the Josianic reformation, the book of Deuteronomy, the New Testament? Should the verses be broken into parts and their prehistory examined, or what is the interpretive significance of considering them in their present literary context? Third, what difference does the context of the interpreter make? How have Jews and Christians read the Shema differently, and how should they read it? Some

---

31. *Prophecy and Discernment*, Cambridge Studies in Christian Doctrine 14 (Cambridge: Cambridge University Press, 2006). On the wider implications of this book (and some of his other writings) for the tasks of theological interpretation more broadly conceived, see especially the review article of Richard S. Briggs, "Christian Theological Interpretation of Scripture Built on the Foundation of the Apostles and the Prophets: The Contribution of R. W. L. Moberly's *Prophecy and Discernment*," *Journal of Theological Interpretation* 4 (2010): 309–18.

32. "A Dialogue with Gordon McConville on Deuteronomy, II: Theological Interpretation of an Old Testament Book: A Response to Gordon McConville's *Deuteronomy*," *Scottish Journal of Theology* 56 (2003): 516–25.

sense of how Walter might address those questions is given in his two essays on the text. The first, "'Yhwh Is One': The Translation of the Shema,"[33] focuses on the textual issues; it was the first academic article written by Walter upon his arriving in Durham to lecture in Old Testament. By his own account, it was only after patiently waiting upon the text for some years that he was then able to move forward to a theologically oriented account of the significance of what the text is actually saying. The resulting article, "Toward an Interpretation of the Shema,"[34] is perhaps one of his most probing examinations of how the text of Scripture, the God of Scripture, and the life of the interpreter are brought into focus together in the demanding but always rewarding practice of interpreting Christian Scripture.

33. "'Yhwh Is One': The Translation of the Shema," in *Studies in the Pentateuch*, Supplements to Vetus Testamentum 41, ed. John A. Emerton (Leiden: Brill, 1990), 209–15; repr. in *From Eden to Golgotha*, 75–81.

34. "Toward an Interpretation of the Shema," in *Theological Exegesis: Essays in Honor of Brevard S. Childs*, ed. Christopher Seitz and Kathryn Greene-McCreight (Grand Rapids: Eerdmans: 1999), 124–44.

Bibliography

Achenbach, Reinhard. *Die Vollendung der Tora: Studien zur Redaktionsgeschichte des Numeribuches im Kontext von Hexateuch und Pentateuch*. Beihefte zur Zeitschrift für Altorientalische und Biblische Rechtsgeschichte 3. Wiesbaden: Harrassowitz, 2003.

Alexander, T. Desmond. *From Paradise to the Promised Land: An Introduction to the Pentateuch*. 2nd ed. Grand Rapids: Baker Academic, 2002.

Alter, Robert. *The Art of Biblical Narrative*. Berkeley: Basic Books, 1981.

Auerbach, Erich. *Mimesis: The Representation of Reality in Western Literature*. Princeton, NJ: Princeton University Press, 1953.

Baden, Joel S. "The Tower of Babel: A Case-Study in the Competing Methods of Historical and Modern Literary Criticism." *Journal of Biblical Literature* 128 (2009): 209–24.

Balentine, Samuel E. *The Torah's Vision of Worship*. Overtures to Biblical Theology. Minneapolis: Fortress, 1999.

Barr, James. "Is God a Liar? (Gen. 2–3)—and Related Matters." *Journal of Theological Studies* 59 (2006): 1–22.

Barrett, Rob. *Disloyalty and Destruction: Religion and Politics in Deuteronomy and the Modern World*. Library of Hebrew Bible/Old Testament Studies 511. New York: T&T Clark International, 2009.

Barton, John. *Reading the Old Testament: Method in Biblical Study*. 2nd ed. London: Darton, Longman & Todd, 1996.

Barton, Stephen C., and David Wilkinson, eds. *Reading Genesis after Darwin*. New York: Oxford University Press, 2009.

Bauckham, Richard, Daniel R. Driver, Trevor A. Hart, and Nathan MacDonald, eds. *The Epistle to the Hebrews and Christian Theology*. Grand Rapids: Eerdmans, 2009.

Beale, G. K., and D. A. Carson, eds. *Commentary on the New Testament Use of the Old Testament*. Grand Rapids: Baker Academic, 2007.

Bellis, Alice Ogden, and Joel S. Kaminsky, eds. *Jews, Christians, and the Theology of the Hebrew Scriptures*. SBL Symposium Series 8. Atlanta: Society of Biblical Literature, 2000.

Berger, Peter L. *The Sacred Canopy: Elements of a Sociological Theory of Religion*. New York: Doubleday Anchor, 1967.

Berman, Joshua A. *Created Equal: How the Bible Broke with Ancient Political Thought*. Oxford: Oxford University Press, 2008.

Bird, Phyllis A. "The Bible in Christian Ethical Deliberation concerning Homosexuality: Old Testament Contributions." In *Homosexuality, Science, and the "Plain Sense" of Scripture*, edited by David L. Balch, 142–76. Grand Rapids: Eerdmans, 2000.

Bonhoeffer, Dietrich. *Life Together*. Translated by John W. Doberstein. San Francisco: Harper & Row, 1954.

Braulik, Georg. "The Sequence of the Laws in Deuteronomy 12–26 and in the Decalogue." In *A Song of Power and the Power of Song: Essays on the Book of Deuteronomy*, edited by Duane L. Christensen, 313–35. Sources for Biblical and Theological Study 3. Winona Lake, IN: Eisenbrauns, 1993.

Brett, Mark G. *Genesis*. Old Testament Readings. London and New York: Routledge, 2000.

Briggs, Richard S. "Christian Theological Interpretation of Scripture Built on the Foundation of the Apostles and the Prophets: The Contribution of R. W. L. Moberly's *Prophecy and Discernment*." *Journal of Theological Interpretation* 4 (2010): 309–18.

———. "Humans in the Image of God and Other Things Genesis Does Not Make Clear." *Journal of Theological Interpretation* 4 (2010): 111–26.

———. "Juniper Trees and Pistachio Nuts: Trust and Suspicion as Modes of Scriptural Imagination." *Theology* 112 (2009): 353–63.

———. "Speech-Act Theory." In *Words and the Word: Explorations in Biblical Interpretation and Literary Theory*, edited by David G. Firth and Jamie A. Grant, 75–110. Nottingham, UK: Apollos, 2008.

Bright, John. *Jeremiah: A New Translation with Introduction and Commentary*. Anchor Bible 21. New York: Doubleday, 1965.

Brown, William P. *The Seven Pillars of Creation: The Bible, Science, and the Ecology of Wonder*. New York: Oxford University Press, 2010.

Brueggemann, Walter. *Genesis*. Interpretation. Atlanta: John Knox, 1982.

Buber, Martin. *Moses*. Oxford: Phaidon, 1946.

Buren, Paul van. "On Reading Someone Else's Mail: The Church and Israel's Scriptures." In *Die hebräische Bibel und ihre zweifache Nachgeschichte: Festschrift für Rolf Rendtorff zum 65. Geburtstag*, edited by Erhard Blum, Christian Machholz, and Ekkehard W. Stegemann, 595–606. Neukirchen-Vluyn: Neukirchener Verlag, 1990.

Calvin, John. *Commentaries on the Four Last Books of Moses Arranged in the Form of a Harmony*. Translated by Charles William Bingham. 4 vols. Grand Rapids: Eerdmans, 1950.

Chaney, Marvin L. "Accusing Whom of What? Hosea's Rhetoric of Promiscuity." In *Distant Voices Drawing Near: Essays in Honor of Antoinette Clark Wire*, edited by Holly E. Hearon, 97–115. Collegeville, MN: Liturgical Press, 2004.

Childs, Brevard S. *Biblical Theology in Crisis*. Philadelphia: Westminster, 1970.

———. *Exodus*. Old Testament Library. London: SCM, 1974.

———. *Introduction to the Old Testament as Scripture*. Philadelphia: Fortress, 1979.

Chirichigno, Gregory C. "The Narrative Structure of Exod 19–24." *Biblica* 68 (1987): 457–79.

Church of England. *The Book of Common Prayer*. New York: Oxford University Press, 1928.

Cody, Aelred. "When Is the Chosen People Called a *Gôy*?" *Vetus Testamentum* 14 (1964): 1–6.

Coggins, Richard. "What Does 'Deuteronomistic' Mean?" In *Those Elusive Deuteronomists: The Phenomenon of Pan-Deuteronomism*, edited by Linda S. Schearing and Steven L. McKenzie, 22–35. Journal for the Study of the Old Testament: Supplement Series 268. Sheffield: Sheffield Academic Press, 1999.

Collins, John J., *The Bible after Babel: Historical Criticism in a Postmodern Age*. Grand Rapids: Eerdmans, 2005.

Cook, Stephen L. *The Social Roots of Biblical Yahwism*. Society of Biblical Literature Studies in Biblical Literature 8. Atlanta: Society of Biblical Literature, 2004.

Crumb, Robert. *The Book of Genesis Illustrated*. Translated by Robert Alter. New York: Norton, 2009.

Davies, Eryl W. *Numbers*. New Century Bible Commentary. Grand Rapids: Eerdmans, 1995.

Davis, Ellen F. "Entering the Story: Teaching the Bible in the Church." In *Sharper Than a Two-Edged Sword: Preaching, Teaching, and Living the Bible*, edited by Michael Root and James J. Buckley, 44–62. Grand Rapids: Eerdmans, 2008.

———. *Scripture, Culture, and Agriculture: An Agrarian Reading of the Bible*. Cambridge: Cambridge University Press, 2009.

———. "Slaves or Sabbath-Keepers? A Biblical Perspective on Human Work." *Anglican Theological Review* 83 (2001): 25–40.

Derrida, Jacques. "Des Tours de Babel." Translated by J. F. Graham. *Semeia* 54 (1991): 3–34.

Douglas, Mary. "The Forbidden Animals in Leviticus." *Journal for the Study of the Old Testament* 59 (1993): 3–23.

———. "The Go-Away Goat." In *The Book of Leviticus: Composition and Reception*, edited by Rolf Rendtorff and Robert A. Kugler, 121–41. Supplements to Vetus Testamentum 93. Leiden: Brill, 2003.

———. *In the Wilderness: The Doctrine of Defilement in the Book of Numbers*. Journal for the Study of the Old Testament: Supplement Series 158. Sheffield: JSOT Press, 1993.

———. *Leviticus as Literature*. Oxford: Oxford University Press, 1999.

———. *Purity and Danger: An Analysis of Concepts of Pollution and Taboo*. London: Routledge, 1966.

Dozeman, Thomas B. *Exodus*. Eerdmans Critical Commentary. Grand Rapids: Eerdmans, 2009.

————, ed. *Methods for Exodus*. Methods in Biblical Interpretation. Cambridge: Cambridge University Press, 2010.

Dozeman, Thomas B., and Konrad Schmid, eds. *A Farewell to the Yahwist? The Composition of the Pentateuch in Recent European Interpretation*. SBL Symposium Series 34. Atlanta: Society of Biblical Literature, 2006.

Driver, Daniel R. *Brevard Childs, Biblical Theologian: For the Church's One Bible*. Forschungen zum Alten Testament 2.46. Tübingen: Mohr Siebeck, 2010.

Driver, S. R. *A Critical and Exegetical Commentary on Deuteronomy*. International Critical Commentary. Edinburgh: T&T Clark, 1902.

————. *An Introduction to the Literature of the Old Testament*. 8th ed. Edinburgh: T&T Clark, 1909.

Dumbrell, William J. *Covenant and Creation: An Old Testament Covenantal Theology*. Exeter, UK: Paternoster, 1984.

Durham, John I. *Exodus*. Word Biblical Commentary 3. Waco: Word, 1987.

Earl, Douglas S. *Reading Joshua as Christian Scripture*. Journal of Theological Interpretation: Supplement Series 2. Winona Lake, IN: Eisenbrauns, 2010.

Farrow, Douglas. "Melchizedek and Modernity." In *The Epistle to the Hebrews and Christian Theology*, edited by Richard Bauckham, Daniel R. Driver, Trevor A. Hart, and Nathan MacDonald, 281–301. Grand Rapids: Eerdmans, 2009.

Fewell, Danna Nolan. "Building Babel." In *Postmodern Interpretations of the Bible: A Reader*, edited by A. K. M. Adam, 1–15. St. Louis: Chalice, 2001.

Fokkelman, Jan P. *Narrative Art in Genesis: Specimens of Stylistic and Structural Analysis*. 2nd ed. Sheffield: JSOT Press, 1991.

Ford, David F., and C. C. Pecknold, eds. *The Promise of Scriptural Reasoning*. Oxford: Blackwell, 2006.

Fowl, Stephen E. *Theological Interpretation of Scripture*. Cascade Companions. Eugene, OR: Wipf & Stock, 2009.

Fox, Everett. *The Five Books of Moses: A New Translation with Introductions, Commentary, and Notes*. The Schocken Bible. Vol. 1. Dallas: Word, 1995.

Frankfort, Henri. *Kingship and the Gods: A Study of Ancient Near Eastern Religion as the Integration of Society and Nature*. Oriental Institute Essay. Chicago: University of Chicago Press, 1948.

Frei, Hans W. *The Eclipse of Biblical Narrative: A Study in Eighteenth and Nineteenth Century Hermeneutics*. New Haven: Yale University Press, 1974.

Fretheim, Terence E. "The Book of Genesis." In *The New Interpreter's Bible*, edited by Leander E. Keck, 1:319–674. Nashville: Abingdon, 1994.

————. *Exodus*. Interpretation. Louisville: John Knox Press, 1991.

————. *The Pentateuch*. Interpreting Biblical Texts. Nashville: Abingdon, 1996.

Gadamer, Hans-Georg. "The Problem of Historical Consciousness." In *Interpretive Social Research: A Reader*, edited by Paul Rabinow and William M. Sullivan, 103–60. Berkeley and Los Angeles: University of California Press, 1979.

Gane, Roy E. "Privative Preposition מִן in Purification Offering Pericopes and the Changing Face of 'Dorian Gray.'" *Journal of Biblical Literature* 127 (2008): 209–22.

Gilbert, Maurice. "Le sacré dans l'Ancien Testament." In *L'expression du sacré dans les grandes religions*, edited by Julien Ries, Herbert Sauren, Guy Kestemont, René Lebrun, and Maurice Gilbert. Vol. 1, *Proche-Orient ancien et traditions bibliques*, 205–89. Louvain-la-Neuve: Centre d'Histoire des Religions, 1978.

Goldingay, John. "Introduction to Genesis and Exodus," in *Genesis and Exodus*, by John W. Rogerson, R. W. L. Moberly, and William Johnstone, 9–34. Sheffield: Sheffield Academic Press, 2001.

Gottwald, Norman K. *The Tribes of Yahweh: A Sociology of the Religion of Liberated Israel, 1250–1050 B.C.E.* Maryknoll, NY: Orbis Books, 1979.

Gray, George Buchanan. *Numbers*. International Critical Commentary. Edinburgh: T&T Clark, 1903.

Greenberg, Moshe. "Hebrew *segullah*: Akkadian *sikiltu*." *Journal of the American Oriental Society* 71 (1951): 172–74.

Grote, George. *A History of Greece*. London: John Murray, 1862.

Grüneberg, Keith. *Blessing: Biblical Meaning and Pastoral Practice*. Grove Biblical Books B27. Cambridge: Grove Books, 2003.

Gunkel, Hermann. *Genesis*. Mercer Library of Biblical Studies. Translated by Mark E. Biddle. Macon, GA: Mercer University Press, 1997.

Habel, Norman C., and Shirley Wurst, eds. *The Earth Story in Genesis*. Earth Bible 2. Sheffield: Sheffield Academic Press, 2000.

Hardy, Daniel W., and David F. Ford. *Praising and Knowing God*. Philadelphia: Westminster, 1985.

Harland, Peter J. "Vertical or Horizontal: The Sin of Babel." *Vetus Testamentum* 48 (1998): 515–33.

Harrington, Hannah K. *The Purity Texts*. Companion to the Qumran Scrolls. London: T&T Clark, 2004.

Hendel, Ronald, ed. *Reading Genesis: Ten Methods*. Cambridge: Cambridge University Press, 2010.

———. "Table and Altar: The Anthropology of Food in the Priestly Torah." In *To Break Every Yoke: Essays in Honor of Marvin L. Chaney*, edited by Robert B. Coote and Norman K. Gottwald, 131–48. Sheffield: Sheffield Phoenix, 2007.

Hiebert, Theodore. "The Tower of Babel and the Origin of the World's Cultures." *Journal of Biblical Literature* 126 (2007): 29–58.

Hillers, Delbert R. *Treaty-Curses and the Old Testament Prophets*. Biblica et orientalia 16. Rome: Pontifical Biblical Institute, 1964.

Hoffman, Ya'ir. *The Doctrine of the Exodus in the Bible* (in Hebrew, with English summary). Tel Aviv: Tel Aviv University, 1983.

Humphreys, W. Lee. *The Character of God in the Book of Genesis: A Narrative Appraisal*. Louisville: Westminster John Knox, 2001.

Jacob, Benno. *The Second Book of the Bible: Exodus*. New York: Ktav, 1992.

Jeremias, Joachim. *The Sermon on the Mount*. Translated by Norman Perrin. London: Athlone, 1961.

Johnson, Luke T. "What's Catholic about Catholic Biblical Scholarship? An Opening Statement." In *The Future of Catholic Biblical Scholarship: A Constructive Conversation*, edited by Luke T. Johnson and William S. Kurz, 3–34. Grand Rapids: Eerdmans, 2002.

Joosten, Jan. *People and Land in the Holiness Code: An Exegetical Study of the Ideational Framework of the Law in Leviticus 17–26*. Supplements to Vetus Testamentum 67. Leiden: Brill, 1996.

———. Review of *Literary Artistry in Leviticus*, by Wilfried Warning. *Revue d'histoire et de philosophie religieuses* 81 (2001): 214.

Kaminsky, Joel S. *Corporate Responsibility in the Hebrew Bible*. Journal for the Study of the Old Testament: Supplement Series 196. Sheffield: Sheffield Academic Press, 1995.

———. "Loving One's (Israelite) Neighbor: Election and Commandment in Leviticus 19." *Interpretation* 62 (2008): 123–32.

Kaminsky, Joel S., and Joel N. Lohr. *The Torah: A Beginner's Guide*. Oxford: Oneworld, 2011.

Kaufman, Stephen A. "The Structure of the Deuteronomic Law." *Maarav* 1, no. 2 (1978): 105–58.

Kelle, Brad E. "Hosea 1–3 in Twentieth-Century Scholarship." *Currents in Biblical Research* 7 (2009): 179–216.

———. *Hosea 2: Metaphor and Rhetoric in Historical Perspective*. Academia biblica 20. Atlanta: Society of Biblical Literature, 2005.

Kiuchi, Nobuyoshi. *Leviticus*. Apollos Old Testament Commentary 3. Downers Grove, IL: InterVarsity, 2007.

Knoppers, Gary N., and Bernard M. Levinson, eds. *The Pentateuch as Torah: New Models for Understanding Its Promulgation and Acceptance*. Winona Lake, IN: Eisenbrauns, 2007.

Koch, Klaus. "Is There a Doctrine of Retribution in the Old Testament?" In *Theodicy in the Old Testament*, edited by James L. Crenshaw, 57–87. Issues in Religion and Theology 4. Philadelphia: Fortress, 1983.

Kugler, Robert A. "The Deuteronomists and the Latter Prophets." In *Those Elusive Deuteronomists: The Phenomenon of Pan-Deuteronomism*, edited by Linda S. Schearing and Steven L. McKenzie, 127–44. Journal for the Study of the Old Testament: Supplement Series 268. Sheffield: Sheffield Academic Press, 1999.

LaCocque, André. *The Captivity of Innocence: Babel and the Yahwist*. Eugene, OR: Cascade Books, 2010.

Lane, Nathan C. *The Compassionate but Punishing God: A Canonical Analysis of Exodus 34:6–7*. Eugene, OR: Pickwick Publications, 2010.

Lash, Nicholas. *The Beginning and the End of "Religion."* Cambridge: Cambridge University Press, 1996.

Lee, Won W. "The Conceptual Coherence of Numbers 5, 1–10, 10." In *The Books of Leviticus and Numbers*, edited by Thomas Römer, 473–89. Bibliotheca ephemeridum theologicarum lovaniensium 215. Leuven: Peeters, 2008.

———. *Punishment and Forgiveness in Israel's Migratory Campaign*. Grand Rapids: Eerdmans, 2003.

Leithart, Peter J. *Deep Exegesis: The Mystery of Reading Scripture.* Waco: Baylor University Press, 2009.

Lemche, Niels Peter. "Justice in Western Asia in Antiquity, or: Why No Laws Were Needed!" *Chicago-Kent Law Review* 70 (1995): 1695–1716.

Leveen, Adriane B. *Memory and Tradition in the Book of Numbers.* Cambridge: Cambridge University Press, 2008.

Levenson, Jon D. "The Conversion of Abraham to Judaism, Christianity, and Islam." In *The Idea of Biblical Interpretation: Essays in Honor of James L. Kugel,* edited by Hindy Najman and Judith Newman, 3–40. Leiden: Brill, 2004.

———. *Creation and the Persistence of Evil: The Jewish Drama of Divine Omnipotence.* Rev. ed. Princeton, NJ: Princeton University Press, 1994.

———. *The Hebrew Bible, the Old Testament, and Historical Criticism: Jews and Christians in Biblical Studies.* Louisville: Westminster John Knox, 1993.

Levering, Matthew. *Jewish-Christian Dialogue and the Life of Wisdom: Engagements with the Theology of David Novak.* New York: Continuum, 2010.

Levine, Baruch A. *The JPS Torah Commentary: Leviticus.* Philadelphia: Jewish Publication Society, 1989.

———. *Numbers.* 2 vols. Anchor Bible 4–4A. New York: Doubleday, 1993–2000.

Levinson, Bernard M. *Deuteronomy and the Hermeneutics of Legal Innovation.* Oxford: Oxford University Press, 1997.

———. *Legal Revision and Religious Renewal in Ancient Israel.* Cambridge: Cambridge University Press, 2008.

Levison, John R., and Priscilla Pope-Levison, eds. *Return to Babel: Global Perspectives on the Bible.* Louisville: Westminster John Knox, 1999.

Lohfink, Norbert. "Darstellungskunst und Theologie in Dtn 1:6–3:29." *Biblica* 41 (1960): 105–34.

———. *Das Hauptgebot: Eine Untersuchung literarischer Einleitungsfragen zu Dtn 5–11.* Analecta biblica 20. Rome: Pontifical Biblical Institute, 1963.

———. "'I Am Yahweh, Your Physician' (Exodus 15:26)." In *Theology of the Pentateuch: Themes of the Priestly Narrative and Deuteronomy,* 35–95. Edinburgh: T&T Clark, 1994.

———. "The 'Small Credo' of Deuteronomy 26:5–9." In *Theology of the Pentateuch: Themes of the Priestly Narrative and Deuteronomy,* 265–89. Edinburgh: T&T Clark, 1994.

Lohr, Joel N. *Chosen and Unchosen: Conceptions of Election in the Pentateuch and Jewish-Christian Interpretation.* Siphrut: Literature and Theology of the Hebrew Scriptures 2. Winona Lake, IN: Eisenbrauns, 2009.

———. Review of *Mitzvoth Ethics and the Jewish Bible: The End of Old Testament Theology,* by Gershom M. H. Ratheiser. *Reviews in Religion and Theology* 15, no. 2 (2008): 237–41.

Lundbom, Jack R. *Jeremiah 21–36: A New Translation with Introduction and Commentary.* Anchor Bible 21B. New York: Doubleday, 2004.

MacDonald, Nathan. *Deuteronomy and the Meaning of "Monotheism."* Forschungen zum Alten Testament 2.1. Tübingen: Mohr Siebeck, 2003.

———. "Did God Choose the Patriarchs? Reading for Election in the Book of Genesis." In *Genesis and Christian Theology*, edited by Nathan MacDonald, Mark W. Elliott, and Grant Macaskill. Grand Rapids: Eerdmans, forthcoming.

———. "The Literary Criticism and Rhetorical Logic of Deuteronomy i–iv." *Vetus Testamentum* 56 (2006): 203–24.

Mann, Thomas W. *The Book of the Torah: The Narrative Integrity of the Pentateuch.* Atlanta: John Knox, 1988.

———. *Deuteronomy.* Westminster Bible Companion. Louisville: Westminster John Knox, 1995.

McBride, S. Dean. "The Essence of Orthodoxy: Deuteronomy 5:6–10 and Exodus 20:2–6." *Interpretation* 60 (2006): 133–50.

Mendenhall, George E. "Covenant Forms in Israelite Tradition." *Biblical Archaeologist* 17, no. 3 (1954): 50–76.

Milgrom, Jacob. *Leviticus: A Book of Ritual and Ethics.* Continental Commentary. Minneapolis: Fortress, 2004.

———. *Leviticus 1–16: A New Translation with Introduction and Commentary.* Anchor Bible 3. New York: Doubleday, 1991.

———. *Leviticus 17–22: A New Translation with Introduction and Commentary.* Anchor Bible 3A. New York: Doubleday, 2000.

Miller, Patrick D. "God's Other Stories: On the Margins of Deuteronomic Theology." In *Israelite Religion and Biblical Theology: Collected Essays*, 593–602. Journal for the Study of the Old Testament: Supplement Series 267. Sheffield: Sheffield Academic Press, 2000.

Moberly, R. W. L. "Abraham's Righteousness (Gen. 15:6)." In *Studies in the Pentateuch*, edited by John A. Emerton, 103–30. Supplements to Vetus Testamentum 41. Leiden: Brill, 1990.

———. *The Bible, Theology, and Faith: A Study of Abraham and Jesus.* Cambridge Studies in Christian Doctrine 5. Cambridge: Cambridge University Press, 2000.

———. "Biblical Criticism and Religious Belief." *Journal of Theological Interpretation* 2 (2008): 71–100.

———. "Christ in All the Scriptures? The Challenge of Reading the Old Testament as Christian Scripture." *Journal of Theological Interpretation* 1 (2007): 79–100.

———. "Christ as the Key to Scripture: Genesis 22 Reconsidered." In *He Swore an Oath: Biblical Themes from Genesis 12–50*, edited by R. S. Hess, P. E. Satterthwaite, and G. J. Wenham, 143–73. Cambridge: Tyndale House, 1993.

———. "A Dialogue with Gordon McConville on Deuteronomy, II: Theological Interpretation of an Old Testament Book: A Response to Gordon McConville's *Deuteronomy.*" *Scottish Journal of Theology* 56 (2003): 516–25.

———. "Did the Interpreters Get It Right? Genesis 2–3 Reconsidered." *Journal of Theological Studies* 59 (2008): 22–40.

———. "Did the Serpent Get It Right?" *Journal of Theological Studies* 39 (1988): 1–27.

————. "The Earliest Commentary on the Akedah." *Vetus Testamentum* 38 (1988): 302–23.

————. "Exemplars of Faith in Hebrews 11: Abel." In *The Epistle to the Hebrews and Christian Theology*, edited by Richard Bauckham, Daniel R. Driver, Trevor A. Hart, and Nathan MacDonald, 353–63. Grand Rapids: Eerdmans, 2009.

————. "Exodus." In *Dictionary for Theological Interpretation of the Bible*, edited by Kevin J. Vanhoozer, Craig G. Bartholomew, and Daniel J. Treier, 211–16. Grand Rapids: Baker Academic; London: SPCK, 2005.

————. "'God Is Not a Human That He Should Repent' (Num. 23:19 and 1 Sam. 15:29)." In *God in the Fray: A Tribute to Walter Brueggemann*, edited by Tod Linafelt and Timothy K. Beal, 112–23. Philadelphia: Fortress: 1998.

————. "How May We Speak of God? A Reconsideration of the Nature of Biblical Theology." *Tyndale Bulletin* 53 (2002): 177–202.

————. "How Should One Read the Early Chapters of Genesis?" In *Reading Genesis after Darwin*, edited by Stephen C. Barton and David Wilkinson, 5–21. New York: Oxford University Press, 2009.

————. "On Interpreting the Mind of God: The Theological Significance of the Flood Narrative (Gen. 6–9)." In *The Word Leaps the Gap: Essays on Scripture and Theology in Honor of Richard B. Hays*, edited by J. Ross Wagner, C. Kavin Rowe, and A. Katherine Grieb, 44–66. Grand Rapids: Eerdmans, 2008.

————. "'Interpret the Bible Like Any Other Book'? Requiem for an Axiom." *Journal of Theological Interpretation* 4 (2010): 91–110.

————. "On Learning to Be a True Prophet: The Story of Balaam and His Ass." In *New Heaven and New Earth: Prophecy and the Millennium: Essays in Honour of Anthony Gelston*, edited by Peter J. Harland and Robert Hayward, 1–17. Leiden: Brill, 1999.

————. "On Learning Spiritual Disciplines: A Reading of Exodus 16." In *Reading the Law: Studies in Honour of Gordon J. Wenham*, edited by J. G. McConville and Karl Möller, 213–27. Library of Hebrew Bible/Old Testament Studies 461. New York: T&T Clark International, 2007.

————. "Living Dangerously: Genesis 22 and the Quest for Good Biblical Interpretation." In *The Art of Reading Scripture*, edited by Ellen F. Davis and Richard B. Hays, 181–97. Grand Rapids: Eerdmans, 2003.

————. "The Mark of Cain—Revealed at Last?" *Harvard Theological Review* 100 (2007): 11–28.

————. *The Old Testament of the Old Testament: Patriarchal Narratives and Mosaic Yahwism*. Overtures to Biblical Theology. Minneapolis: Fortress, 1992; repr., Eugene, OR: Wipf & Stock, 2002.

————. "Patriarchal Narratives." In *Dictionary for Theological Interpretation of the Bible*, edited by Kevin J. Vanhoozer, Craig G. Bartholomew, and Daniel J. Treier, 564–66. Grand Rapids: Baker Academic; London: SPCK, 2005.

————. "Pentateuch." In *New Interpreter's Dictionary of the Bible*, edited by Katharine Doob Sakenfeld, 4:430–38. Nashville: Abingdon, 2009.

————. *Prophecy and Discernment*. Cambridge Studies in Christian Doctrine 14. Cambridge: Cambridge University Press, 2006.

————. "Review of *The Garden of Eden and the Hope of Immortality*." *Journal of Theological Studies* 45 (1994): 172–77.

————. *The Theology of the Book of Genesis*. Old Testament Theology. Cambridge: Cambridge University Press, 2009.

————. "Toward an Interpretation of the Shema." In *Theological Exegesis: Essays in Honor of Brevard S. Childs*, edited by Christopher Seitz and Kathryn Greene-McCreight, 124–44. Grand Rapids: Eerdmans, 1999.

————. "What Is Theological Interpretation of Scripture?" *Journal of Theological Interpretation* 3 (2009): 161–78.

————. "Why Did Noah Send Out a Raven?" *Vetus Testamentum* 50 (2000): 345–56.

————. "'YHWH Is One': The Translation of the Shema." In *Studies in the Pentateuch*, edited by John A. Emerton, 209–15. Supplements to Vetus Testamentum 41. Leiden: Brill, 1990.

Moran, William L. "The Ancient Near Eastern Background of the Love of God in Deuteronomy." *Catholic Biblical Quarterly* 25 (1963): 77–87.

Mosis, Rudolf. "Exod 19, 5b–6a: Syntaktische Aufbau und lexicalische Semantik." *Biblische Zeitschrift* 22 (1978): 1–25.

Muilenburg, James. "The Form and Structure of the Covenantal Formulations." *Vetus Testamentum* 9 (1959): 347–65.

Nelson, Richard D. *Deuteronomy: A Commentary*. Old Testament Library. Louisville: Westminster John Knox, 2002.

Neusner, Jacob. *Handbook of Rabbinic Theology: Language, System, Structure*. Leiden: Brill, 2002.

Nicholson, Ernest W. *God and His People: Covenant and Theology in the Old Testament*. Oxford: Clarendon, 1986.

Noth, Martin. *The Deuteronomistic History*. Journal for the Study of the Old Testament: Supplement Series 15. Sheffield: JSOT Press, 1981.

————. *Gesammelte Studien zum Alten Testament*. 3rd ed. Part 1. Munich: Kaiser, 1966.

————. "Nu 21 als Glied der 'Hexateuch'-Erzählung." *Zeitschrift für die alttestamentliche Wissenschaft* 58 (1940/41): 161–89.

Olivier, Johannes P. J. "Restitution as Economic Redress: The Fine Print of the Old Babylonian *Mēšarum*-Edict of Ammiṣaduqa." *Zeitschrift für altorientalische und biblische Rechtsgeschichte* 3 (1997): 12–25.

Olson, Dennis T. *The Death of the Old and the Birth of the New: The Framework of the Book of Numbers and the Pentateuch*. Brown Judaic Studies 71. Chico, CA: Scholars Press, 1985.

————. *Numbers*. Interpretation. Louisville: John Knox, 1996.

Origen. *Homélies sur le lévitique: Texte latin, introduction, traduction et notes*. Edited by Marcel Borret. 2 vols. Sources chrétiennes, 286–87. Paris: Cerf, 1981.

————. *Homilies on Numbers*. Ancient Christian Texts. Translated by Thomas P. Scheck. Downers Grove, IL: InterVarsity, 2009.

Otto, Eckart. *Das Deuteronomium im Pentateuch und Hexateuch: Studien zur Literaturgeschichte von Pentateuch und Hexateuch im Lichte des Deuteronomiumrahmens*. Forschungen zum Alten Testament 30. Tübingen: Mohr Siebeck, 2000.

———. "Programme der sozialen Gerechtigkeit: Die neuassyrische *(an-)durāru*-Institution sozialen Ausgleichs und das deuteronomische Erlaßjahr in Dtn 15." *Zeitschrift für altorientalische und biblische Rechtsgeschichte* 3 (1997): 26–63.

Patai, Raphael. "The 'Control of Rain' in Ancient Palestine: A Study in Comparative Religion." *Hebrew Union College Annual* 14 (1939): 251–86.

Patrick, Dale. "The Covenant Code Source." *Vetus Testamentum* 27 (1977): 145–57.

Perlitt, Lothar. "Deuteronomium 1–3 im Streit der exegetischen Methoden." In *Das Deuteronomium: Entstehung, Gestalt und Botschaft*, edited by N. Lohfink, 149–63. Bibliotheca ephemeridum theologicarum lovaniensium 68. Leuven: Peeters, 1985.

———. "Priesterschrift im Deuteronomium?" *Zeitschrift für die alttestamentliche Wissenschaft* 100 (1988): 65–88.

———. "Wovon der Mensch lebt (Dtn. 8,3b)." In *Die Botschaft und die Boten: Festschrift für Hans Walter Wolff zum 70. Geburtstag*, edited by Jörg Jeremias and Lothar Perlitt, 403–26. Neukirchen-Vluyn: Neukirchener Verlag, 1981.

Persky, Joseph. "The Ethology of *Homo Economicus*." *Journal of Economic Perspectives* 9 (1995): 221–31.

Petersen, David L. "Genesis and Family Values." *Journal of Biblical Literature* 124 (2005): 5–23.

Rad, Gerhard von. *Genesis*. Old Testament Library. Rev. ed. London: SCM, 1972.

Radner, Ephraim. *Leviticus*. Brazos Theological Commentary on the Bible. Grand Rapids: Brazos, 2008.

Ratheiser, Gershom M. H. *Mitzvoth Ethics and the Jewish Bible: The End of Old Testament Theology*. London: T&T Clark, 2007.

Redford, Donald B. *Egypt, Canaan, and Israel in Ancient Times*. Princeton, NJ: Princeton University Press, 1992.

Rendtorff, Rolf. "Is It Possible to Read Leviticus as a Separate Book?" In *Reading Leviticus: A Conversation with Mary Douglas*, edited by John F. A. Sawyer, 22–35. Journal for the Study of the Old Testament: Supplement Series 227. Sheffield: Sheffield Academic Press, 1996.

———. "Leviticus 16 als Mitte der Tora." *Biblical Interpretation* 11 (2003): 252–58.

———. *The Old Testament: An Introduction*. London: SCM, 1985.

———. *The Problem of the Process of Transmission in the Pentateuch*. Journal for the Study of the Old Testament: Supplement Series 89. Sheffield: JSOT Press, 1990.

Reno, Russell R. *Genesis*. Brazos Theological Commentary on the Bible. Grand Rapids: Brazos, 2010.

Ricoeur, Paul. *Interpretation Theory: Discourse and the Surplus of Meaning*. Fort Worth: Texas Christian University Press, 1976.

Rowe, C. Kavin. "Biblical Pressure and Trinitarian Hermeneutics." *Pro ecclesia* 11 (2002): 295–312.

Sarna, Nahum M. *Exploring Exodus: The Origins of Biblical Israel.* New York: Schocken Books, 1996.

Schmid, Konrad. *Erzväter und Exodus: Untersuchungen zur doppelten Begründung der Ursprünge Israels innerhalb der Geschichtsbücher des Alten Testaments.* Wissenschaftliche Monographien zum Alten und Neuen Testament 81. Neukirchen-Vluyn: Neukirchener Verlag, 1999.

———. *Genesis and the Moses Story: Israel's Dual Origins in the Hebrew Bible.* Translated by James D. Nogalski. Siphrut: Literature and Theology of the Hebrew Scriptures 3. Winona Lake, IN: Eisenbrauns, 2010.

Schneider, Tammi J. *Mothers of Promise: Women in the Book of Genesis.* Grand Rapids: Baker Academic, 2008.

Schreiner, Josef. "תולדות [*toledot*]." In *Theological Dictionary of the Old Testament,* edited by G. Johannes Botterweck, Helmer Ringgren, and Heinz-Yosef Fabry, translated by David E. Green, 15:582–88. Grand Rapids, Eerdmans: 2006.

Schüle, Andreas. *Der Prolog der hebräischen Bibel: Der literar- und theologiegeschichtliche Diskurs der Urgeschichte (Genesis 1–11).* Abhandlungen zur Theologie des Alten und Neuen Testaments 86. Zurich: Theologischer Verlag Zurich, 2006.

Schut, Michael. *Money and Faith: The Search for Enough.* Denver: Church Publishing, 2008.

Schwartz, Baruch J. "Leviticus." In *The Jewish Study Bible,* edited by Adele Berlin and Marc Zvi Brettler, 203–80. New York: Oxford University Press, 2004.

Seitz, Christopher R. "The Canonical Approach and Theological Interpretation." In *Canon and Biblical Interpretation,* Scripture and Hermeneutics Series 7, edited by Craig Bartholomew et al., 58–110. Grand Rapids: Zondervan and Carlisle: Paternoster, 2006.

Singer, Isidore, and Cyrus Adler, eds. *The Jewish Encyclopedia.* 12 Vols. New York: Funk & Wagnalls Co., 1901–6.

Ska, Jean-Louis. *Introduction to Reading the Pentateuch.* Translated by Pascale Dominique. Winona Lake, IN: Eisenbrauns, 2006.

Smith, Adam. *An Inquiry into the Nature and Causes of the Wealth of Nations.* Dublin: N. Kelly, 1801.

Smith, Mark S. *The Early History of God: Yahweh and the Other Deities in Ancient Israel.* Grand Rapids: Eerdmans, 2002.

———. *The Pilgrimage Pattern in Exodus.* Journal for the Study of the Old Testament: Supplement Series 239. Sheffield: Sheffield Academic Press, 1997.

———. *The Priestly Vision of Genesis 1.* Minneapolis: Fortress, 2010.

Speiser, E. A. "'People' and 'Nation' of Israel." *Journal of Biblical Literature* 79 (1960): 157–63.

Sperling, S. David. "Modern Jewish Interpretation." In *The Jewish Study Bible,* edited by Adele Berlin and Marc Zvi Brettler, 1908–19. New York: Oxford University Press, 2004.

Stackert, Jeffery. *Rewriting the Torah: Literary Revision in Deuteronomy and the Holiness Legislation.* Forschungen zum Alten Testament 52. Tübingen: Mohr Siebeck, 2007.

Steiner, George. "The Good Books." In *The New Yorker*, January 11, 1988. Repr. in *Religion and Intellectual Life* 6 (1989): 9–16.

———. *Real Presences: Is There Anything in What We Say?* London: Faber & Faber, 1989.

Stökl Ben Ezra, Daniel. *The Impact of Yom Kippur on Early Christianity: The Day of Atonement from the Second Temple to the Fifth Century*. Wissenschaftliche Untersuchungen zum Neuen Testament 163. Tübingen: Mohr Siebeck, 2003.

Telushkin, Joseph. "Sacrifices." In *Jewish Literacy*, 46–48. New York: William Morrow, 2008.

———. "Yom Kippur." In *Jewish Literacy*, 638–41. New York: William Morrow, 2008.

Thiselton, Anthony C. "The Supposed Power of Words in the Biblical Writings." *Journal of Theological Studies* 25 (1974): 282–99.

Thompson, George H. P. "Called—Proven—Obedient: A Study in the Baptism and Temptation Narratives of Matthew and Luke." *Journal of Theological Studies* 11 (1960): 1–12.

Tigay, Jeffrey H. *Deuteronomy: The Traditional Hebrew Text with the New JPS Translation*. Jewish Publication Society Torah Commentary 5. Philadelphia: Jewish Publication Society, 1996.

Tolkien, J. R. R. *The Lord of the Rings*. Part 1, *The Fellowship of the Ring*. 1954. Reprint, London: HarperCollins, 1992.

Trible, Phyllis. *God and the Rhetoric of Sexuality*. Overtures to Biblical Theology. Philadelphia: Fortress, 1978.

Turner, Laurence A. *Announcements of Plot in Genesis*. Journal for the Study of the Old Testament: Supplement Series 96. Sheffield: JSOT Press, 1990.

Uehlinger, Christoph. *Weltreich und "eine Rede": Eine neue Deutung der sogenannten Turmbauerzählung (Gen 11, 1–9)*. Orbis biblicus et orientalis 101. Freiburg: Universitätsverlag, 1990.

Van Seters, John. "Conquest of Sihon's Kingdom: A Literary Examination." *Journal of Biblical Literature* 99 (1972): 182–97.

———. *The Life of Moses: The Yahwist as Historian in Exodus–Numbers*. Louisville: Westminster John Knox, 1994.

———. "The Tower of Babel as Lookout over Genesis 1–11." In *Words Become Worlds: Semantic Studies of Genesis 1–11*, 84–109. Biblical Interpretation Series 6. Leiden: Brill, 1994.

Van Zyl, Daniel C. "Exodus 19:3–6 and the Kerygmatic Perspective of the Pentateuch." *Old Testament Essays* 5 (1992): 264–71.

Vaux, Roland de. *The Early History of Israel*. Vol. 1, *To the Exodus and Covenant of Sinai*. London: Darton, Longman & Todd, 1978.

Veijola, Timo. *Das fünfte Buch Mose: Deuteronomium. Kapitel 1,1–16,17*. Das Alte Testament Deutsch 8. Göttingen: Vandenhoeck & Ruprecht, 2004.

Vervenne, Marc. "The Question of 'Deuteronomic' Elements in Genesis to Numbers." In *Studies in Deuteronomy: In Honour of C. J. Labuschagne on the Occasion of His 65th Birthday*, edited by F. García Martínez, A. Hilhorst, J. T. A. G. M.

van Ruiten, and A. S. van der Woude, 243–68. Supplements to Vetus Testamentum 53. Leiden: Brill, 1994.

———. *Old Testament Theology*. Vol. 1. New York: Harper & Row, 1962.

———. *Studies in Deuteronomy*. Studies in Biblical Theology 9. London: SCM, 1953.

Walton, John H. *The Lost World of Genesis One: Ancient Cosmology and the Origins Debate*. Downers Grove, IL: InterVarsity, 2009.

Warning, Wilfried. *Literary Artistry in Leviticus*. Biblical Interpretation Series 35. Leiden: Brill, 1999.

Watson, Francis. *Paul and the Hermeneutics of Faith*. London: T&T Clark, 2004.

Watts, James W. *Reading Law: The Rhetorical Shaping of the Pentateuch*. The Biblical Seminar 59. Sheffield: Sheffield Academic Press, 1999.

———. *Ritual and Rhetoric in Leviticus*. Cambridge: Cambridge University Press, 2007.

———. "The Torah as the Rhetoric of Priesthood." In *The Pentateuch as Torah: New Models for Understanding Its Promulgation and Acceptance*, edited by Gary N. Knoppers and Bernard M. Levinson, 319–31. Winona Lake, IN: Eisenbrauns, 2007.

Weinfeld, Moshe. *Deuteronomy and the Deuteronomic School*. Oxford: Clarendon, 1972.

———. *Deuteronomy 1–11: A New Translation with Introduction and Commentary*. Anchor Bible 5. New York: Doubleday, 1991.

———. "Pentateuch." *Encyclopaedia Judaica* 13 (1972): 231–61.

Wells, Bruce. "What Is Biblical Law? A Look at Pentateuchal Rules and Near Eastern Practice." *Catholic Biblical Quarterly* 70 (2008): 223–43.

Wells, Jo Bailey. *God's Holy People: A Theme in Biblical Theology*. Journal for the Study of the Old Testament: Supplement Series 305. Sheffield: Sheffield Academic Press, 2000.

Wenham, Gordon J. *The Book of Leviticus*. New International Commentary on the Old Testament. Grand Rapids: Eerdmans, 1979.

———. *Exploring the Old Testament: A Guide to the Pentateuch*. Downers Grove, IL: InterVarsity, 2003.

———. *Genesis 1–15*. Word Biblical Commentary 1. Waco: Word, 1987.

———. *Genesis 16–50*. Word Biblical Commentary 2. Waco: Word, 1994.

———. *Numbers*. Tyndale Old Testament Commentary. Leicester, UK: Inter-Varsity, 1981.

———. *Numbers*. Old Testament Guides. Sheffield: Sheffield Academic Press, 1997.

———. "The Religion of the Patriarchs." In *Essays on the Patriarchal Narratives*, edited by Alan R. Millard and Donald J. Wiseman, 157–88. Leicester, UK: Inter-Varsity, 1980.

Werrett, Ian C. *Ritual Purity and the Dead Sea Scrolls*. Studies in the Texts of the Desert of Judah 72. Leiden: Brill, 2007.

Westermann, Claus. *Blessing in the Bible and the Life of the Church*. Translated by Keith Crim. Overtures to Biblical Theology. Philadelphia: Fortress, 1978.

―――. *Elements of Old Testament Theology.* Translated by Douglas W. Stott. Atlanta: John Knox, 1982.

―――. *Genesis 1–11: A Commentary.* Translated by John J. Scullion. Minneapolis: Fortress, 1984.

―――. *Genesis 12–36: A Commentary.* Translated by John J. Scullion. Minneapolis: Fortress, 1985.

Wette, Wilhelm M. L. de. "Dissertatio critico-exegetica, qua Deuteronomium a prioribus Pentateuchi libris diversum, alius cuiusdam recentioris auctoris opus esse monstratur." DPhil diss., University of Jena, 1805.

Williams, Rowan. "Archbishop's Article on the Financial Crisis." In *The Spectator*, September 27, 2008, http://www.archbishopofcanterbury.org/articles.php/629/archbishops-article-on-the-financial-crisis.

Wolde, Ellen van. "Facing the Earth: Primaeval History in a New Perspective." In *The World of Genesis: Persons, Places, Perspectives.* Journal for the Study of the Old Testament: Supplement Series 257, edited by Philip R. Davies and David J. A. Clines, 22–47. Sheffield: Sheffield Academic Press, 1998.

Wolff, Hans Walter. *Hosea.* 3rd ed. Biblischer Kommentar 14. Neukirchen-Vluyn: Neukirchener Verlag, 1976.

Wright, Christopher J. H. *Deuteronomy.* New International Biblical Commentary 4. Peabody, MA: Hendrickson, 1996.

―――. *The Mission of God: Unlocking the Bible's Grand Narrative.* Nottingham, UK: Inter-Varsity, 2006.

Wright, G. Ernest. *The Old Testament against Its Environment.* Studies in Biblical Theology 2. London: SCM, 1950.

Wright, Terry R. *The Genesis of Fiction: Modern Novelists as Biblical Interpreters.* Aldershot, UK: Ashgate, 2007.

Wyschogrod, Michael. *The Body of Faith: God in the People Israel.* Northvale, NJ: Jason Aronson, 1996.

Yee, Gale A. "'She Is Not My Wife and I Am Not Her Husband': A Materialist Analysis of Hosea 1–2." *Biblical Interpretation* 9 (2001): 345–83.

Author Index

Scripture Index

References in bold indicate a substantive discussion of the whole passage as the subject matter of one of the chapters of this book. All verse numbers refer to English translations rather than MT.

OLD TESTAMENT

Genesis
1 9, 21, 25–26, 28, 39, 47, 96
1–3 181
1–11 22, 24–27, 29–31, 35–38, 43, 45–47, 181
1:1 21, 116
1:3–5 21
1:26 39
1:28 13, 38, 45, 47
1:29–30 97
2–3 48
2:3 60
2:4 21, 22
2:24 26
3 183
3:22 39
4 182
4:15 182
4:16 37
5:1 22
6 30, 48
6:2 20
6:5 182
6:9 22
8:21 182
9:1–7 97
9:19 38, 47–48
10 26, 37, 41

10:1 22
10:5 37
10:9–10 37
10:10 41
10:18 38, 47
10:20 37
10:31 37
11 39, 43, 46–47
11:1 37, 40, 43
11:1–9 37–49
11:2 37
11:3–4 39
11:4 40, 47
11:5 40
11:6 40
11:7 39–41
11:8 38–40
11:9 38, 40–41, 43, 46
11:10 22
11:27 22
12 52
12–25 22
12–50 11, 22, 29, 179, 181
12:1–3 13, 20, 30–32, 181
12:2 32
12:2–3 32
12:6 24

12:7–8 153
13:10–12 123
15 20
17 20
18:17–19 27
19 27
22 13, 178, 180
22:12 163
22:15–18 180
25:12 22
25:12–18 31
25:19 22
25:23 13
27 33–34
27–35 22
27:4 33
27:29 33
27:34 33
27:35 33
28:9 33
29:25 33
31:19 34
31:34 34
31:35 34
32:22–32 22
32:25 48
32:26 22, 32
32:28 22
32:29 32
32:31 48

35:1–7 153
36:1 22
36:9 22
37–50 22
37:2 22–23
38 23
46:8–27 53
48–49 32
49:28 32
50 11
50:24 53
50:24–25 53

Exodus
1 11
1–15 51
1–15:21 54
1–18 56
1–24 55
1:1–7 56
1:9 57
1:15–2:10 59
1:20–21 59
2:23 59
2:24–25 59
3 35, 57, 60, 65, 67–68, 71, 81, 182
3:1 58
3:1–6 60

3:2 60
3:5 60
3:6 53
3:7 58
3:7–10 60
3:15 60
3:16 53
5:7 38
6 35, 63, 182
7–11 68
7:3 59
12 53
12–13 54
12–15 56
12:40 64
13:2 62
13:19 53
14–15 54
15 54, 141–42
15–17 141
15–18 126
15:1 134
15:1–21 54, 142
15:22–16:36 142
15:22–18:27 54
15:26 133
16 59, 183
16:5 164
16:16–18 164
16:19–21 164

207

NEW TESTAMENT